Jason Om is a Walkley Award-winning reporter with the ABC's *7.30* program. Previously, he's been a presenter on the ABC News Channel and a reporter for *ABC News Breakfast*, *Lateline*, ABC Life and ABC Radio.

In 2017, he won widespread praise for his personal story about his dad's sixteen-year struggle to accept him as gay. The article and TV piece ran Australia-wide, attracting a million views. Viewers were moved to tears, and the story earned Jason a nomination in the 2018 NSW (LGBTI) Honour Awards. *All Mixed Up* is his first book.

all mixed up

a memoir

jason om

ABC BOOKS

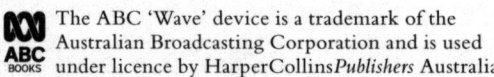 The ABC 'Wave' device is a trademark of the Australian Broadcasting Corporation and is used under licence by HarperCollins*Publishers* Australia.

HarperCollinsPublishers
Australia • Brazil • Canada • France • Germany • Holland • Hungary
India • Italy • Japan • Mexico • New Zealand • Poland • Spain • Sweden
Switzerland • United Kingdom • United States of America

First published in Australia in 2022
by HarperCollins*Publishers* Australia Pty Limited
ABN 36 009 913 517
harpercollins.com.au

Copyright © Jason Om 2022

The right of Jason Om to be identified as the author of this work has been asserted by him in accordance with the *Copyright Amendment (Moral Rights) Act 2000*.

This work is copyright. Apart from any use as permitted under the *Copyright Act 1968*, no part may be reproduced, copied, scanned, stored in a retrieval system, recorded, or transmitted, in any form or by any means, without the prior written permission of the publisher.

A catalogue record for this book is available
from the National Library of Australia

ISBN: 978 0 7333 4191 5 (paperback)
ISBN: 978 1 4607 1393 8 (ebook)

Cover design by George Saad
Cover image of the author by Narong Om
Author photograph by Sanjeev Singh
Typeset in Sabon LT Std by Kirby Jones
Printed and bound in Australia by McPherson's Printing Group

For Mum

All Mixed Up is a work of non-fiction, based on recollections, interviews and found documents. The names of some people and some details have been changed.

This book contains sensitive themes. If it raises any issues for you, you can contact Lifeline (13 11 14), Beyond Blue (1300 22 4636) or QLife (1800 184 527).

Prologue

The sound was alien. Repetitive. Guttural. It was coming from Mum's bedroom.

I was on the couch, watching the Wimbledon Championships on late-night television.

'Mummy?'

No answer. Only the strange noise. It drowned out the polite clapping and the soft *pock pock* of the tennis balls.

Normally Mum kept me company at night because I was easily spooked. 'Stay with me, Mummy,' I would beg her, tugging on her arm like a bellringer.

'Why, are you afraid of the bogeyman?' she would tease.

Of course I was. There were shadows moving under the trees along our dimly lit street. Our dog's wild barking, at noises only canines could hear, made me jump out of my skin.

Mum was usually my protector on the lonely nights when Dad was working in the city or out with friends. Snuggling up to her warm body was a comfort, but on this night she'd gone to bed early.

The noise from her bedroom continued. It sounded as if a wild animal were attacking her.

I called out a second time. Still no answer.

Forcing my legs into action, I crossed the polished floorboards and ran down the darkened hallway.

Mum's door was open, as usual, but the room was pitch-black. My fingers searched for the light switch.

The brightness revealed Mum flailing about in the double bed, the covers shrink-wrapped around her body. She was reaching out as though trying to grab me. Beside her on the bed, looking alarmed, was Spike, our little dog.

'Mummy, what's wrong?' I cried, falling to her side.

Mum was fighting for air.

All I could do was hold her hands. 'What's wrong?' I pleaded. 'What's wrong?'

She was fading fast. Eventually, the sound from deep inside her throat stopped, and the room fell silent.

Mum became a statue. The colour drained from her face, her eyes shut, and her body sank into the sheets. Spike shrank away in fear.

I panicked. I ran to Dad's study and stood in front of our rotary phone, paralysed. If I called the ambulance, my worst fears would be realised. My world would be ending.

Perhaps things were okay. Perhaps Mum would wake up again.

Nan Ruby, Mum's mother, lived a short drive away. I spun the dial on the phone.

'Hello?' she answered in her slow, suspicious way. An unexpected call late at night might be from unwelcome market researchers.

'Nanny!' I panted through the receiver. 'Mum's not breathing.'

'What? Your mother is bleeding?'

'Breathing!' I screamed through tears, emphasising the 'r' and the 'th'. 'She's not breathing!'

Why couldn't Nan understand? Was she pretending to be deaf?

'Oh,' she said, *'breathing!'*

Time was running out. Minutes had passed. Nan was no use.

I hung up and called triple zero, hooking one finger at a time on the dial. I dialled twice, terrified the first two zeros had failed to go through. I needed to do it perfectly.

The call connected to a woman's calm, clear voice. She told me to check on Mum, who was still unconscious. After I'd done this and reported back, I took in every word of the woman's instructions for CPR.

Jumping onto the bed, I did as I'd been told: pinched Mum's nose, blew into her mouth, pumped her chest with my hands. I exhaled into her dry mouth as hard as I could, like they did on *Baywatch*. Her head felt like a ripe melon in my small hands.

After the first puff, Mum's body convulsed. Her throat gurgled, a sign that my attempts were working, my stale air circulating in her lungs, rebooting her system. A foul stench came out of her.

I blew a few more times, but my breaths were meagre. I staggered off the bed. 'I can't do this,' I said out loud to myself. 'I can't do it. I don't know what to do!' *I give up. I'm hopeless. I'm useless.*

'I can't do it!' I wailed to the woman on the phone.

'The ambulance is on its way,' she said, then told me to fetch an adult.

I bolted into the blackness of our street, my bare feet springing on the asphalt, my wet cheeks chilling in the winter air. I ignored the shadows – there was only one way to end my terror, and that was to find a grown-up who could comfort me.

No one answered next door, so I darted across the street and tried an old couple, Ian and Joan. Walking up the steps to their front door, I saw the flicker of a television between the metal blades of white venetians and sensed someone moving around.

The porch lit up. Ian, a gentle man with steel-wool hair and dark-lensed spectacles, emerged, blinking down at me.

'It's Mum. She's not breathing. I've called the ambulance.'

As we returned to the house, red flashes illuminated the end of the street like a lighthouse beacon cutting through the darkness, but there was no siren.

'The ambulance is coming, it's coming,' I said to Ian.

Suddenly, the house was illuminated. Two large ambulance officers entered our narrow hallway, lugging medical kits and strange devices. While the adults took charge, I hovered as far from Mum as I could. I heard the men exchanging instructions and pumping air into her mouth.

My father arrived in his white Camry. He'd been attending a Cambodian wedding reception, celebrating with friends. As Ian headed home, Dad burst through the front door.

By the time he reached Mum, the paramedics were about to leave. 'There's not much we can do here – we have to get her to the hospital,' one of them said to Dad.

My father didn't sweep me into his arms or ask if I was okay. Instead, he was spluttering, 'She is sick. My wife is sick.' He spat out the words in his Cambodian accent, with a mix of anger and disgust. 'Sick!' Dad was erupting while I flitted around the house without any bearings.

After the ambulance officers stretchered Mum outside and into the van, one returned and sat me down on the couch. 'Tell me what happened,' he said gently. He had soft eyes and dark hair, and next to me he seemed like a giant.

'I was watching TV, then I heard a growl. It sounded like an animal —' I tried to find the right description '— like a pig.'

The minute the word left my mouth, I realised how harsh it sounded. I thought the ambulance officer would burst out laughing, but his face was grave.

'Then I found her and called the ambulance.'

Mum's older brother Uncle Johnny lived with Nan Ruby, and after my phone call he'd come straight over on his pushbike. For the rest of the night, he minded me while Dad sat by Mum's bed in the intensive care unit.

At some point, I snuck back into Mum's desolate bedroom. The bed had been moved. The doona was splayed open. Paper wrappers and little glass bottles with metal caps littered the carpet. I sat on the floor among the mess for a while, my head spinning. *What had just happened? How could this be happening? Why was God doing this to me? Why was he such a bastard?*

Back in my room I cried into my pillow, exhausted and numb. The door opened, and Uncle Johnny poked his head in, a shadow against the light from the kitchen. He told me he had to get to his job as a hospital assistant; it was already early morning, and his shift was about to start.

'When's Dad coming back?'

'He's still at the hospital. He'll be there for a while.'

In the darkness, I put my hands together and prayed. 'I'm sorry, God. I'm asking you to help me get through this. Please, God, help me get through this. Please help Mum and Dad, me and the rest of the family pull through. Oh God, *please*.'

*

The following day, Dad took me to see Mum in the hospital. I approached her bed cautiously. Tubes and cords came out of her body, an apparatus helped her breathe, and a machine beeped beside her. She was more machine than woman.

'Why are her fingers so fat?' I asked, touching her hand, which was smooth and bloated like a rubber glove engorged with water. I put my hand on hers. *Mummy. Mummy?* Her eyes were closed. 'Can she hear me?'

'Yes, she can hear you,' somebody said.

How could that be? Mum was comatose, trapped between life and death.

Maybe she *could* hear me but was stuck inside her body, climbing up the walls, screaming, 'Let. Me. Out!'

'What happened to her?' I asked.

Dad explained that Mum had suffered an inflammation of the heart. 'Myo … myo-car-something. What was it?'

Myocarditis, the Victorian Coroner would later conclude. A heart attack.

I sat quietly on a stool and stared at the machine woman as the rest of the hospital hummed around us. When someone handed me a tissue, I wiped my eyes. Then I smoothed it out on my knee and slowly tore off vertical strips, letting each piece fall like ticker tape onto the floor.

'Oh, Jason,' somebody muttered in the background.

I wanted a nurse or someone else to tell me off, to smack me on the nose. But nobody protested. I wanted to scream and shout and run away. My world was shaking in a cataclysm, my rage clamouring for an outlet, but there was no vent. I sucked it all in and poured it into a reserve where it pooled.

Later the doctors explained that Mum was brain dead. The only thing keeping her alive, if you could call it that, was the life support machine. Dad told me she might be brain damaged if she woke up, and we'd have to care for her for the rest of our lives. 'She wouldn't be the same Mummy, without any quality of life.'

He was left to decide whether to flick the switch on his wife of nineteen years. Six days passed. Without any signs of recovery, the machine woman was turned off, and Mum was gone. She was forty-four. I was twelve.

Chapter One

I remember my parents getting up early in the morning so Dad could drop Mum off at the factory. A sleepy-eyed three-year-old, I would be curled up by the slate hearth of the gas heater in my favourite spot, a lambskin rug on the floral carpet of our small lounge room. All the rooms in the house had sky-blue walls except the kitchen, which was sunflower yellow, a colour Mum had chosen because it was cheerful.

In the darkness, Dad would come over to switch off the flames, and he'd give me a gentle nudge. 'Come on, Jeh, we go.' My parents would stand in the shadows by the front door, waiting for me to follow.

They worked at a potato chip factory – Mum on the morning shift, Dad changing over in the afternoon. Mum had found the job first, after losing her job at General Electric. Later she helped Dad secure a position there as a machine operator, after he lost his job at the Philips appliances factory. Both were on the production line among the Greeks, wearing uniforms and hairnets.

Mum and Dad met in the era when some young people placed dating ads in newspapers and waited days with crossed fingers for a reply. In 1973, when Dad was twenty-eight, he searched for a perfect match by advertising in a Melbourne paper.

A single mother was first to respond, but there was no spark on their first date. Next was a nurse, but when Dad arrived on her doorstep for their date, her parents told him she was 'sick'. A third date ended in humiliation – a university student laughed in his face after revealing she'd replied as a prank.

Not to be deterred, Dad inspected a fourth reply, ostensibly written by a 24-year-old woman called Patricia, a recent arrival in Australia from Malaysia. Impressed by her lovely handwriting, Dad arranged to meet her on the steps under the clocks at Flinders Street Station, a popular meeting place in Melbourne.

Before setting off from his share house, Dad combed his hair and dressed smartly in a white shirt with red pinstripes, a navy cardigan, trousers and polished black shoes. His semi-rimmed glasses sat firmly and evenly on his nose.

W-class trams and Holden Kingswoods rolled past as he waited dutifully for his blind date. Patricia hadn't included a photo with her letter, but he knew that spotting an Asian face in the mainly white crowd would be easy.

Soon enough, a lithe woman with long wavy black hair appeared, wearing a bold red shirt with white polka dots, a blue woollen cardigan and white slacks. She had a pointy nose, pink lips and a joyous smile. Dad was mesmerised. The Eurasian woman reminded him of the beautiful protagonist in the movie *Love is a Many-Splendored Thing* based on the book by Han Suyin. 'I thought she was adventurous, having come all the way from Malaysia,' Dad said, not acknowledging his own daring in coming to Australia as a teenager.

After a bit of chit-chat, they took a red rattler train back to Dad's share house in the south-eastern suburb of Caulfield. Walking from the station, they went across a sports oval opposite the college where Dad studied engineering. The grass was sprinkled with hundreds of small yellow flowers, their tightly packed petals resembling fireworks. Patricia bent down to inspect them, entranced. 'Flowers in the field!' she exclaimed, her voice lilting. The dandelions were widely seen as a weed that blighted lawns around Melbourne, but Patricia saw beauty in them, one that Dad had been oblivious to until she showed him.

His share house was a squat red-brick California bungalow on a street lined with plane trees. 'No girls allowed,' the landlady had warned, but on that day Dad threw caution to the wind. He took Patricia through the back of the house to his small room, furnished with a single bed, a chair, a heavy wooden desk, a wardrobe and an art deco dresser. An old photo of his mother and a T-square engineering ruler hung on the wall.

Wanting a memento of their first date, he screwed his Petri camera onto his tripod. He and Patricia cuddled up to each other and smiled at the camera, the timer counting down, three, two, one, then a flash. Their beaming faces imprinted on a roll of film.

They married in 1974 and had me in 1980.

They scraped together whatever money they could from their modest factory jobs, building the future that lay before me, while helping to fire up Australia's economy, the promise of wealth for toil in their eyes.

*

Born in Kralanh, a rural town in north-west Cambodia, my father, Narong, had come to Australia in 1961 when the White Australia policy was still in force. Despite the 'prohibition of all alien coloured immigration', the Menzies Government welcomed him as a student under the Colombo Plan scholarship program, designed to strengthen relationships in the Asia-Pacific region. The initial length of the scholarship was seven years: three in high school and four in higher education.

Dad was sixteen when he said goodbye to his father, two older brothers and two younger sisters. His mother had died in 1954 when he was at a tender age. Grandma Sieng had apparently suffered blood loss from a previously unknown pregnancy. As she began bleeding at home, she asked Dad to hop on his bike and fetch medicine from a herbalist a few kilometres away. When he returned, she was already in the hospital. 'I want to see my children before I die,' she said from her bed, but by the time Dad arrived at the hospital, she was gone.

During the mourning period, Dad had his head shaved like that of a monk and went commando in orange robes according to Buddhist practice. He watched the flames as his mum was cremated on a pyre in front of a temple. A man prodding the body with a long poker told Dad he'd seen the remains of a baby boy that somehow did not burn.

When Dad set off for Australia, he boarded a plane to Sydney with five other Cambodian boys. He stayed with some of them in a boarding house near the glistening white sands of Coogee Beach, and Dad delighted in the new flavours of his first hamburger.

To Dad, Australia was a stunning dreamland compared to the poverty of Cambodia. Living there, he told me, had

All Mixed Up

been like being a frog at the bottom of a deep well, gazing longingly at the sky.

Dad attended Trinity Grammar in Summer Hill, a suburb in Sydney's Inner West, and was later transferred to Manly Boy's High School. In the mid-1960s he moved to Melbourne to complete a diploma in mechanical engineering at Preston Technical College. After he failed some subjects, the Colombo Plan scholarship money was cut off, but the Australian government allowed him to remain as a private student, so he worked in a fast food shop to support himself as he attained the diploma. Then, in the early 1970s, he completed a bachelor's degree in engineering at Caulfield Institute of Technology.

During that time, Dad watched from afar as his beloved homeland was engulfed in civil war. Then, in 1975, the communist Khmer Rouge, led by the dictator Pol Pot, gained power and disembowelled the country. An estimated two million people – almost one quarter of Cambodia's population – were killed or died of starvation and forced labour.

As well as factory work, Dad had a job as a part-time radio broadcaster, reading the news in his mother tongue at 3EA – later rebranded SBS Radio – where he'd set up the Khmer language program in 1979.

Dad had no previous broadcasting experience. But a year earlier, he'd seen radio programs produced and edited during a visit to the Voice of America in Washington, DC, when his cousin generously gave him a trip to the States. Back in Australia, Dad had simply walked into the 3EA studios in South Melbourne and pitched a radio show to help the Cambodian refugees. He saw an opportunity and seized it. 'I've seen how they use reel-to-reel tape machines in the

US,' he reassured the 3EA manager, who hired him after an audition.

One of the first projects he led in 1979 was a radiothon to help Cambodians affected by famine. For a whole day, the broadcasters from the forty-odd language groups at 3EA rallied together under the one roof, raising a hefty sum of eighty-five thousand dollars. The Melbourne Greeks, Dad said, were the most generous, trying to outbid each other in the hundreds of dollars. One old woman stopped by the studio with a thousand dollars in cash.

Dad said 3EA was like a family and always busy with people dropping by to say hello. He loved the job there because it was helping people and he put in a lot of hours – so many hours that cynical Nan Ruby came to suspect he had a girlfriend. The two of them never got along.

When I was little, Dad took me on the odd visit to the 3EA studio. The broadcasters sat hunched over typewriters, their cigarette smoke seeping into the grey carpet. The largest groups were the more established European migrants in Melbourne: Greek, Italian, German, French and Yugoslavian. The world, I realised, was much bigger than Australia.

I knew less about Mum and her family. Patricia, or Patsy as she preferred, was born in Penang, an island in north-west Malaysia. Mum grew up in a large Portuguese-Eurasian Catholic family: Nan Ruby, Grandpa Leo, three brothers and two sisters. Of the girls, Mum was in the middle. After one of the sons died, everyone migrated to Australia except Mum and one sister. Mum followed in 1972, moving to Melbourne at twenty-three on family reunion grounds.

Mum's family lived in a small flat near the centre of the south-eastern suburb of Oakleigh, but it wasn't long before some of them went their separate ways. Grandpa Leo returned to Malaysia after he and Nan Ruby divorced. Mum's younger sister, Aunty Madeleine, ended up in Tasmania while Uncle Johnny and Uncle Alex stayed in Melbourne.

In Malaysia, 'Eurasian' is a term for the minority group with European and Asian ancestry in the Muslim-majority nation. Their numbers are tiny: tens of thousands in a population of around thirty-two million. They're colloquially known as rojak, after a popular salad of fruit and vegetables mixed together in a spicy sour sauce.

In Australia, mixed-race people are sometimes called mixies or halfies. When you're half, you never feel whole. We're largely unrecognised in the public imagination, and we're treated as whatever race we look like to whoever is looking at us. Why didn't Australia's mixed race people collectivise and form their own community?

*

Mum, Dad and I lived in a modest cream brick-veneer home in Oakleigh, hemmed in by busy roads, golf courses and quarries. The only oasis was a small public library. All around us the suburbs spoke with the constant *zzzzz* of electricity and the distant *woarrrrrr* of traffic. South of our house, warehouses hummed and tall transmission towers buzzed. To the north was a big intersection with a Macca's, Red Rooster and Pizza Hut, a bus depot and a few petrol stations – the usual suburban wasteland of fast food and fast cars. Dad would drive around squinting at the signs as he shopped for fuel. 'Aiyah,' he'd moan when the prices shot up.

Our neighbourhood was predominantly European, a mix of Italians, Hungarians, Anglo-Australians and Russians. As far as I know, we were the only Asians in our street. At the end of it was a typical Australian shopping strip of red-brick buildings: a milk bar, a bakery, a pizza shop, a hairdresser and a fish and chip shop run by a Greek family who made mouth-watering lamb souvlaki and crispy yellow potato cakes. This was a regular pit stop for truckies who parked on the main road before jumping back in to travel to the sand quarries further to the south-east. Sometimes the trucks tore down our street, much to Dad's annoyance: 'Why they drive so fast?!'

A stroll to the shops with Mum was a regular ritual. She spoiled me, getting anything I desired: mixed lollies in white paper bags twisted at the top, purple Hubba Bubba bubblegum, a Drumstick from the freezer. While I stared at the chocolate bars lined up on the child-height shelves, Mum perused the pastel-toned greeting cards in the front window. When she turned around to pick up a Bounty bar – she was from the tropics, so it made sense she liked coconut – I'd be baring my fangs at her, a minty denture-shaped lolly hanging from my two front teeth.

Mum wore her thick black hair in a neat bob parted slightly to the side, and in the summer she donned colourful floral dresses. She seldom wore make-up or the chunky necklaces, gold chains and sparkling earrings she locked away in a shiny black music box. I used to beg her to bring it out so I could play with the treasures. The jewellery was reserved for special occasions, such as the time she and Dad got dolled up to see their favourite singer, Shirley Bassey, live in Melbourne.

Large limbed, Mum was like a big soft tree that I liked to climb when she was in a good mood. I poked her belly and played with her toes; she stroked my hair and massaged my head and scooped me up in her arms.

Mum was the only person in my family who hugged and kissed. Just once, when I was little, did I see my parents embrace. In the kitchen, Dad stood in his burgundy dressing-gown at the sink when Mum came floating in and briefly put her arms around him. 'Thank you, Narong, thank you.' What Dad had done for her was unclear.

I revelled in attracting Mum's attention. I'd fool around by plucking a pink hibiscus flower from our garden and placing it behind my ear, or crouching down and eating dry pellets from our cat Yo-yo's orange food bowl. After school, I'd run to the couch and yank off my sweaty socks, lifting my feet to my nose and inhaling the fromage aroma with an 'Mmm, yum!', which always put a smile on Mum's face.

She let me run wild, whereas Dad was the stern enforcer of rules, backed up by a thin bamboo stick cut from an overgrown thicket in our backyard.

'You need discipline,' he used to bark. 'I'll send you to boarding school!'

'Don't sit so close to the TV! Ruin your eyes.'

'Don't put your feet on the chair. Smell.'

'Don't play with your belly button!'

Mum's parenting technique was, 'I'll tell Dad.'

I came to fear Dad's bamboo stick, which he kept behind the door of his study. One time I ran off with it and lobbed it next door over the fence.

'Be careful, Narong, don't provoke him,' Mum pleaded with Dad. 'He might run away.' I then learned to say 'I'll run away' as an empty threat so Dad would back off.

Dad was authoritarian; Mum was anarchic. Always out of tune with each other, they never worked towards a consistent parenting style.

Both spoke English at home. Mum would sprinkle in the odd Malay word here and there, though she wasn't fluent. Dad's Khmer was incomprehensible to me and often came in the form of loud, laughter-filled conversations with his Cambodian friends over the phone in his study.

Straitlaced and practical, Dad liked to wear blue-grey woollen cardigans and square glasses, and he shuffled around the house in socks and thongs. In summer he occasionally wore a lime-green sarong, and I dreaded his *Basic Instinct* leg cross on the couch. He used mint toothpicks to fiddle with his gums and carried Quick-Eze in his pocket. His trips to the toilet usually came with an announcement, 'I go pee-pee', or 'I go make poo' as if he were a factory.

His only extravagance was a silver Seiko digital watch that he tinkered with. He was obsessed with keeping time and collected all kinds of clocks: analogue, digital, and brass mechanical ones with spinning dancers. They crowded the mantelpiece, the walls, the shelves, the desks. Decades later, he put one on the toilet wall so he could time his poos. Our house ticked and chimed, but the cuckoo clock was broken.

One of Dad's favourite clocks was a clever analogue piece in a glass square. It displayed the time around the world, including in obscure places like Iceland, Anchorage, Guam and Karachi. Kuala Lumpur was on there, but not Phnom Penh. The second hand was a little red aeroplane that circled the globe.

Dad seemed most at ease when fiddling with his gears and gadgets. He taught me about different types of screwdrivers, from tiny to ginormous, and how to clean battery acid from toys. As part of his radio work, he kept a large reel-to-reel tape machine in his study, and he let me play around with his microphones and cassette recorders.

The locker in his study was bursting with camera gear. I'd been in front of the lens ever since I was in the womb, and he still buzzed around me like a paparazzo.

'Stand there!' he ordered me in Mum's bedroom one day.

'But Daaaaad!'

'Stay still! I check the light.' *Click*.

'But I'm tired. Can I leave now?'

Click. 'Jeh! Stay still!'

Dad took photos at every occasion, no matter how happy or unhappy, or proud or embarrassing. Once he took a photo of me in the lounge room as I screamed and cried like a trapped rabid animal because I didn't want to go to kindergarten.

Mum had been raised Catholic and Dad was Buddhist, but at home my parents didn't enforce any religion. My father's Buddhism was casual. He'd help out the monks in Melbourne now and then, but as a child I didn't see him pray in the house. Because Dad had been educated in the Christian system in Australia, he maintained an interest in Christianity and kept a Saint Christopher magnet in his car for safe travels. And next to the clocks on our shelves sat Christian idols, including a phosphorescent Virgin Mary and a heavy ceramic statue of Jesus, Mary and Joseph. Their vacant eyes were always watching, and I believed they brought bad luck on our family.

By the mid-1980s, Mum struggled to hold down a job. One time she managed to secure work as a cleaner at an aged-care home, but she quit within days; she said the other workers looked down on her.

'Why you throw away a job?!' Dad asked, raising his hands in bewilderment.

Although Mum desired to keep working, she declared herself a proud housewife.

Chapter Two

Mum could be affectionate and loving, but she could also be cruel and strange. I would find myself questioning her love for me and sometimes I even believed she hated me.

'You were a mistake,' she once told me, her words elongated. 'You were a mistake, Jeh-sun.'

She would whisper rude words in my ear and tell me explicit stories that children should never hear. She got excited when she talked about cats and dogs on heat. Updates on the ins and outs of her menstrual cycle came frequently, as did the story about why she couldn't have any more kids, which she recounted to anyone within earshot. 'Mummy's tubes are tied, means no more babies,' she would declare solemnly.

Great, thanks for that, Mum!

One afternoon when I was six, I was playing with my Matchbox cars in the front yard when Mum came out to talk to me. As we stood on our porch next to the cherry-red camellia tree, she broke the news. 'You have a half-sister in Malaysia.'

In normal families, such a life-shaking announcement would be carefully managed. The concept of a new sibling would be gently introduced after meticulous planning. But as was Mum's way, there was no further explanation, and no involvement from Dad. She simply dropped a bomb on me and walked back into the house, leaving me to figure it out.

Perhaps this was how Astro Boy had felt on discovering he had a new robot sister. But my version was all too real, and I was far less enthused.

At the time, all Mum would tell me was that my half-sister's name was Sarah and that she currently lived in Malaysia. I would discover over the following few years that she was a decade older than me, had been born and raised in Malaysia, and lived in the capital, Kuala Lumpur. She was from Mum's previous marriage to a man called Adel.

Eventually I saw Sarah's face for the first time in a photo she sent us. A pretty young woman with short black hair like Mum's, she wore a traditional lime-green outfit and gazed out at me with a radiant smile. Her light brown skin contrasted with my paler features, and we looked quite different from each other. *Who does this girl think she is?*

Sarah – or the image of her – was gatecrashing my solitary life in suburban Melbourne, and I petulantly loathed the idea of sharing Mum with some strange foreign girl. But to my relief, Sarah continued to live in Malaysia, and my daily routine carried on as usual. At bedtime, Mum or Dad tucked me in beside my favourite companion, a white soft toy named Monkey. With wide eyes and an exaggerated voice, Dad called me the Master of the House, stoking my acute case of only-child syndrome.

Mum was often in a mood, and when she was, she walked around the house muttering to herself. 'Fed up, fed up. So fed up.' It was as if her mind were stuck in first gear, sputtering like a broken-down engine. She also used a Cambodian phrase she'd learned from Dad, roughly anglicised as 'tung oss', which means 'to give all of something to someone' – but Mum used the phrase in a way that meant 'too much' or 'fed up'.

When people asked her how she was, she would reply, 'Up and down.'

'Tsk,' she would cluck while sitting on the couch with a vacant expression on her face and one leg jiggling over the other. 'Tsk, tsk, tsk,' she uttered while going about her business in the kitchen. She often seemed disappointed with something or someone.

Our washing machine spoke to her in peculiar ways. 'Jason, it goes *cha-chung, cha-chung, cha-chung.*'

Mum slept a lot. Even on a warm afternoon, she would go to her room and black out the sun with the gold curtains while leaving the door open. And she slept, and slept, and slept. Sometimes she would lie there staring at the ceiling. If I got bored, tired or hungry, I'd shake her arm under the doona, but she would shoo me away. She preferred to hide in the darkness, or maybe her body refused to let her out of bed.

When I had friends over, Mum wandered around the house aimlessly or slept in bed without providing entertainment like the other mums did. This must have appeared weird to my friends, when to me it was completely normal. But I started to avoid inviting them over and instead went to their houses. Their mums would welcome me in and sprinkle me with questions, or we'd go for a drive somewhere nice, or they'd ask me to stay for dinner as if I was part of their family.

One night an Italian friend had a house full of relatives, and their pasta dishes and other delights were steaming on the stove. I sat squashed between them at a table overflowing with food and alcohol. Head down, I ate quietly, overwhelmed and slightly embarrassed by their warmth. I was their guest of honour.

Once, when I was about nine years old, I was watching TV in my room with my younger Cambodian cousin, Nicky. The door was open and Mum appeared out of the blue, completely starkers. 'Nicky, you like?' she asked. I slammed the door in her face and collapsed, crying.

Late one afternoon when I was ten, I heard loud laughter from the front yard. Peering through the sheer curtains in Mum's room, I saw her lying on a blanket in the grass next to the purple magnolia bush, stomach down and heels in the air.

'Dad!' I yelled. 'Something's wrong.' We went to investigate.

Mum's face was flushed. 'Hee, hee, hee,' she chortled, each 'hee' coming out in a gust of air.

'What's the matter?' Dad asked through gritted teeth.

I put up my emotional force field and watched from a safe distance, desperately hoping no one was observing us through our front gate.

Mum ignored Dad and continued to have a delightful picnic by herself in the dying daylight. The joke seemed absolutely hilarious, except the punchline was a secret. 'Hee, hee, hee.'

'Patsy, you are too much,' Dad said with a sigh. 'That's enough.'

Dad was always open about Mum's condition – perhaps he was ahead of his time. 'She has mental illness,' he told my favourite primary school teacher. Perhaps he was appealing for sympathy, for the school to go easy on me. 'She is sick,' he said. 'She had a nervous breakdown.' The teacher replied with comforting noises.

Mum also liked to inform me of this, usually in the third person: 'Mum had a nervous breakdown.' To a child, this was baffling. What had really happened to her? Had she collapsed in a heap, or had her head exploded one day? BOOM! When and why had it happened? No one gave me an explanation, but I witnessed the symptoms.

Mum had a habit of giving things away or throwing stuff out for no reason, and sometimes this had a traumatic effect on me. Once I lifted the lid of the kitchen bin and found a wicker duck filled with potpourri – a gift I'd bought from a school fete for Mother's Day. I was crushed.

Dad told Mum off. 'How could you do this to your own son?'

Another incident involved a new pet kitten, little Monty. One day I was romping around with him when Mum erupted. 'Jason, stop it!' she shouted. 'Jeh-SUN!'

That evening I gently put Monty into a cardboard box in the laundry, forgetting about him while I ate dinner and watched TV. Mum announced she was going out for a wander. An hour or so passed. I went to check on Monty, but his box was empty. Mum had taken him with her and presumably dumped him somewhere.

When Dad came home he was livid, and we hit the streets, shining torches into people's gardens. Through tears, I yelled, 'Monty! Mon-teeeeee!'

Mum refused to tell us the kitten's fate.

In those moments she may not have been herself, but I couldn't tell the difference. Every bizarre act pushed me further away until I was on the other side of an ocean of shame and embarrassment. On the opposite shore she appeared as a blur, waving at me.

The stigma surrounding her illness was overwhelming and utterly corrosive. She was a 'crazy person'. Dad grew fearful about going out of the house with her, because he worried she might lose control in public.

*

When you live in an anxious household, you learn to stay alert. Your toes are curled as you sit on the edge of the couch, waiting for the next disaster. Things will go wrong, as they always do. That's just the way life is.

From a young age, I was aware of the tensions in my parents' marriage. I'd wake up in the dark and hear muffled angry words through my bedroom wall, or I'd be sitting on the kitchen floor while my parents disappeared behind the door, arguing as if they thought I wasn't paying attention. One row made me hide under my desk.

My parents slept apart. Dad had a single bed in the corner of his study. Opposite was Mum's larger room with mustard carpet, a double bed, a dresser and two heavy white wardrobes.

I never questioned this arrangement until one of my older Cambodian cousins, Dit, asked me why my parents didn't sleep in the same bed. His parents did; so did the ones on TV. I took the question to Dad and was sceptical of his answer: 'Mummy make too much noise when she sleeps.' So that was why he preferred to camp out with his electronics and books?

One night I woke to light from Mum's bedroom spilling into the open doorway of mine. Dad huffed out and retreated to his study. At the time Mum kept a rotary phone on her bedside table, and I heard it being dialled. She greeted a close family friend, then said, 'You know what? Narong is an itchy man. A very, very itchy man.'

'Patsy!' Dad barked at her through the wall.

Tucked into the corner of a photo frame in Dad's study was a passport-sized headshot of a pretty Japanese woman, porcelain pale with her shiny black hair done up. Dit seized on this as evidence of an extramarital affair, and one day we confronted Dad about it. 'Who is that woman?' my cousin demanded. 'Is she your other wife?'

'Oh,' Dad said with a sideways smirk, 'she's my girlfriend. I love the Japanese. So *byootiful*.'

My jaw dropped. Surely he was joking.

He certainly had a penchant for all things Japanese, like his Toyota. He raved about buying a Japanese paper room divider, but it was way too expensive, and he dreamed of owning a futon, also too dear. Perhaps he had just snipped the photo of the woman from a magazine.

Out of the two of them, Mum took the trophy for tall stories – or were they?

'What Dad doesn't know,' she told me once, as I cuddled up to her on the couch, 'is that sometimes I take the man from the street.' She had a good chuckle to herself while gazing into space.

Did she mean she secretly invited road workers in high-vis into our house? Was she cruising our street?

I saw no evidence of this, though she did have a male friend who turned up one night on our doorstep. His hair was like Dickie Knee's from *Hey, Hey It's Saturday*, and he wore blue shorts and a white singlet. I answered the door as he stood under the porch light. 'Is your mum home?' He spun a story about going for a run and wanting to stop by, while I eyed his scuffed runners suspiciously.

*

As an only child I learned to entertain myself and was comfortable with solitude, and I escaped the chaos around me by retreating into my imagination. I read books, played in imaginary worlds and took tea with my stuffed animals. Another escape was a Lego town I built on a glass coffee table in the sunniest spot in my room, next to the large corner window with bamboo-print curtains. For hours I'd sit on the warm carpet, constructing an empire that included a TV reporter and live-broadcast van.

My toys were abundant. But as a result of this largesse, everyone in my extended family described me as spoilt, sometimes a spoilt brat, which made me feel undeserving. Perhaps by showering me with almost anything I begged for, Dad was trying to make up for the fact that he was at work for long stretches – usually six days a week, sometimes at night – while Mum was often confined to her bed.

Our ancient television in the lounge room was my de facto babysitter. You could say television was in my blood. As a household, we skewed towards commercial TV, and like many families in Melbourne we tended to watch the most popular network, Channel Nine: *National Nine News* with Brian Naylor, *A Current Affair* and *60 Minutes*. The ABC and SBS were of lower priority.

Occasionally a letter from Sarah would appear in our mailbox. Mum wrote to my sister often, and I came to know her vaguely through her friendly replies. I was too young to write back to her, but on the odd occasion she sent me messages. Her envelopes were badged with exotic-looking stamps of Malaysian flowers and butterflies. *Happy tenth birthday! Love, Sarah*, she wrote in a blue card titled 'For a Special Brother' with an illustration of a campfire scene. Another card read: *Happy belated b'day! Take care and study hard and make Mum happy. Love Sarah.* She was waving to me from across the seas.

Sarah was Muslim, but she sent us Christmas cards, despite her religious beliefs. One year she impressed us by decorating her own card. On the front was a green-and-gold wreath, probably cut from a department store catalogue. At the bottom, a brown teddy bear peeked over some red tartan paper.

Dear Mum, Merry Christmas to you, Narong and not forgetting Jason. I made this card specially for you. Hope you'll have a good time with the family. Take care, luv ya, Sarah. Hugs and kisses from me!

As endearing as these messages were, I kept wondering why Mum cared so much for this mysterious girl from Malaysia. To me she was Suddenly Sarah and remained an abstract concept.

Chapter Three

I was about nine and sprinting for my life, fleeing from my Cambodian cousin, Dit, who was chasing me up the road near his house in Oakleigh. He waved around a worm on a stick, threatening to put it on me. I felt my body rising from the ground like a Qantas plane taking off, the wheels lifting into my belly, as Dit cackled behind me.

Soon the worm would be on my head. Then in my ear. Then inside me, where it would writhe around and lay eggs. Then there would be baby worms in my body.

The lactic acid in my side was building up into a stitch. I turned my head and saw my cousin gaining on me. My legs spun faster, but the hill conquered me. Defeated, I waited for the worm to arrive.

'I'm so proud of you!' Dit hooted.

Proud? I swung around to see his expression of unrepentant glee. But I wasn't laughing, my face red and grim. There was no worm. He'd made it up. Another one of his pranks.

Dit chucked the stick onto the footpath.

'Fuck off,' I spat.

'I've never seen you run so fast!' he said triumphantly, slapping my back.

This was my cousin's idea of improving my athletic performance, not that I was training for any kind of competition. Being an avid runner, he was obsessed with fitness.

I went over to Dit's place frequently. His mum was Aunty Touch, my dad's sister, and Dit lived with her, his stepdad, two brothers and three sisters. Their house had a cream faux-brick facade and sat on Atherton Road near the heart of Oakleigh. It was usually in need of more love, with a hole in an exterior wall or a broken back door. Their Hills hoist in the concrete backyard was rusty and wonky, and we made it worse by swinging on it like a carousel.

'Why don't we ever do this at your house, Jason?' my cousins would ask, accusingly.

Our Hills hoist was pristine. Dad would have killed us if we'd wrecked it.

My cousin's house was loads of fun. Three of us – Dit, Nicky and I – wandered the streets unsupervised, picking fruit and flowers from people's gardens. In summer, we'd sprint after the tinkling gelato van in a fun race then seize our prizes and lick up the ice cream furiously as it dripped onto the footpath.

One day we went on a short adventure to a nearby lake and fished for yabbies. Dit tied raw meat to white thread – pinched from Aunty Touch's garage workshop – and dunked the line into the murky water. Warehouses loomed in the distance as Dit crouched in the long dry grass until there was a tug.

I was stranded at the edge of the lake, fearful of moving any deeper. I couldn't see beyond my feet. 'There might be syringes!'

To my horror, when we got back to my cousins' house, Dit cooked the poor creatures alive.

'You can't do that!' I screamed, as he stood by a pot of boiling water on the stove.

'How else are we going to eat them?' Plop, in they went, making a squealing sound. 'They're screaming!' Dit said with a laugh.

Being older than me, Dit had an aura of influence, and I usually obeyed whatever he said. Nicky was also held hostage.

He forced us to go jogging with him around the wide streets.

'Do we have to?' I grumbled.

'Just to the end of the street,' Dit promised, though I knew he was lying.

Another day we were all playing in the hallway, and for some reason we had a watermelon.

'Okay, now lie down on the floor.'

'Dit, why are we doing this?' Nicky asked.

'Just do it,' he ordered. 'Now, put your arms around the watermelon.'

Lying on the dark brown carpet on my belly, I pulled the round fruit close to me in a hug. On my left Nicky did the same.

'Now, put your other hands under your chins. Open your mouths. Look up and smile.'

He pulled out a camera. *Snap!*

'Dit!' I screamed.

Despite my cousin's gags, I was in awe of him. He was the best at everything. He blitzed us at *Monopoly*, card games, and *Frogger* on the IBM. He was lightning fast at tiggy and pulled off a supreme disappearing act in hide-and-seek. He could blow bubbles from Hubba Bubba, and he pummelled me in the arcade game *Street Fighter* at the mall. His favourite character was the muscular Ryu from Japan, the main protagonist. 'You can play Chun-Li, the girl from China,' Dit teased.

Dit knew all the cool music and taught me how to sing along to Belinda Carlisle and Madonna, and he had a different spin on Roxette's latest hit: 'Listen to your *fart*,' he crooned before pooting one out.

In Dit's bedroom the shelves groaned under the weight of Little Athletics and other trophies with grandiose titles like 'Best and Brightest' and 'Best Male Athlete of the Year', while I only ever won burgundy 'Competitor' ribbons. In tennis, he destroyed me with his powerful first serves.

He was taller than me, his brown arms bulged, and he spent time working on his abs. In the mirror I sized up my pale body and wondered if I'd ever grow bigger. My arms were too skinny, and I had knobbly knees on my chicken legs.

'Come on, I'll show you how to do a sit-up,' Dit offered. 'Lie down on your back with your knees up, and pull up with your stomach.' It seemed simple. As he demonstrated, his torso swung back and forth effortlessly in a metronome movement, but my attempts left me in a panting heap. Next, some stretches. 'Can you touch your toes?' he barked. 'Show me.'

I bent over, my fingertips barely reaching my shoelaces, my belly unyielding.

'Oh my god, you can't even touch your toes!'

To my father, Dit was the standard-bearer for all good Cambodian sons, standing shirtless with his muscly chest puffed out and a gold wreath on his head, the Australian flag flying behind him. Perhaps he would become one of our nation's great Olympians.

'Be like Dit, Jason,' my dad said. 'Why can't you be like him?'

*

On the main street of Springvale, or 'Chingvale' as my cousins jokingly called the suburb because it was full of Asians, Aunty Touch ran her clothing shop. A talented seamstress, she toiled over her sewing machine out the back, creating shimmering sequinned gowns and puffy white wedding dresses. Once she made me a full-body dingo costume out of orange felt for a primary school fair.

Dad and I would drop by Springvale to pick up cans of rambutans and lychees for Mum, or the dried salty sour plums only he liked to eat, which put a cat's bum expression on my face.

In the cramped grocery store with the sticky lino, I eyed the stacks of fake money sitting on the floor: joss paper. 'Dad, can I play with these?'

'No, they're for burning.'

Why would anyone want to burn money? Dad had told me it didn't grow on trees.

My cousins and I were glad we lived in Oakleigh, which wasn't so Asian. We desperately wanted to fit into Australian culture, because that's what the culture did to us: we were expected to strip ourselves of our heritage and put on masks. One time Dit's older brother drove through Springvale screaming out the car window 'Ching-chong! Ching-chong!' at random Asian people. Our loathing of our own heritage went unchecked, and it was folly: even if you were born in

Australia, the culture often rejected you because no matter what you did, you weren't seen as Australian.

'Why doesn't Jason have to go to Cambodian school?' Dit asked Dad as we drove home from Springvale one day. 'It's unfair.'

Dad shuffled in the driver's seat, concentrating on the road.

Unlike me, Dit and Nicky were forced by their parents to attend Khmer classes where they reluctantly learned how to speak and write the curly language.

Dad shuffled some more before eventually answering Dit's question. 'I asked Jason to go, but he doesn't want to.'

I'd fought vehemently against attending the Khmer classes. Being Asian was enough of a curse, and I was born in Australia, so why should I have to learn someone else's language? I was Australian but wore a different skin, and I wanted to avoid being any more of a misfit than I already was.

This must have been embarrassing for Dad, who at the time was producing his Khmer language program on SBS Radio. His gravelly voice travelled over the airwaves into the living rooms and cars of Australia's tiny Cambodian community. Whenever we visited Springvale, shopkeepers recognised him instantly from his voice. And yet his own son barely spoke Khmer.

I could have used the lessons. My Khmer rolled off my tongue clumsily, the English competing to flatten out the Cambodian pronunciation. The Khmer words I knew were 'yes', 'no', 'thank you' and 'let's go' – and 'penis', which my cousins had taught me: 'kdor'. I also knew the word 'kon', meaning 'son', which Dad called me.

My efforts to speak the language were routinely mocked by my relatives.

'Duh rip suah,' I said to them once, trying to pronounce a traditional greeting. Pressing my palms together into the Buddhist prayer pose, I bowed slightly as you're supposed to … only to be met with hysterical laughter from my cousins and aunties.

'It's "chum reap suor, chum reap suor"!' they whooped. 'Do it again!'

My two Cambodian aunties, who saw me as a cute foreign oddity, would grab my cheeks and rub them as if they were trying to start a fire. '*Oi-yoh*, your skin so beautiful, byoo-ti-fool!' Aunty Touch whinnied. 'Like a baby's bum! Ha-ha-ha.'

Dit and Nicky giggled at my woeful attempts at using chopsticks in our favourite Chinese restaurant, where one of the few dishes acceptable to me was bog-standard chicken chow mein. Dad regularly took the three of us there, ordering sizzling steak and whole steamed fish, and occasionally expensive bird's nest. The first time the dish came out, Dit laughed at my disappointment. 'It's not a real bird's nest, Jason!'

Dad's appetite was voracious. He ate anything and everything, even the fish head and eyeballs. 'Are you finished with that?' he'd ask me, salivating over my leftovers.

'No, you can have it,' I'd reply, and he'd hoover them up.

The meal usually ended with banana fritters or fried ice cream. Content and full, Dad would use a toothpick as he repeatedly made a tsk-tsk sound. In Cambodia, you scraped together an existence; in Australia, you had the luxury of sitting back with a fat belly.

Because I was an Australian-born child to a Cambodian father and a Eurasian-Malaysian mother, Dad made exceptions for me. Along with being allowed to skip

Cambodian school, I was always called Jason as opposed to my Khmer middle name, and I had no nickname like my cousins. When I was a guest in Cambodian households, I was even exempt from the Asian custom of removing your shoes at the door.

'Teu Jason ches niyeay Khmer te?' the Cambodians asked my dad curiously as I stepped across a mountain of shoes and sandals while still wearing my white runners.

'Ot ches te,' Dad replied. 'Me vear cheat Malaysie.' Which meant, 'No, he doesn't speak Khmer. His mother is Malaysian.'

Later, my dad explained why I was treated differently: 'You are mixed.'

But my Cambodian cousins put it more bluntly. 'You're too Australian for your dad,' they said. *You're not Cambodian enough.* 'And your mum is white. Look at her! And look at your nan!'

The thought had never crossed my mind, because to me, the idea that they were white was preposterous. Curious, though, I crept into the lounge room and eyeballed Mum, who was sitting on the couch. She had pale skin, thick dark hair with a wave in it, heavily lidded eyes, a pointy nose and rosy cheeks. Then I thought of Nan, with her curly chestnut hair, whom I supposed could pass as European.

The Cambodian cousins were wrong, though – Mum and Nan Ruby definitely weren't white, especially not in the Anglo-Australian sense of the word. While Mum's side of my family had Portuguese, English and French blood further up their tree, they were not continental Europeans: they were Eurasian, born and bred in Malaysia.

And we were definitely different from the families who lived just to the west of us in posh suburbs like Brighton. Those families had pools in their backyards, four-wheel drives, and mums who wore lots of make-up and smelt like fresh flowers when they walked past. They ate Boston buns for morning tea, then sat down for tea again at five or six o'clock in the evening. I glimpsed them at tennis matches where they wore head-to-toe white and lugged large bags overflowing with racquets when my dad could only afford to buy me one.

But if we weren't like them, then who were we?

The Greeks and Italians in Melbourne adorned their conspicuous brick houses with concrete lions, while the extent of our household's Asian-ness was Dad's picture of Angkor Wat and the concrete statue resembling a Buddhist temple he'd installed in the backyard. Sometimes we enjoyed Mum's Malaysian recipes, but we mostly ate chops and mashed potatoes for dinner, and bacon and eggs for breakfast.

My Cambodian relatives cooked mouth-watering sour soups and used pungent fish sauce. They even owned a stool designed to shred coconut flesh; you squatted on it and scraped the coconut halves on a serrated blade between your legs.

Except for Nicky, all of my Cambodian cousins in Australia were plane refugees from Pol Pot's killing fields, and they spoke Khmer fluently. Given Dad had arrived twenty years earlier, he was 'more Australian' than his sisters and their families. 'I'm like a banana: white on the inside, yellow on the outside,' he would joke.

He'd certainly quickly come to relish the Australian way. While learning English at the education department in Sydney's CBD in the early 1960s, he and his gang of five Cambodian boys – the ones he'd travelled over with – had stumbled across a milk bar. The menu board above the counter was incomprehensible to them, but they knew the

French word 'jambon' and consulted their dictionary for an English translation. 'Ham sandwich!' they said to the woman behind the counter, pointing at the board. Over several weeks, that's all they ate.

Later, they'd broadened their tastes after seeing a big billboard with a picture of a meat pie. 'I'm sick of ham sandwiches,' they said in Khmer among themselves. 'Why don't we try that?' On the billboard, a flock of blackbirds was bursting out of the pie crust. 'Yeah, crow meat in a dumpling!' Back in Cambodia, crows were put on the barbecue. At the milk bar they motioned to the dumplings in the pie warmer, then handed over nine pence each. Sinking their teeth into the pastry, they quickly realised the meat wasn't crow, but the salty mince gravy of a famous Four'n Twenty pie.

This was the Cambodian world in suburban Melbourne that I was parachuted into and helicoptered out of. When I went home to Mum, my cousins started their chores and cooked their food because they had to do it themselves. They washed leafy green vegetables at the sink and put on the rice cooker. I was exempt from slogging into the night like my cousins, who sat on the cold concrete floor of Aunty Touch's garage workshop, cutting loose threads from piles of clothes with labels like Country Road and JAG – rich people's clothes that we couldn't afford.

In this world, the older children looked after the younger, and everyone was put to work. The women's roles were in the kitchen, and the men were freewheeling. When you were Cambodian, your duty was to honour your family and protect its name. Above all, obeying your parents was mandatory.

*

Mum's family, with Nan Ruby in charge, was very different. When I made the odd visit to Nan's house, she would offer me Royal Dansk biscuits in a round blue tin. Excited, I would eye the buttery treats sprinkled with coarse sugar, thinking about how many I'd pick. Only one, she would decree, bringing me back down to earth.

In her backyard, brown chickens scuttled around in a wire pen, and birds tweeted in a cage above her doorstep. I was overwhelmed by the aroma from the overgrown red geraniums by the fence and the tantalising smell of curry that often wafted from her neat, spartan kitchen.

Uncle Johnny lived with Nan for years. He'd drop by our house sometimes, heralding his arrival with a ring of his bicycle bell. The dinging and the screech of the front gate always made me jump up to the window. Mum would greet him at the door, crying out, 'How are you?' in Malay: 'Apa kabar?' Her eyes would often seep tears of joy.

Uncle Johnny used to give us haircuts under our lemon tree. He wasn't a trained barber but had learned the skill at boarding school in Malaysia. He would set Mum up in the garden on a vinyl chair from the kitchen while I'd run to the bathroom drawer to retrieve the scissor kit and a white sheet that Uncle Johnny had sewn into a cape. Sitting under the cloth, Mum would ask him to cut her hair 'short, but not too short', and he would oblige. I usually got a crew cut, having been sorely disappointed when Uncle Johnny wasn't allowed to give me a mushroom like Dit's, because Dad thought the style was too radical.

Nan rarely came to our house. On one occasion, while Dad was away, she forced me to gargle salt water because she believed it was healthy and ordered me to swallow strange little pills from Mum's cupboard. I overheard her many tense phone calls with my mother, which usually ended with Mum slamming down the receiver and bursting into the lounge room in tears. Years earlier, Nan had helped Dad get a factory job, but now they clashed, and he later said she'd asked him for money to babysit me.

As I grew older, I realised Nan was a divisive figure both within and outside my family. Some saw her as a heroic survivor of the Japanese occupation during World War II. Others thought her a cold, vindictive meddler. But I felt ambivalent: I found my grandmother odd and distant, and couldn't work out why she acted that way.

My cousins on Mum's side were also distant from me. They lived interstate or in Kuala Lumpur, and I saw them very rarely.

A cloak of vagueness separated me from Mum's family, whereas my boisterous Cambodian cousins were in sharp, colourful focus.

Chapter Four

The TV news was a source of inspiration for my antics with Dad's contraptions. My go-to device was a spare cassette recorder in a worn-out black leather case, which in my small hands felt as heavy as a brick. I carried it around as I waited for the next opportunity to accost an interviewee: the cat, the dog, or Mum while she sat on the couch. 'Say something!' I would demand, brandishing the recorder in her face. Foot-in-door tactics. She'd say something with a wave of her hand: 'go away' or 'get out of my sight'.

One day I had an idea for a whole TV show, albeit on the recorder.

It was 1990, and Treasurer Paul Keating's 'recession Australia had to have' took on a personal dimension for us when Dad came trudging home one day. I went out to the porch to greet him, but he stared straight ahead as if I were invisible, gripping his black briefcase by his side.

'What's wrong, Dad?'

'I've been retrenched,' he replied through gritted teeth.

Five years earlier, Dad had quit the potato chip factory and returned to the appliances factory, where he'd been quality testing fridges on the production line. This was the second time he'd been sacked from the factory because of restructures.

'What?!' I scoffed, not understanding.

'Don't laugh, this is serious,' he said, stomping into the house.

A pit of worry opened up in my belly.

Amid the recession gloom, we all needed cheering up. I summoned Mum and Dad into the lounge room and ordered them to sit at a blue folding table. I hit the record button and fired off a high-pitched introduction. 'Hello, I'm Jason Om, and we're going to interview Narong and Patsy, Jessie the cat, the birds, quails, pigeons, chicken and the duck. Okay, now we're going to interview Narong and Patsy. Where do you live?'

'Australia,' my father replied.

'Where?'

'Melbourne.'

'What do you do for a living?'

'Unemployed,' he said, sounding deflated.

I turned to my mother. 'Okay, Patricia, what do you do for a living?'

'Housewife.'

'Any job?'

'No job,' she said in a singsong voice.

Then I inquired about their ethnic backgrounds. 'A question for both of you. What internationality are you? Narong.'

'Nationality,' Mum corrected.

'Cambodian.'

'What are you?' I asked, turning to Mum.

'Eurasian.'

I wrapped things up. 'Okay, that's the latest update, back to your local scene.'

Decades later, I rediscovered this cassette. It remains the last known recording of Mum's voice.

*

Under the soaring ceiling of the Catholic church, I sat next to Dad in my school uniform. Mum's body lay in an open casket in front of the altar, looking like a million dollars in one of her favourite dresses. On her wrist was a Seiko watch Dad had bought her as a gift.

Empty and detached, I let the service wash over me. As I listened to the priest's words and my piano teacher playing the organ, my eyes were bone-dry.

Nan stood up to deliver the eulogy. Dad was surely better placed to write the speech, but in his grief-stricken stupor he had deferred to Nan.

'And her dog, Spike, will miss her very much,' Nan uttered from behind the lectern. Dad and I didn't rate a mention.

'Evil witch, that woman!' a family friend said to us later.

When the service was over, I jumped in the front passenger seat of the hearse with the coffin in the back. It rained all the way to the cemetery.

During the wake at our house, a procession of Cambodian Buddhist monks in orange robes floated up the driveway and sat cross-legged on mats in the lounge room. Paying their respects, they chanted into the afternoon. I shut out the noise and hid in my bedroom with Dit and Nicky, watching game shows. There was nothing to say, so I let the bright chatter of commercial television fill in the gaps.

That day I buried Mum in more ways than one. Survival meant building a wall around her, along with the bad memories from my childhood. Brick by brick, I hid her from view, mixing a dollop of stigma in with the grout. Part of me was relieved we no longer had to deal with a 'crazy person' in our lives and that the family dramas would surely end. I blocked out the night I'd called the ambulance. I even avoided visiting her grave.

For the next twenty years that wall let me carry on with my life and fill my mind with distractions. The grief and the ill-feelings were contained, or so I thought.

*

Sarah didn't attend Mum's funeral, and after a few months I began to wonder about her. I rummaged through Mum's belongings for Sarah's address and wrote to her for the first time.

Dear Sarah,
I'm not a very good writer because there's mostly nothing to write about. Everything down here is boring.

I have just seen *Jurassic Park* recently. Do they have *Jurassic Park* in Malaysia and have you seen it?

I will be 13 in December this year.

Last term, I was elected class captain. I didn't like it very much because I had to do a lot of things. Next year, I'll be in Year 8.

I have two pets, a cat and a dog named Meldrum and Spike.

Did you hear that Sydney got the Olympic bid for the year 2000?

I collect stickers and *Jurassic Park* cards. I especially like cute stickers with cats and dogs on them.

My dad got me this aerogram, I don't usually write overseas. I have to go now. Bye!

From Jason.

I slipped the envelope into a red mailbox near the milk bar and waited for a reply, but the letter bounced back. I tried again, and a few weeks later I received a letter in Sarah's neat handwriting.

Dearest Jason,
Hi! How are you, boy? Hope you're in the best of health. Sorry I haven't written to you for quite some time. I've been extremely busy with work. However, I have received your second letter recently.

Dear Jason, I know it's your birthday today, I haven't forgotten. I just posted your birthday card two days ago. Sorry if it didn't reach you on time. But I guess it's better late than never.

How are studies? Don't play too much okay? Jason, please send me your latest photo if possible, okay? How is your father? Please do send my regards to him.

Hope you'll have a happy celebration during Christmas. As for me, I'm going to take a few days off and probably visit my father.

Other than that, I'm always busy with work. I'm planning to save some of my earnings until perhaps the end of next year, and perhaps spend my holiday vacation in Melbourne.

We will meet one day, I promise you! Okay, I got to go now, you take care, okay, and study hard?

Regards to your dad, grandma (if you happen to see her), Aunty Madeleine and others.

Love, Sarah.

Neither of us mentioned that Mum had just died, our friendly chatter literally papering over a family cataclysm. Sarah never took that vacation in Melbourne, and she never explained why she hadn't come to Australia when Mum was in hospital, or why she'd been absent from the funeral. We wrote to each other a couple more times, but a distance grew between us.

Nan Ruby and Uncle Johnny also disappeared from my life, yet Dad and I drove past their house every day. Sometimes we saw one of them on the footpath or standing at the bus stop nearby, but Dad never tooted the horn or waved hello. Whenever I probed him about their absence, I was met with a long, morose silence.

Dad, too, put up a wall around Mum. On the rare times when I tried to talk about her, he swiftly shut me down with a grunt. We fell into a strange, lonely void, and a frost spread everywhere.

*

There was nothing in the fridge except leftover lamb chops. Into the microwave they went, coming out black, spitting oil and grease everywhere. They were joined by some potatoes I boiled and bits of cooked-to-death grey-green broccoli.

Dad was out of the house as usual; that night he was working at SBS.

Sitting down at the kitchen table, I sliced into the chops. One piece went into my mouth, then two. Then something caught my eye. It wriggled out of the meat and into a pool of grease. A maggot.

'Fuck!' I recoiled, jumping out of the seat. 'Uggghhh. Eeewww!' I dry-retched and grabbed my stomach. *Oh my god. Did I eat it? Did I eat it!?* I ran for the Mortein and sprayed it all over the plate until it foamed.

Then I rang up Dad. 'There was a maggot in the chops!'
'A what?'
'A maggot. There was a maggot!'
'How did it get there?'
'There must have been a fly!'
'Can't understand how it got there,' Dad said, baffled.
'You need to be more careful.' I was crying. 'Cover it with Glad Wrap.' *Why is everything like this!? Faaarrrk!*

This was the reality with Mum gone. Lonely tomatoes and old lettuce leaves in the fridge. Overcooked food from undercooked recipes.

When Mum used to cook, she would cry out, 'Makan, makan!', meaning 'Come and eat!' in Malay. The kitchen had been full of tantalising aromas and spicy, salty, sugary flavours. Standing on a soft vinyl chair in my bare feet, I would help her make cakes, meat patties and her signature curry puffs. I'd watch her drop plastic-like discs into a pot of bubbling oil, where they unfurled into airy pink prawn crackers.

Dad almost never cooked, and I didn't know where to start. Under the stark fluorescent light in the kitchen, standing on the tiles that no one mopped, I tried to remember what she used to prepare: Milo, Tang, Cottee's cordial, barley water, John West sardines on toast, grilled Kraft singles on toast, Don Strasburg and cheese sandwiches, bread with Vegemite or Kraft peanut butter or Cottee's jam, Heinz baked beans,

Continental packet chicken noodle soup, bacon and eggs, Birds Eye fish fingers, Asian packet noodles, rice, curry meatballs, curry puffs, chicken curry (kari ayam), fishcakes, mince cutlets, lamb chops and mashed potato, canned lychees and rambutans with ice cream, cakes, Aeroplane Jelly, rice or cornflake crackles, and coconut ice.

I tried to replicate the way Mum had cooked, yet my experiments were usually disastrous. I started with something simple: boiling an egg. The stove was an alien contraption, but somehow I managed to get the pot going. The egg came out with a runny yolk, or cracked and jizzed in the water. Sometimes it ended up hard as a rock. Other times I forgot about the pot, distracted by Apple Macintosh computer games or a TV show, and the water evaporated and burned.

'Jeh, the pot!' Dad would yell out.

Eventually I started trying to boil pasta, which ended up either soggy or super al dente. I mixed the overcooked or undercooked pasta with teaspoons of basil pesto out of a bottle. I learned from *Burke's Backyard* that you could dip bread in olive oil because that was how the Italians ate it. Authentic.

I tried to copy Mum's Eurasian curry puffs from memory, but mine were no match for hers. The frozen sheets of puff pastry went gloopy on the kitchen table while the filling of minced meat and potato was heaped in piles that were either too big or too small. The puffs came out of the oven uneven, slightly undercooked or overcooked. I missed Mum's piping hot and golden version.

At least I knew how to use the newfangled microwave that Dad bought. I made popcorn in a bag and zapped pre-prepared meals of grey beef in watery gravy, limp green beans and boiled potatoes.

Dad and I desperately needed help. It was an emergency. Enter Betty. When Dad was studying in Melbourne in the late 1960s, this kindly college librarian had taken him under her wing, and soon became a trusted confidante and de facto mother to him.

Betty was a forthright Jewish woman with thick Coke-bottle spectacles and a curly bouffant. Her husband, Leon, also Jewish, had a thick grey moustache like a giant furry caterpillar. He reminded me of the character Max from the board game Guess Who?

Betty and Leon lived in a big old house in a Jewish area of Melbourne, about a fifteen-minute drive from our place. Our family would often be invited over for dinner, and after Mum died, the visits became more frequent. In the kitchen Dad and I would sit at a table in a cramped wood-panelled alcove with retro floral wallpaper, basking in the glow of light, heat and steam.

Betty's menu usually started with a freshly made vegetable soup and oval slices of rye bread with butter. Pasta or a casserole would follow.

'Now we're eating real food,' Dad recalled me saying.

I would eye the fancy rye bread and wonder where we could buy it. I never saw it at Coles.

Each night in the alcove, two cultures ravaged by genocide came together. After dinner we retired to the lounge room and watched TV in the dark, except for the light streaming in from the kitchen. We pulled the levers on the cushy armchairs and leaned back with our feet up while Betty ranted about Middle East politics. When I got bored, I snuck away and practised on an old piano in the front room.

Betty had a solution for our food woes. 'Now, all you need is a can of tomato soup, doesn't matter what brand it is. Grill the chops, peel and cut the potatoes. Put them in a casserole dish, pour the soup on top and bung it in the oven until it's cooked.'

Good old Betty. She sorted things out.

'You can make a big batch and put the leftovers in here. See?' She opened the freezer, revealing stacks of frosted plastic containers full of food.

We always took home a bounty of Betty's bolognese sauce, casserole and soup to reheat during the week.

After her pep talk, I drew up a shopping list and devised a weekly schedule of meals we could manage. It was mainly pasta and frozen food such as crumbed fish and potato chips. Sometimes we still resorted to the rubbery meat and overcooked veggies of microwave dinners. On Saturdays we took home roast chicken and potato salad from the Safeway deli for lunch.

Later, I became fussy and demanded that we buy brown bread and fresh green vegetables. I'd eaten too much McDonald's and KFC when I was little, I told Dad – that's why I was so undernourished. I needed more meat and veg to be big and strong like the 'wog' and 'skip' boys at school.

Sometimes Dad's relatives would leave metal pots of wondrous stews or soups on our doorstep, with rice noodles, mounds of pickled carrot and cabbage, and crispy spring rolls.

There was grandness in these gestures. Without Dad's family and Betty to feed us, we would have relied on sickly grey microwave meals for the rest of our lives.

Chapter Five

It was yet another gloomy Melbourne day, beckoning me through the thin lichen-green venetians. What was the point of getting out of bed? There didn't seem to be one when your mother was buried six feet under.

Three years had passed since Mum died, and I was in Year 10.

'Jeh, time to go,' Dad said sternly at my bedroom door. He was in his burgundy dressing-gown, dishevelled with sleep in his eyes.

Five more minutes. Need more sleep.

'Come on. We will be late.' Stern voice again.

What's the point of going to school?

I sleepwalked into the shower, brushed my teeth, then put on my Catholic boys school uniform: a grey shirt, grey pants, a forest-green blazer and black shoes. In my wardrobe, a green tie hung in a tight double Windsor knot, permanently done up because I struggled to do it myself. Dad had shown me once: 'Then you do like this, then like this, and then like this,' he'd said, as though demonstrating a magic act. *Why don't I know how to do a tie? What's wrong with me?*

I put on my specs. *Why are my eyes so bad? I wish I didn't have to wear glasses. My genes must be faulty.*

I pulled my black hair back into a ponytail, but I detested how it parted down the middle. The unruly waves refused to obey. *Why is my hair like that? Why can't it be different?*

I looked my thin body up and down. Too bony. *I'll never be as big or strong as the other boys.*

'Jeh, come on, you take too long,' Dad muttered, shuffling away in his thongs.

Why am I so slow? Why am I like this?

Dad warmed up the Camry in the driveway, its exhaust white in the morning chill. Then we took our places as two men in the peak-hour traffic on busy Warrigal Road, ignoring each other, triple j or the ABC news on the radio, all the way to school, past Nan Ruby and Uncle Johnny's house, the sea of red skirts at the Catholic girls college, the Oakleigh overpass and the train station, 'Chaddy' shopping centre, and beyond the old Aspro factory.

My Catholic school sat on two hills divided by a freeway lined with buzzing electricity pylons. In the grove where the sports oval sloped down towards the cars, the bad boys would go for a puff. Next to the oval, a long pedestrian overpass connected the main campus to the second hill, home to a couple of neglected sports fields and the compound where the priests lived.

By the time I arrived, I was fifteen minutes late. The boys were already onto their morning prayers. 'Sorry,' I mumbled as I slunk into class.

Why do I always come late? Why can't I get up earlier? I'm so lazy.

This was now my standard morning routine: a complete character assassination. By the time I sat down and unpacked my books, I was so small I needed no one else to cut me down.

The teachers turned a blind eye to my tardiness. Repeat offenders usually copped a detention, but not me – I served time only once in my six years of high school.

In the afternoons I would be deflated, and sometimes I ended up in the sick bay. The narrow room opposite the assembly hall was run by a Catholic sister, a thin woman with a warm, ruddy face and white hair.

'Did she give you Eno?' one of my friends would ask.

'Um, yeah!'

The joke was that her antidote to all our ailments was to reach for the fizzy antacid drink before even laying an eye on us. Hit in the head by a soccer ball? Quick, get the Eno. Broke your leg on the oval? Here, have some refreshing Eno. Demolishing yourself because you couldn't save your mum? Eno!

When the final bell rang, I lugged my spine-bending backpack down the hill towards the old Aspro factory and plonked myself at the bus stop next to a noisy intersection. I never bothered with the busier bus right outside my school, which was stuffed with rowdy boys, their bodies pressed against the windows.

I took my place in a single seat towards the back as the bus made its way to Chadstone Shopping Centre. 'Chaddy' was said to be the southern hemisphere's largest mall, and it spread like a cancer over the years, swallowing up a nunnery and other surrounding properties.

More schoolboys piled onto my bus at the stop in Chaddy. The older Italian boys sat with their thick legs wide open, fists on their knees. I stared out the window, thinking about the articles I'd been reading in *Voiceworks* magazine.

The journey felt interminable, the bus stinking of an army of teenagers wilting in the summer heat. A couple of times on this route, I happened to see Uncle Johnny either stuck in a throng of schoolkids or sitting near the front. He'd been MIA ever since Mum's death. We never spoke until he got off, scurrying towards the door like it was an emergency exit on a sinking ship.

'Jason.' He nodded as if he hardly knew me.

The other boys stared.

'Mmm,' I managed.

As he alighted, Uncle Johnny chirruped to the bus driver, 'Thank *yoouuu*.'

'Thank *yoouuu*,' the boys on the back seat mimicked, sniggering.

My face burned. I didn't know why Uncle Johnny treated me like a stranger, but I missed him.

*

Like me, my fellow school students were predominantly the Australian-born children of migrants of all different colours. The school was a microcosm of group dynamics and the way racial groups exerted power over each other. In my year, the Greeks, Italians and Eastern Europeans were known as 'the wogs' and outnumbered everyone else – it was a 'wog' school. The second-largest group were 'the skips', but they couldn't even muster up the numbers for an Aussie Rules footy team during PE. 'What are you having for dinner, canned food again?' the 'wogs' would mock the 'skips', because they thought Anglo-Australians were uncultured. The 'gypos' were a smaller group of Middle Eastern boys; other groups included the Sri Lankans and Anglo-Indians and the odd

South American. As for me, I was one of the East and South-East Asians, who were so few in number you could count us on two hands.

Bullies and adult-thugs-in-training came in all different races. On the quadrangle, you could get spat at, tripped, kicked in the shins, punched in the arm, dacked, 'stacked on' or pushed around like a pinball if you weren't careful.

It was the mid-1990s at the height of Pauline Hanson's political prominence when she declared that Asians were threatening to swamp Australia. A time when racist vandals scrawled *Asians Out* on neighbourhood fences. At school, I was called a 'gook' – sometimes a 'fucking gook'. Another word thrown around was 'kinezo', which I learned meant 'Chinese' in Greek. Lots of Australians mistakenly thought 'Chinese' and 'Asian' were interchangeable.

During a volleyball match, a lanky Greek boy muttered 'bloody kinezo' after I missed the ball.

'Hey!' I said, getting right up in his face. 'I'm not Chinese.'

Startled, he tottered on his heels as he suddenly realised that an Asian could understand what he was saying. 'What *are* you then?' he retorted.

My brain whirred. There wasn't a short answer; it was always a mouthful to explain. 'Cambodian-Malaysian and I'm mixed. Eurasian on the Malaysian side.'

'Er, okay.'

At least I didn't have an accent like poor Mrs Chan, who was ridiculed mercilessly in chemistry class, a grown adult cut down by children. I ducked my head, glad not to be the target, a guilty wave of relief washing over me.

I was called other words too.

'Faggot,' the boys barked in class.

'Poofter,' they grunted in the quadrangle, followed by a gob of spit on the concrete.

I felt more like a gook than a faggot or a poofter. The racist slurs stung more because I knew I was Asian – I could see that in the mirror. What I couldn't see so lucidly was that I was gay, even though I'd liked guys since primary school.

Those undetermined feelings stirred whenever I saw one particular boy in my year. His name was David, a Canadian who played hockey and was fondly teased for the way he pronounced water: 'Wah-terrr.' His big brown eyes made me melt, and I admired his gravity-defying black quiff. Dad and I drove past his house every day on the way to school, and I wondered what he got up to in his bedroom. One day, while running late for morning prayers, I couldn't resist stealing a look at him through the window of his home room. His hands were clasped loosely in front of him, his eyes meeting mine. There seemed to be a glint of recognition. Perhaps a knowing look.

In high school, I learned there was a gay vegetable. 'Finnochio' was the Italian word for fennel, and it had a derogatory dimension too: it meant 'faggot'. 'Finnochio' was also the favourite word of a skinny Italian boy, Robbie, who made trouble for everyone, even the poor teachers.

Whenever I opened my mouth to voice an opinion in class, he wailed, *'Finnochio!'* like a town crier. *'Fin-no-chio!'* He sat at the front of class with his amico Nicolo, who sniggered along; they were like the hecklers in *The Muppets*.

When my new textbooks disappeared from the cubbyhole in my desk, I immediately suspected Robbie had taken them. But it could have been any of the various bullies in my class. Mitch with curly blond hair, who shot spitballs behind me, or facetious Dane to my left, or skulking Stavros to my right, who smeared some sort of cloudy substance, probably spit, on my new spectacles when I left them inside my desk.

I stopped storing my things in the cubbyhole and took them home every day. That's why my backpack was so spine-bending when I trudged down the road after school.

The stolen books had to be replaced. 'Why buy second hand?' Dad said. 'Buy them new. Last longer.'

*

After school, Robbie and his acolytes roamed around harassing kids, including my overachieving Greek friend, Dimitrios. He was standing on a backstreet kerb, waiting for his sister to pick him up, when they lobbed missiles at him for entertainment. Dimitrios held on to his backpack, immobilised, the sticks and stones raining down on him until the thugs got bored and walked away.

When his sister pulled up, Dimitrios jumped in the car and shut the door, before breaking down, bawling his eyes out.

'Why didn't you stand up for yourself?' his sister asked, a quizzical look on her face under her bleached-blonde locks.

'I don't know,' Dimitrios wailed. 'I was afraid I'd get into trouble.'

They drove home, Dimitrios's eyes red, his sister's mind ticking over. She decided to call upon the Oakleigh Wogs. They were said to be a Greek gang who tagged the shopping mall and the overpasses with graffiti, marking their territory. They maintained a bogeyman status that struck terror into every child who knew about them – even Dit, who I'd thought was fearless.

Dimitrios's sister knew one of the Oakleigh Wogs, and soon enough Robbie the town crier was rendered mute and laid off Dimitrios.

'She made the bullies go away,' he told me many years later.

I had no such luck. There were no tough guys to protect me; instead, words became my weapon. I couldn't match the bullies' punches – and their punches hurt like hell – but eventually I worked out a way to shut them up.

I turned to Mitch, putting on my most sarcastic tone. 'Oh, have a whinge, Mitch, why don't you?' I dripped with scorn. 'You're a whinger, aren't you?'

He was gobsmacked. Nobody likes being called a complainer. It was enough for him to lay off a bit, knowing I would at least push back.

*

At fifteen I started dating girls, though I knew little about the realities of sex with them.

When no one was listening, I loved belting out Alanis Morissette's deliriously deranged and sweary lyrics. 'You Oughta Know' has a sensational line that probably makes drivers swerve while listening to the radio – a line I didn't understand.

'You don't know what that means?' Dimitrios asked me.

'Nuh, what?' I wondered, truly ignorant.

'She goes down on him.' He laughed nervously. 'She sucks his dick at the movies.'

My mind exploded. I found it hard to imagine the mechanics of this act at the back of a theatre in the Chaddy Hoyts cinema complex.

Our school held activities with a sister school: dancing classes, end-of-year formals and religious retreats. While we all grumbled about having to attend the inter-school retreats, they allowed us to swap our blazers for jeans and T-shirts, and mingle with the girls. The Year Ten retreat, held on the school's second hill, was one such opportunity.

After being split into groups, we were tasked with workshopping the topic of the day, perhaps 'What does it mean to be ethical?' or 'How can we be compassionate?' These religious discussions were never punitive but gentle if earnest ruminations on big-picture themes such as life, the world and personal values.

'I'm Casey,' a blonde girl told me as we sat on chairs facing each other. She was an unpretentious girl-next-door type with a bob of wavy hair and endearingly impacted front teeth. She wore baggy cotton pants and seemed tomboyish.

Towards the end of the retreat, when the girls were about to jump on a bus, I asked Casey, 'Do you wanna hang out? Can I have your number?' I felt awkward as I tried not to stammer, a nervous habit. But Casey said yes, and we swapped our landline numbers, writing them on our hands.

Our first date was a blur. At Chaddy we watched that year's blockbuster, *Twister*, which featured cows flying around in a tornado. For our second date, I suggested that Casey bring her tennis racquet for a hit or two at the clay courts in a nearby suburb. After the first round I was down, and in the end she slaughtered me.

Afterwards, we walked to a discreet section of the park and sat on a bench in front of a clump of large bushes that hid us from the road.

It was time for me to make a move. My very first kiss.

But I was clueless. The kissing I knew only existed on *Neighbours* and *Home and Away*. I'd also seen the TV personality Andrew Denton sucking on the flesh of an orange – apparently that was how actors practised.

'Can I kiss you?' I asked clumsily.

A car went past. The birds tweeted. Casey was waiting.

I was going in for the kill, leaning towards her, when disaster struck. I froze. My eyes fixated on her lips. Her quivering mouth and impacted teeth became the only things that existed; everything else collapsed and disappeared into space.

My mind raced. *What would happen if I kissed her? Would we automatically become boyfriend and girlfriend?* Deep down, I wished she were David.

The moment came and went. The opportunity for the kiss was lost. Casey and I took our racquets and left the park, never to speak again.

But 'picking up chicks' earned kids prestige at my school, and the story of my dates with Casey was doing the rounds. How had Jason managed *that*?

The true story of Casey and the park bench remained secret. And instead of wanting to boast, I felt an overwhelming sense of failure and an unassailable fear that eventually my tsunami of feelings for guys would crash over me.

Chapter Six

Frozen fast-food burger patties would make excellent frisbees, if throwing them across the room weren't a waste of food. Pink and crimped in a factory, the thin discs I worked with at Hungry Jack's were a far cry from the juicy flame-grilled fakery in the menus above the front counter. But knowing the truth never deterred me from wolfing down the end product, tasty morsels dripping in mayo and sauce. They were one less meal Dad had to worry about, and better than the ageing leftovers on the barren shelves of our fridge.

My friend Tanya worked at Hungry Jack's and had helped me get a job there. After school, I jumped off the bus and swapped my green school blazer for a burgundy pinstripe shirt. I tucked my ponytail underneath a hairnet and cap, clipped on a tie, and pinned a name tag neatly on my chest.

Our store sat beside the eight-lane Princes Highway, and everyone worked in unison on the production line to feed the hungry residents of Oakleigh. All of us played our part, from the juniors laying down the pink frisbees on the broiler to the more senior boys at the burger assembly station.

Gooch was the oldest among us; he must have been in Year Twelve or older. I watched his big hairy arms work deftly as he taught me how to wrap up a freshly made Whopper burger. 'That's how you do it,' he said when he was done, pushing the warm parcel down the chute. 'And if you stuff it up, I'll come over to your place and spray Mortein in your cat's eyes,' he added, deadpan.

I quickly got used to the staff's dry humour. At the employee induction, Pete the manager had cheerfully warned us against amputating ourselves accidentally when we lobbed black bags of garbage into the skip. 'The lids are very heavy, and I don't want you coming back to me and saying, "Look, Pete, no fingers,"' he said, wiggling his fingers. 'Cool bananas, everyone?' This was his go-to phrase to gauge whether we understood the gravity of workplace safety – and anything else in general.

At peak times, service was mad. 'Come on, everyone, keep it going,' Pete would yell, egging us on like a football coach. Slouching against the benches was frowned upon. 'Time to lean? Then it's time to clean.' I was fastidious, wiping away the never-ending torrent of sesame seeds that scattered everywhere.

For a while my domain was the brightly lit chicken and fries station, which stood between me and the girls on the front counter. Communicating through a hole in the wall, we felt like spies. The overhead heater partially obscured their bodies and tightly framed their faces.

'Hey, how are ya?' I'd say, trying to chat them up. 'What's your shift today?'

'I think you need to put more fries down in the fryer,' they usually replied.

Everyone at work thought my friend Tanya and I were an item, but I wasn't interested in her. I had a crush on another girl at Hungry Jack's – at least, that's what I thought.

One day at work, I was furiously making chicken burgers when the duty manager approached me. 'Hey, Jason, a couple of people are here to see you.'

I looked up from my oat buns and ranch sauce. 'Who?'

'Dunno. But you can go out, I'll cover you.'

Putting down my spatula, I walked past the fry baskets and slid out the side door into the corridor. The sun was sinking on the horizon, bright yellow light streaming through the restaurant windows. I scrunched up my eyes, trying to make out the features of two shadows waiting by the front door.

'Hello, Jason!' the taller shadow said brightly.

I was stunned – it was Uncle Alex.

'We were thinking of you and heard you worked here. How are you?'

Apparently on the spur of the moment, Uncle Alex, who I hadn't seen or heard from in more than three years, had jumped in his car to come say hello in the middle of my shift. Didn't he realise I was busy? He was like Mum, I thought, a bit 'crazy'.

The shadow standing next to him was a younger man. 'Do you remember me?' he said, beaming. 'I'm Daniel, your cousin. I haven't seen you since we were kids. It's so good to see you.'

My memory whirred. Daniel was Aunty Madeleine's eldest son, and as far as I knew he lived in Tasmania. His father was Vietnamese, he was older than me, and we'd played together once when I was very little.

My neck burned with embarrassment as the girls at the front counter watched me speak to these strangers.

'We really wanted to catch up with you,' Uncle Alex said. 'There's a lot of confusion.'

Confusion?! 'Mmm,' I replied. *Fuck off.*

'Anyway, if you ever want to come and visit, I'm just up Ferntree Gully Road. You know it?'

'Yep.' *Fuck right off.*

'Okay?'

'Okay.'

'Bye.'

As I went back to work I bumped into the duty manager, who raised his eyebrows. 'Who were they? You okay?'

'Just some relatives.'

Since Mum's death, I'd not heard from them. Some of them lived interstate or in Malaysia, making it convenient for them to lose touch. But Nan, Uncle Johnny and Uncle Alex lived in Melbourne so really had no excuse.

I remembered how Uncle Johnny used to cheerfully ring his bicycle bell as he approached our house, and cut Mum's hair under our giant gnarled lemon tree in the backyard. Not any more. Without Mum around, it seemed he had no reason to see me or Dad. We didn't exist to them, and they did not exist to us.

I had no plans to travel up Ferntree Gully Road to visit Uncle Alex in the hills on Melbourne's outskirts. Why would I have done that? There was nothing to talk about and no 'confusion'. Mum was dead, and that was that. I took a deep breath and pushed all my feelings down while watching the fries bubble in the hot oil.

*

Having a job gave me space from Dad, and as long as I was occupied, I could avoid remembering that Mum was gone. The wall in my mind was doing its job. I packed my schedule with as many shifts as I could, working three to four days a week while juggling school, tennis, drama classes and piano lessons. Some days I finished after the restaurant shut only to wake up early the next morning for school. From the highway at night, I was a lone figure against the bright lights, mopping the chequerboard tiles of the ersatz 1950s dining room while 'Mama' by the Spice Girls played on a neon jukebox.

My side hustle was acting, which removed me from the burden of my reality: I could be sailing on a seventeenth-century tall ship one day, crewing a futuristic space station the next. The work came through an agent who specialised in ethnically diverse talent, because in the 1990s people who looked like me were rarely considered at the mainstream agencies.

Audition notifications arrived via Dad's fax machine, and I would venture into the city after being granted a leave pass from school. My first break came in a tiny role in an ABC TV drama series, *Raw FM*. Curiously, the Filipino character I played was also named Jason, and he had a twin sister called Sunny. When the scenes were in post-production, I eagerly waited for the series to air, ceremoniously cutting out every article about the show from *TV Week* and *The Age*'s 'Green Guide'.

In work I found purpose and structure, and felt appreciated for my contributions. There was a tangible outcome to my efforts and a reward at the end of the day. I desired to make the most out of life because I knew how short it could be.

At Hungry Jack's I worked my way up to the prestige of front counter and drive-through, branching out into customer service and becoming the only boy – apart from the duty manager – to face the outside world.

'How come Jason gets to do front counter?' the boys out the back complained.

The front counter became a grand stage where I stepped out into the spotlight. I put on my friendliest smile and learned how to speak to complete strangers. The built-in microphones allowed me to practise orders in my best presenter's voice. 'Bacon Deluxe, no mayo. Whopper, no onion, extra pickle.'

On drive-through duty I projected my brightest voice through the headset and played around with intonation, imagining I was on TV or the radio. 'Welcome to Hungry Jack's Oakleigh, how can I help you?'

It was arguably the best enunciated burger menu in Melbourne.

*

Dad said, 'You can't make money being an actor,' but the jobs I scored were pulling in several hundred dollars for just a few hours' work. My eyes bulged when I opened my payslips.

The money from my jobs was creating a safety net for whatever was around the corner. My chest tightened when I thought about the future. Mum was already gone, so what would be the next disaster?

'Learn to save,' Dad intoned. 'What happens if you lose your job? What happens if *I* die, what will you do then? You never know.' He sounded like a prophet of doom. *What if, what if, what if?*

My money also provided the freedom to buy what I wanted, when I wanted.

Throughout my childhood Dad had scrutinised my music choices, and I'd had to find ways around his strict rules. Perhaps the cartoon cat on the cover of Paula Abdul's 'Opposites Attract' persuaded him it was okay for children – never mind that in the video clip Paula gets together with a hard-partying, cigarette-smoking animal. Later, by some miracle, Madonna's controversial album *Erotica* slipped past Dad, and we sailed out of the store with the CD. He somehow hadn't seen the ads promoting her racy new book about sex. I never played the album when he was home – Madonna moaned too much.

Dad also tightly controlled what I watched on TV, following a literal interpretation of the government-sanctioned classification codes. Movies and shows rated Adults Only (AO) – the equivalent of today's M – were banned in our house. An exception was *Alive*, a movie about the true story of a Uruguayan rugby team who survived a plane crash in the Andes and resorted to cannibalism. 'Teach you about life,' Dad reasoned.

He was unaware I got my fill of AO movies at my Cambodian cousins' house, where we watched *Aliens*, *A Nightmare on Elm Street* and other terrifying films on VHS. 'This is AO – Dad says I can't watch this,' I would tell my cousins, but they'd howl me down, saying the ratings meant nothing.

Dad even rushed to switch off *Neighbours* and *Home and Away*. 'Too many arguments,' he said through gritted teeth. He thought the trite conflicts of Ramsay Street and Summer Bay were creating problems in the home.

'What about the arguments in real life?!' I cried.

As a teenager, while I still had to live by my father's rules, I was free when I had my music on. At night I crept into the lounge room – ignoring Dad as he watched TV – and sat in front of the stereo. Turning my back to him, I put headphones on, closed my eyes and dreamed of another reality. My personal anthem for that era was 'Only Happy When It Rains' by Garbage – the golden age of grunge suited my mood.

'I wish I were like you and your music,' Dad said. 'I can't even whistle.'

*

After my late shifts Dad reliably picked me up from Hungry Jack's, but whenever I thought of him I felt anger as hot as the bubbling oil in the fryers. He was often morose, hiding in his study, or absent, working long hours at SBS Radio in the city.

Dad's peculiarities irked me. His fixation on security, as he repeatedly checked the front gate and door. The way he *poot-poot*-ed his farts around the house, or while seated, lifting his arse cheek to let one out. His literal understanding of idioms: 'What do you mean you can't wait?' His Cambodian-ness and his accent, and the *mwah-mwah-mwah* of his foreign language – why couldn't he just speak English?

In turn, Dad found ways to ignore me while I spoke to him, inspecting the latest catalogues in the mail without looking up, or feeding scraps of meat to our dog at the kitchen table, so the sound of Spike gnashing at them was between us as we ate.

'I got ninety-six per cent on the science test,' I'd tell him. No reply.
Or when I tried talking to him, he'd respond:
'Can't you see I'm driving?'
'Can't you see I'm watching TV?'

All Mixed Up

'Can't you see I'm trying to do a poo – in peace!' (Through the toilet door.)

After my shifts, we usually ignored each other in the car. We were two men facing forward, going somewhere, but we either kept tight-lipped or yelled before sitting in silence for the rest of the journey. Dad would be hunched over the controls, his teeth clamped, his fingers massaging the steering wheel. We reached home, went to our rooms, then woke up to do it all again. For many years that was how we arranged ourselves.

Chapter Seven

'Okay, let's go,' I said to my Cambodian cousin Din, Dit's 23-year-old sister, as I hopped in the car.

I had just stormed out of the house, leaving Dad to brood in his study. It was like talking to a brick wall.

Din wore a Breton stripe dress, her face shining in the dim light of Aunty Touch's rundown gold Mitsubishi Sigma.

'Where's your dad?' Din asked.

'I don't care,' I muttered. 'Just drive.'

The car sprang into action as Din hit the accelerator awkwardly. 'Ha-ha-ha. I can't even reach the pedals!'

'Oh my god, are we going to be okay?' I said, looking over at her pregnant belly.

'It's fine.' She leaned forward to extend her legs.

I sank into the passenger seat, glad to be driving out of the suburbs towards the city lights.

I had saved up a whole fifty dollars to see my favourite band, Deep Forest, live in concert. The new-age world music outfit was travelling all the way from France to Melbourne on their first Australian tour, and this would be my first time at a gig.

But on the night they were playing, after I showered and dressed up, Dad had other ideas. 'You're not going.'

'What?!' I shouted. 'What do you mean?'

'You're out of control. That's it.' He wandered off to his room and shut the door, refusing to drive me into the city.

Didn't he understand that Deep Forest had come halfway across the world? Didn't he know how important the concert was to me?

I was determined to find a way there, but I knew I wouldn't make it in time if I caught public transport. A taxi would have cost more than the concert ticket. So I called the next person I knew who had a car.

What did Dad know about music anyway? He had no rhythm. No verve.

Din pulled up near the venue as traffic began banking up on the Princes Bridge in the city centre. As I got out, she agreed to pick me up around ten.

A wall of silver-haired men in blazers and women in shawls blocked the entrance – the well-heeled time-rich demographic who went to see 'the arts'. I made my way through the throng, feeling conspicuous, a lanky Asian teenager with a ponytail coming to indulge in culture and not steal handbags. I'd dressed up, smelling sweetly of Lynx.

The Melbourne Concert Hall was posh. Its concrete exterior was brutalist in design, but the interior was a plush contrast of gold leaf, brushed red carpet and soft lighting that made the mirrored surfaces gleam like treasures in an Egyptian tomb.

I sidled along a row close to the stage and took my seat among a sea of white hair and white faces. There would be no thrashing about in a mosh pit that night.

The lights dimmed and everyone applauded as Éric Mouquet, Michel Sanchez and their ensemble appeared with benign smiles. I eased into a night with my favourite band, feeling like this was compensation for everything that had gone wrong.

When 'Sweet Lullaby' began, a melody of churning water, pan flute samples, and a mother singing in a foreign tongue to her child, I stifled a whoop of joy and redirected the energy into my feet, which tapped to the beat. Closing my eyes, I felt like the child being rocked in his mother's arms, and when I opened them again, Michel Sanchez seemed to be looking me in the eye. This performance was for me and no one else. The world disappeared. Dad disappeared. Or I wished he would disappear.

'Of course you're a burden,' he'd said.

Had that been lost in translation? Did he understand the hurtful meaning of the word 'burden'?

'You're out of control.'

Yes, I spoke back, but my grades were decent. Drugs and drinking were not my thing. I listened to world and classical music, not Metallica. Prim and proper.

When the show was over, I loitered around the entrance until Din returned in the bomb, now carrying my younger cousin, Nicky, and her friend Angela.

'How was it?' Din asked.

'Awesome! Can I go see the band afterwards? I really want their autographs. Meet me out the back.'

My stomach giddy, I waited outside the stage door with one other hardcore fan and a bouncer. The two long-haired Frenchmen emerged with benevolent smiles. They scribbled messages for me on a Deep Forest postcard: *Amities! Dear Jason! For Jason!*

I left the Concert Hall beaming, chest out, a kick in my stride. Au revoir, Deep Forest, au revoir!

Din drove us back to the suburbs along the Princes Highway. Lit windows in apartment blocks. Tram lights. The Deep Forest postcard glowing in my hands.

When we reached the Oakleigh cemetery, we stopped behind a car turning right into a side street. Din's eyes were fixed on the rear-view mirror. 'Oh god, oh god,' she murmured. 'Oh my god.'

'Aaaahhhhhhhh!' I squealed, thinking she was joking. I kicked my feet in front of me excitedly.

Then B-A-A-A-A-N-G.

A slow roar, the scrape of metal against metal. It lasted five seconds but felt like an eternity. Seatbelt tightening around me, my body pushed forward like a crash test dummy, a smoky metallic taste in my mouth as if a gun had been fired.

What the fuck just happened?

'Is everyone okay?' was the first thing I said when the car stopped shaking.

I turned to the back seat where Nicky and Angela were struggling with their seatbelts. 'Yeah, yeah,' they muttered, grimacing.

We tumbled out of the car, Nicky and Angela hobbling like bent paperclips. Petrol began pooling on the asphalt under the wrecked boot. The old bomb was totalled.

'Stand back, stand back,' I warned the others.

A tall man emerged from the car behind us. His bonnet was barely smashed. 'I'm sorry,' he said. He was completely out of it, probably wasted. I wanted to yell at this dickhead, but I bit my tongue.

'It's okay,' Din said quietly. 'It's okay, it's okay.'

'No, it's not okay!' I snapped. 'We could have died! We could have burned!'

We ended up at the nearby Oakleigh cop shop, housed in an Art Deco building.

Din turned to me in the foyer. 'Why did you make that sound in the car?'

'Dunno. I didn't think you were serious.'

'Oh.'

*

I was the last of the four of us to leave. I gave my home phone number to a cop behind the clear perspex at the counter, then waited on a plastic seat to be collected. The foyer was beige with nothing to look at except the cop moving around behind the counter. He had nice firm arms. I admired the shape of his strong back and broad shoulders while he spoke to a colleague out the back. Something stirred inside me.

Dad appeared outside the glass entrance. His face was igneous rock, with magma underneath. He refused to come inside; he couldn't front the officer.

I followed him to the Camry, parked out front. One word between us, 'Shame!' More of a violent grunt than a word.

I tiptoed across the nature strip into the front seat. Dad's gritted teeth. Jaw clenching. Silence all the way home. Deep Forest postcard in my hands.

I slept badly, and the next day Dad and I didn't speak to each other. That afternoon, I went to make lunch and realised the fridge was empty.

'Why is there no food in the house?' I huffed, slamming the fridge door.

Dad entered the lounge room and sat on the couch, clearing phlegm in his throat.

I pulled out a pot, filled it with water, and whacked it on the electric stovetop with a clatter.

'Jeh!' Dad barked.

I tried to work out the dials. 'We never have anything to eat!' I cried. More clattering. Slamming of cupboards. I rummaged for a packet of San Remo spaghetti.

Dad kept clearing his throat. He was facing the TV, so I could only see the back of his head.

I barked at him over the kitchen counter. 'Why?' I shoved the spaghetti into the pot while the water was still cold. 'Why is everything like this?!'

'Learn how to cook!' Dad rumbled. Dad was standing up now, turning to face me as my pasta slowly sank into the tepid water.

'You can't learn if no one teaches you,' I snapped.

'Jason! I will disown you! I. Will. Disown. You!'

We yelled over each other.

'You are not my son!'

'What do you –'

'Not my son!'

'– mean I'm not your son?'

'I disown you!'

Chapter Eight

At school, we'd been asked to start thinking about our careers and organise work experience placements. A future of daily grind and adult responsibilities seemed like an eternity away, but because I was good at writing I had a vague idea that I might become a journalist.

My school had no connections with the media industry, but I had the most obvious link: Dad. Up until then, I'd paid little attention to his SBS radio work because it was in Khmer. The path into mainstream journalism was as opaque to me as it was to the career counsellor at school.

I ended up being assigned three days' work experience at SBS, housed in the Australian Ballet Centre at Southbank. I'd been there a few times with Dad, and every time we passed the small entrance, we stopped and said hello to the receptionist. 'Remember Helen?' Dad would say. 'She knew you when you were little. Even before, when you were in the tummy.' I'd smile politely without any recollection, and Helen called me a '3EA boy'.

Helen helped run the admin office, and that was where

All Mixed Up

my placement would be, not the radio or TV newsrooms. I wouldn't be working with Dad.

When I turned up on my first day, the first thing I noticed was how clean it smelt – no more chain-smoking like in the old days. Computers had replaced typewriters, and the number of foreign language groups had expanded from forty to sixty-eight.

Very quickly I became so efficient that they ran out of things for me to do. I twiddled my thumbs until I was introduced to the Melbourne TV news bureau. Soon I was out on the road with the journos and the camera crew. The first time, they did one interview and then picked up lunch at a cafe. Seemed like a pretty easy gig.

The second job was with the sports reporter, and we headed to a press conference at the North Melbourne Football Club. While I followed tennis – always watching the Australian Open with Dad, who sat calmly with a crossed leg even as the crowd erupted in elation – AFL was of no interest to me. I saw it as a rough team sport played mainly by Anglo-Australians. At school, I couldn't kick a footy to save my life.

We arrived at the manicured oval and went deep inside the spartan change rooms, empty except for the media. As we waited for the players to arrive, the crews from the various networks set up their lights and cameras. Most of the microphones were placed on a small table in front of a bench where the players would sit. I was given the fluffy boom mic to hold while I crouched below the cameras.

The three players being interviewed filled up the space, a wall of muscle and blondness in blue-and-white stripes. My eyes were level with their powerful legs. I held the boom mic out as the questions began, my arm sore within moments. The big men spoke the language of sport, a drawl of monosyllables and jargon.

The boom pole began leaning onto the table of microphones. *Pull up, pull up,* I thought. I pulled and pulled, but the pole snagged on a tape recorder.

Click. The stop button pressed down.

I froze. The press conference was ruined for whoever owned that recorder – they would miss the crucial, life-changing events of AFL. A legion of fans would riot in the streets. But if I alerted the journo, would the blame fall on me? Would I be thrown out?

I acted like it hadn't happened. From the scrum, an arm, then a head, slowly poked out next to me. The journo pressed the record button.

My neck burned as I waited for a barrage of expletives, but he didn't say anything. We packed up and returned to base.

*

As I explored the world of journalism, I learned I would need to build up a portfolio of work. Through my acting jobs, I already had some knowledge of TV production, as well as an ease in front of the camera. That was drama, though, not journalism.

Few writing opportunities existed for teenagers, but one way of getting published was through the letters pages of *The Age*. I started sending in my views on topical issues, and sometimes my hand-drawn cartoons to the public callout section.

An editor called up once to verify my letter; she probably had to check the unusual surname to make sure I wasn't a crank. 'You write like you're twenty-five years old,' she told me, which made my heart backflip.

Several of my letters and cartoons were published, and I lovingly cut them out for my portfolio.

In my final year at school, I proposed reviving the student newspaper, which had been out of circulation for years. With the backing of my teachers, we published a small run of two editions on a photocopy machine. Dimitrios was a co-editor, and we spent a few hours each day after school working on the submissions and laying out the pages in QuarkXPress.

*

By Year Twelve I had assembled my own crew: an Indian-Singaporean, a Filipino, and Dimitrios the Greek. On Saturday nights we went cruising from nightclub to nightclub along Chapel Street, dressed up to make ourselves look older. A black suit from Roger David and a collared shirt were all I needed to sail past the burly bouncers.

Dimitrios was the only one of us who owned a car, bought with savings from his department store job at Chaddy and a contribution from his folks. A second-hand bronze 1988 Mitsubishi Magna with boxy edges, it lumbered along like a tank. But there were no complaints from us as we crawled at a snail's pace with all the other teenagers who thought sitting in a traffic jam was the coolest thing to do.

Winding down the windows, we would crank up Dimitrios's mixtape, a collection of commercial hits dubbed from his sister's CDs. His favourite song was a remix of Tori Amos's 'Professional Widow'.

We'd egg him on. 'Do a burnout, Dimi! Burnout! Burnout!'

'I'm not going to do that, it'll wreck my tyres.' That was our school captain speaking.

We were in the wrong part of Chapel Street for burnouts anyway. That section was near KFC, where the hoons hung out. '*Chapoooool*,' they barracked. Unlike them, we cruised like the good Catholic schoolboys we were, checking out the high heels and short skirts on the footpath amid the glare of headlights and the stink of exhaust fumes.

One night we decided to head out of the city and go for a drive around Port Phillip Bay. We hit the coast-hugging road that led back to the south-eastern suburbs.

'Let's go somewhere, anywhere.'

'Yeah, let's go!'

'I know a place,' Dimitrios said, putting his foot on the accelerator.

The red and white lights of the Melbourne skyline sank behind us as we ventured towards the unknown, the charcoal expanse of the bay stretching out to our right. To our left, row after row of white-cubed mansions – the homes of the bayside bourgeoisie – scrolled past, the darkness interrupted only once by the blaze of a service station.

After passing long stretches of coastal heath, we turned down a narrow side street that led to a yacht club. Dimitrios parked the tank, and the four of us jumped out and stood under a white streetlight. In the cool breeze we scanned the lights of the Rialto Towers and the West Gate Bridge, which appeared like faraway stars.

The place we'd landed was Half Moon Bay, a name so romantic it seemed fictional – and it was the name of a place in my favourite sci-fi fantasy novel, *Obernewtyn* by Isobelle Carmody. Suddenly I felt like I was the protagonist, Elspeth, standing wistfully on a peninsula, wind in my hair, staring into the abyss of the squid-ink horizon.

'This is where my dad comes to fish,' Dimitrios explained. 'We spend ages out here in his boat.'

No wonder his dad was so weathered, with deep lines in his face. From 2 pm to 2 am they would bob around on the bay, hunting red snapper, whiting and flathead. While waiting for their next catch, they conversed in Greek about what was happening at school, or about the goings-on in their extended family. When night came, they watched the stars, figuring out that the fast-moving lights in the sky were satellites.

They were two men bonding in a small boat that floated near the wreck of HMVS *Cerberus*, a navy vessel scuttled as a breakwater after being decommissioned in the 1920s. In Greek mythology, Cerberus was the three-headed hound that guarded the gates to the underworld.

My dad and I never did such things.

As I stood with my crew under the streetlight, my mind meandered towards the uncertainty of the future. There were widespread fears that because of the Y2K computer glitch, planes would fall out of the sky and nuclear power plants would melt down. The world was ending, and soon I'd end up like Mum. My head throbbed. *What if, what if, what if.*

'Let's go,' I said. 'There's nothing here.'

We piled into the Magna and re-entered the cultural desert of outer suburbia. Soon we arrived at a large roundabout near a level rail crossing.

'Weeeee!' Dimitrios squealed as he turned the wheel, the tank straining on the curve. We tilted, and the world became lopsided.

Weeeeee ...

We were going the wrong way.

'What are you doing, Dimi?'

'I'm going around the roundabout.'

Weeeeeeeee …

'We're supposed to be going home.'

'I know.'

Weeeeeeeeeee …

On the second time around, we erupted into whooping. We went around a third time. Then a fourth. By the fifth, I could barely breathe. My ribs were about to burst.

'What if the cops come?'

'Yeah, the cops?'

'Doesn't matter.'

'Keep going! Keep going!'

Skin pulled back, eyes shut tight, my face was screwed up in joy, the face of a spaceman in a centrifuge. Around and around we went.

Weeeeeeeeeeeeeeeeeeeeeeeeeeeee …

We exited the roundabout and crossed the train tracks with smiles on our faces and our heads spinning, the wide open road in front of us. I was totally breathless.

*

Towards the end of high school, I bumped into my crush, Canadian David, on the bus home. His black quiff was now tinted with flame-coloured highlights. 'Hey, it's Jason Om,' he said with a dreamy smile.

'How's it going?' I mumbled.

'I'm moving back to Canada.'

'Oh,' I said, trying to hide my disappointment. 'Why's that?'

'I'm going to play ice hockey.'

Giddy, I thought of running after him, packing my bags for the land of the maple leaf. 'So, is that forever?'

'Um. Yeah, for a while.' He smiled again.

The bus pulled up at his stop near the quarry, opposite the Macca's.

'See ya,' he said, hopping off.

'Bye.'

The door closed.

*

I sat on a kerb under the red-and-yellow Hungry Jack's sign, waiting for a lift.

'What are you going to do when you finish Year Twelve?' asked Jen, one of the front counter girls, who was sitting next to me on her break.

'I don't know.' I suddenly felt drained. 'I've looked at lots of courses. I'll apply for a few and see what happens. But I really want to get into journalism.'

Mandie, the senior manager, saw us from the drive-through window and came out for a smoko. 'We were thinking of making you a manager,' she said, in between puffs.

'Oh,' I said. 'I didn't think about that. I wouldn't know how to do it.' *Manager? Me? No, no, no. As if.* It was too much responsibility.

'Don't worry, we'll give you training and everything,' Mandie said, still puffing away. 'There's a course you can do. It's also more pay.'

Did the future really start *here*? Was I proud enough of the HJ's uniform to wear it for the rest of my life? Maybe it was an option. Like Dad said, take what you can get. At least the job would be a fallback if everything else went to shit. Everything always did go to shit, so I guessed it was a good opportunity.

'Anyway, have a think about it,' Mandie said, walking inside to prepare for the busy dinner shift.

Turning back to Jen, I sighed, stroking my ponytail. 'I don't think I'll ever get into journalism.'

'But you don't know,' she said gently. 'You haven't even tried.'

*

My last exam was Maths Methods, a subject I'd reluctantly chosen after Dad explained it would allow me to apply for science courses. With minutes to go and a pang of regret, I filled out random numbers, assailed by anxiety.

You couldn't save your mum. You will fail.

But my VCE score turned out to be decent, and I applied for arts courses and the coveted journalism degree at the Royal Melbourne Institute of Technology. It was the top course in the nation – RMIT handpicked only thirty or so lucky students each year from hundreds of high school graduates around the country.

The traditional path into the Australian news business was through cadetships, or going straight from high school into a bottom-rung job. Many journos of that era would tell you how they fell into the industry by accident, or started as gofers running errands in newsrooms. By 1998, when I graduated from high school, there was a push to professionalise the trade and require journalists to have a university degree. This had a huge impact on the types of people entering the industry, which was already largely white and would now also become the domain of the middle- to upper-class echelons.

To enter RMIT, I had to compete against students from the posh suburbs and elite colleges, the kids who wore boaters and tended to have higher marks than me. My score sat just at the cut-off, but it wasn't the only prerequisite. An entrance exam – testing general knowledge, news trivia and writing skills – whittled out the weak. If you passed that, you went through to an interview process. I passed.

Because of my letter writing and work on the student newspaper, I thought I was in with a good chance, and I proudly brought my portfolio to the interview in the city. In a small room, two interviewers – a lecturer and a journalism student – scrutinised my efforts with upturned noses. I'd practised answering all the questions I expected them to ask, but was unprepared for the most basic: 'Why do you want to be a journalist?'

I shifted in my seat, rattling off a half-arsed story about how Dad worked at SBS.

'So you want to be a journalist because your dad was a journalist?'

'Um, ahh,' I tongue-twisted.

'I don't think that's a good enough reason,' the lecturer said snootily.

Couldn't they see my burning desire and absolute determination to be a journalist? Hadn't I ticked all the boxes?

Soon after, two letters arrived in the mail. One was from RMIT: a rejection. The other was from Deakin University: an acceptance into an arts course at Burwood in the outer suburbs.

Chapter Nine

After missing out on RMIT, I began my first year at Deakin University on the cusp of the millennium. I wasn't going to give up on journalism easily, and figured the arts course could still land me a career in that world. I'd bide my time, taking the bus from Oakleigh, past Chaddy, up to Burwood – my axis in the suburbs wouldn't change.

As I attended classes at the tiny Deakin campus, which was dominated by a white tower popularly known as the cheese-grater building, my mind was freed from the narrow parameters of high school. I encountered fresh concepts such as Othering, which helped explain the racism I'd faced, and a new view of religion as a human construct.

During this time I continued to date women at my own peril, testing the veracity of my gayness. In one of my tutorials, a woman with long curly brown hair caught my attention, and we went on a date at the Chaddy Hoyts cinema. I rolled my eyes at the film, unable to engage with its absurd storyline and cheap special effects. Then I looked over at my date in the darkness of the theatre, the light bouncing off her face, and felt deeply uneasy. I was a fraud.

All Mixed Up

She drove me back to my house while I tore into the film. When she pulled up at the front gate, she kept the car idling. I quickly jumped out, avoiding any opportunity for a kiss, and went inside. From the front window I spied on her as she drove off. I felt guilty for misleading her. I saw her again on campus, but ignored her.

It was time. Time to overcome the denial that was eating away at me. Time to acknowledge all the desires I'd vehemently suppressed. David the Canadian. The cop with the nice arms. The photos of champion swimmers in the school annual. The music video in which a pair of manly legs playfully teased Fiona Apple while she bobbed around in a bathtub. The guy with a cute smile who goofed around playing pool in the rec room at uni. The dirty late-night movies on SBS in which men coalesced in the darkness under bridges on the Seine. Even as I waited for naughty pictures to download over the dial-up internet, pixel by pixel, and then printed them off on the ink-jet while I worried about wasting too much colour, I tried to ignore all of the evidence.

*

I met Kavindi when I struck up a conversation with her during a campus orientation tour. She would later tell me that when she first laid eyes on me, she thought I was 'one of those handsome guys too stuck up to speak to anyone else', but with her silver cargo pants and black-and-white Skechers, I reckoned she was cool. A Sinhalese Sri Lankan from the outer suburbs, Kavindi worked casually in the inner city as a go-go dancer at Dome nightclub – she busted a move in the techno room on Asian night. With me in my black puffer jacket and hair gel, the two of us were as thick as thieves around Burwood.

'You're a mixie!' she said to me. 'I knew it the minute I saw you.' Other Asians sensed these subtle racial ambiguities.

Eventually we set up a music show at the student radio station, which wasn't really a station because it didn't broadcast beyond the main student building. We put our CD collections together and DJ-ed from a glass booth in the rec room, playing a mixture of grunge, electronica and R&B. Third Eye Blind rubbed against Lauryn Hill many a time.

I began dropping not-so-subtle hints about my gayness, testing the waters with Kavindi.

'That guy's pretty handsome.' I nodded towards him as he grinded to Blue Boy against the pool table in the rec room. 'I think he likes our music.'

'What?! You think he's handsome?' Kavindi's mouth was agape. She wasn't yet joining the dots, but at least her response wasn't disgust.

I trusted her instinctively, and after my disastrous date at Chaddy I decided to confide in her. We were at my house, about to trek into the city for a dinner date with a friend, when I plucked up the courage.

'You're *gay*?' Kavindi said, mouth agape again. 'Are you sure?! Are you *sure*?!'

I held back tears. 'Yes, I just told you. We better go, we'll miss the bus.' If there was going to be this much fanfare every time, I'd want to run back into the closet.

Kavindi picked her jaw off the floor, and we walked to the bus stop, sitting on a bench a nose length from roaring traffic. As we waited, my heart thumped, and my mind galloped with anxiety. I'd just taken a huge psychological leap into the unknown, and I didn't know when I'd reach the bottom. There would be no going back. This was my world now – the real world where the truth lived. Smiling through gritted teeth would become less of a reflex.

But what if, I fretted, Kavindi secretly no longer wanted to be my friend? What if I'd never see her again?

As we stepped onto the bus, the evidence was before me: she wasn't running away. She sat next to me, then on a train into the city, then at dinner, and stuck with me on the journey for many more years.

Eventually I would have to tell Dad.

*

At the end of my first year at Deakin, having built up even more journalism experience, I had a second go at RMIT. Again I passed the exam and secured the interview, and again I rehearsed my answers, but now I had better knowledge of what questions to expect.

This time the two interviewers seemed more amenable. As we wrapped up, they asked whether I had anything I wanted to add.

'Yes,' I said, smiling. 'I've applied for this course once already, and if I don't get in this time, I will keep coming back, just so you know.'

'Righto,' the lecturer said. 'Great to hear.'

The letter of acceptance arrived in the mail. After I opened it, my heart burst with happiness. I walked quietly into the kitchen and announced the news to Dad.

He sat in silence at the table. Then he murmured, 'That's good.'

I went to my room, knowing this was all I'd get from him. Balloons wouldn't be falling from the ceiling any time soon. But as I held the letter in my hands, reading it over a few times, I savoured the moment. I'd done well, and from that point I knew my destiny lay beyond the suburbs.

The course was three years, but I ended up studying for three and a half, going part-time to work as an editor on the student newspaper.

RMIT gave me a firm grounding in theory and practice. It had its own student TV station that broadcast on community Channel 31, and radio studios that aired the news on Triple R, a station that broadcast around Melbourne.

The staff taught us to be hard-nosed journalists: 'foot-in-door tactics' and 'not taking no for an answer'. My favourite tenet, though, was 'do not presume anything, and always ask if you don't know something'. Some journalists make the mistake of being too smart by half. How can you pursue the truth if you prejudge the facts?

The importance of the media as the fourth estate of democracy was drilled into us. We would hold the powerful to account and give them hell while standing up for the public. As we read the *Herald Sun* and *The Age* with black ink smudging our thumbs, we all laughed at the idea of digital news taking off. Mobile phones were text-only in chunky pixelated fonts.

I discovered that not all of my fellow students had needed to fight to make it into the course – and some took it for granted. When asked what they wanted to do after graduating, they would tilt their heads back as if they were thinking about what to have for breakfast. One of them said, 'I don't really know, maybe journalism isn't for me.'

'If you don't want to be a journalist,' I said, 'then why are you here?'

They snorted as they left the room.

*

In my second year at RMIT, 2001, I moved out of home to a share house in North Melbourne to escape from Dad and be closer to uni. I also started going out with my first boyfriend.

The first time we kissed, I was sitting on a swivel chair when he pulled me towards him, the chair rolling across the carpet, our lips smacking. Such assertiveness was a revelation. This was the furthest I'd got with anyone, and the kiss felt weird and gross and exhilarating. I later broke down in tears in my boyfriend's arms, which probably made him run a mile because the relationship was over within months.

I'd grown up being called a mistake by Mum and ignored by Dad, so feeling desirable was exciting and new to me. But some gay men, I would soon learn, were scared of intimacy. They were still caught up in a world that rejected them, a world in which any kind of acceptance felt abnormal. Constantly being told 'you're not good enough' was a comfort to them, because that's what they were used to. But my denial of my sexuality was falling away, and I felt lighter.

Two years had passed since I came out to Kavindi, and it was now time for me to tell Dad. The stakes were high, but the risks were low. When I was a teenager, he'd threatened to disown me over my disobedience, and the chance of being thrown out of the house – over anything – had seemed very real. Already disobedient, and not Cambodian enough, I was an imperfect son. I'd thought of ways to leave and where to go if I were ever forced out. It had never come to that, but beneath my denial I'd known that telling him I was gay would open up that risk. Now, at twenty, I had work. I had money. I had my share house. I was safe.

My coming out to Dad was planned with military precision – when you're primed for disaster, you're quick with survival plans. All the scenarios were thought through. I had already run tests on my gayness, and I was absolutely sure that it was part of who I was.

Dad had just dropped me back at North Melbourne after a weekend visit to his place, when I broke the news. We were in the kitchen, and he gripped the back of a chair. I braced myself for yelling and the word 'disown'.

It didn't come.

'But we sent you to a Catholic school' was the first thing he said, as if the Catholic Church was the height of moral authority.

Then he went quiet, standing like a statue.

'It's not a phase,' I told him before he drove back to Oakleigh. 'This is who I am.'

'Okay,' he murmured, with the smile of a prisoner about to face the firing squad.

A few months later, Dad and I were sitting in our family doctor's office. I wasn't feeling ill, but Dad had said we should go for a check-up, and I hadn't wanted to make a fuss.

'So, your dad tells me you are a gay?' Dr Wong said slowly in his Chinese accent. *You. Are. A. Geh?*

My father had just left the consulting room.

'Yes,' I said. 'It's not a phase.'

Dr Wong sat behind a glass-topped desk with charts underneath, a jar of rainbow jelly beans to one side. He wore a blazer and had thin unruly hair and big square spectacles, which made him look like a nutty professor. His practice was in a converted suburban house.

What I liked about Dr Wong was that he prescribed us antibiotics without a fuss and avoided over-diagnosing our variety of ailments. But I was starting to dislike him as he lectured me on safer sex.

'Well, be careful because the lining of the anus is *very* sensitive,' he imparted.

'Well, of course I would use a condom if it came to that,' I said.

'Good.'

Had Dad arranged our appointments that day with the hope there could be a diagnosis for his 'sick' son? Did he wrongly think that being gay was a mental illness, and that I'd got 'gay' from his 'crazy' wife?

*

My wall around Mum had been holding up well, despite the occasional crack here and there. Whenever that happened, I held my breath and patched it up. But in 2002, my third year at RMIT, I was at the cinema when a scene of a mother lying in a coma transported me back to the ICU and my wall suffered a major structural collapse. I immediately ran for the entrance, leaving my second boyfriend baffled. 'Are you okay?' he asked, but I brushed him aside. In an alcove on the street, I choked and blubbered, the words to explain myself struggling to come out. All I could comprehend was that my body had reacted involuntarily, and like everything about Mum, it didn't make sense to me.

I began thinking about my sister again. In my last years of high school I'd stopped writing to her, and she hadn't tried to keep in touch either. I'd felt that losing Mum had been painful enough to deal with, especially as I was a growing teenager, and decided I had no time for a half-sister whom I'd never even met. My goal had been to push through Year

Twelve without dwelling on my loss. But now I wanted to get back in touch with Sarah, and I managed to re-establish contact through a Malaysian cousin. I was twenty-one; Sarah was thirty-one. Email was around back then, but she still penned letters.

> I heard you've been trying to reach me. Well, here I am! I've been wondering about you too. It's really amazing how we know each other, but we have never even met. It's like getting to know some celebrity or a public figure. I think it's about time that we really get to know each other. I mean, it's really nice to know that I have a brother in another country (even though of a different father, we came out of our mother's womb). I would love to see you and get to know you better. Having a brother of a different background, religion and belief system is really something unique.

We agreed to meet in person for the first time. I discovered that Sarah was living in Melbourne on a scholarship for her PhD in design; she later told me she'd decided to apply partly because it might provide a chance to make things right between us.

We arranged to meet on the steps of Flinders Street Station. When I arrived at the grand sandstone-coloured arch beneath the green dome, I scanned the afternoon commuters for her familiar face. Under the clocks, as the crowds buzzed around me, I took a deep breath as I approached the woman I knew from the photo my mum had given me. 'Sarah?' Her black hair was longer and wavy around her neck. Up close, she had the same rosy face as Mum and was plump like her.

Sarah's head tilted upwards as she held the straps of a small backpack on her shoulders. 'I can't believe I finally get to meet you,' she said, looking awestruck.

There was no dramatic hug or emotional soundtrack. We didn't break down in tears. We simply slipped into an easy rhythm as if we were old friends. I knew of a nice cafe up Swanston Street, so we crossed the busy intersection, going past the Young & Jackson pub while the trams dinged. As we strolled along the crowded footpath, I leaned over to Sarah with wet eyes and a sudden realisation. 'This is what Mum would have wanted,' I whispered.

Mum didn't live to see the day her children, born into two different cultures, bridged the immense divide to finally meet each other. The childish recriminations of the past dissipated and I was ready to accept Sarah for who she was, my sister.

I led Sarah upstairs to the cafe, and we took seats at a bench by an open window overlooking the lawns of the State Library. Over a teapot of freshly brewed chai, we discovered we were both in creative fields and had common interests in art, graphic design and nature. Sarah explained she was married and had a son who was only a few years old – my family was expanding as we spoke. I revealed to her that I was gay, having come out to Dad the year before, and she told me she was Muslim. But sitting there that day, I felt we were the same.

During that first meeting and over the years as we grew to know each other better, Sarah never failed to ask me, 'What was Mum like?' She was desperate to squeeze out any details of the life she'd never had with Mum.

'Um, I don't really know,' was my weak response. I struggled to express myself because my memory was blank.

Although cracks were beginning to show, the wall still did its job. Kind words escaped me amid my confused feelings about Mum, the shame and embarrassment of her illness coming up again. By the age of twelve, I hadn't yet been mature enough to get to know her deeply as a person; to me, Mum had spoken gibberish a lot of the time.

But Sarah's question needled me. I kicked myself for being unable to answer it properly.

Soon after our first meeting, I visited Sarah in Malaysia over the summer break and met my brother-in-law, Hammad, and three-year-old nephew, Ayman, an impish boy.

My life in Australia fascinated my brother-in-law. He'd heard about Pauline Hanson and wondered whether all white Australians were racist. 'We call them "gweilo",' he said, using the colloquial word for white person.

'Some are, some aren't,' I replied optimistically, 'but we do have a racist history. We had the White Australia policy and almost wiped out the Indigenous people in a genocide.'

Malaysia had its own difficulties with race. There were tensions between ethnic groups: the majority Malays, the Chinese, the Indians and the Eurasians.

I didn't know whether Hammad knew I was gay, but I talked freely to Sarah about my boyfriend back in Melbourne. During a trip to a tropical island, I drew his initials in the sand next to mine in a love heart before the waves washed over them. Outside our rundown cabins, flooded by mosquitoes and ants at night, Sarah and I sat on the damp sand and watched the sun go down. A muscly Japanese-looking guy in black shorts was chest-bumping the crashing waves. 'What do you think of that one, eh?' Sarah said, nudge-nudge, wink-wink. I was becoming familiar with her smiling face and gentle jibes; she was playful and affectionate.

I laughed. 'Yeah, he's a bit of an *orright*, as we say in Australia.'

In Muslim-majority Malaysia, homosexual acts were illegal, but the law seemed to have little bearing on my sister's attitude to me. Sarah seemed more open to me being gay than Dad was. As we sat on the bed in her cabin, we shared secrets like a brother and sister would.

*

During uni, I had no shortage of work. I was overloading myself again. *Keep moving, don't stop.* As well as the editing job at the student newspaper, I worked in market research casually, and I was a reporter at SBS Radio, filing digital audio pieces for the *Whatever* website and later for the youth show *Alchemy*. I clocked in at the Australian Ballet Centre, then at Federation Square when SBS moved into its shiny new offices.

Dad had long finished at SBS, having lost his job in my final year of high school. Three times in his working life, he'd been sacked. It felt strange to be following in his footsteps unintentionally. He had no desire for me to do so, and pulled no favours. 'I don't want what happened to me to happen to you!' he cried.

But my opportunities would be different, and it felt like home. I'd grown up at SBS. Some of the other foreign language broadcasters – Thai, German and French – remembered working with Dad fondly; they treated me like family and would come round to the *Alchemy* area with warm smiles. 'Oh, Narong's son!' they would say.

I kept working for *Alchemy* until my final year at uni, when I started applying for cadetships. I would have killed to secure a coveted ABC cadetship, but in 2003 the national broadcaster suspended the program because of twenty-six million dollars in budget cuts. That left *The Age* and SBS. Like everything in journalism, the competition was fierce, and hundreds of people around Australia applied for both. SBS had just three TV cadet positions.

I was twenty-two when I graduated uni with distinction in 2003. I also won a university award that year for my radio studies. Dad came in to pose for graduation photos, and we waited in the atrium of RMIT's garish Storey Hall, the epitome of Melbourne architecture. The entrance resembled a cave, painted in bright lime-green and purple, with a cladding of green geometric shapes that spread to the top like barnacles. I thought it was stunning.

My favourite lecturer, Doug, came sailing across from the hall to say hello. He was a former ABC Washington correspondent.

'Mr Om, so nice to meet you,' he said, smiling as he shook Dad's hand.

My face burned as Doug heaped praise on me – I always felt embarrassed when people said nice things about me.

'You must be so proud of your son,' Doug said.

It suddenly felt like we were at a media conference, the lights and cameras in our faces. I glanced at Dad's expression, which was the usual: no expression. The whole room seemed to fall silent, waiting for his answer.

'Come on, Mr Om,' Doug repeated. 'Mr Om?'

The cameras rolled. The crowd was hushed.

Dad's reaction may have been silence, or a murmur, 'Mmm.'

We posed together for photos, standing side by side in front of a backdrop. In my black gown and pink sash, I held a certificate tube as a prop and smiled as best as I could.

The ceremony, which included all RMIT graduates, was held at a football stadium. After the pomp and light show, I took my certificate and walked around the crowded stadium with Dad. On the far side in the stands, away from the action, we took photos with my Sony Cybershot. They came out a little blurry.

Up until that point he'd said very little, as was his way.

'How are you feeling?' I asked nervously.

Another of Dad's long pauses.

'Yes, I am proud,' he whispered.

*

My heart was in broadcast, and I knew my chances of getting an SBS cadetship were strong: I was already in the organisation, and I smashed all the boxes.

I made it through to the interview and audition stage, and flew up to Sydney. The panel quizzed me on my general news knowledge. Then they tossed me a curve ball. 'What's the toughest thing you've faced?'

I took a deep breath and paused.

I was weighing up whether I should tell them about Mum. Would it appear sleazy if I did? Was I prepared to open up about something so deeply private, something I didn't even discuss with my own father? How could I take a brick from the wall without letting everything on the other side come flooding back? I realised that although the interview was going well so far, I had to throw all my might at it and clinch the prize. Journalism was my destiny – I was determined to make a go of it. I could no longer wait my turn.

'Losing my mum at twelve years old, and seeing her die.'

Silence. Blank faces all round. I stared back at them. I bet they hadn't had many candidates talk about loss and grief, but I hoped they sensed my honesty.

Not long after the interview, I got the call. I packed my things to move to the big smoke, Sydney, in 2004.

Chapter Ten

My new home in Sydney – all twenty-four square metres of it, in a Depression-era apartment block – was a short walk from the beating heart of the gay community, Oxford Street, and not far from the famous Wall where sex workers waited for their next clients. That year, though, I would live like a monk, having broken my boyfriend's heart by leaving him for the job, something I immediately regretted when I arrived. But with even more distance from Dad, I felt that Sydney allowed me to be whoever I chose to be.

The rent in Darlinghurst cost me more than a quarter of my humble cadet's salary before tax, and the basic living expenses ate into my savings. Sydney was a never-ending drain, but that was the price you paid to simply exist in a place locals believed to be the centre of Australia. For those who wanted to make it in journalism, this was where it was at. The next stop was London or New York.

The two other cadets in my year were white women. I would be one of four Asian journalists in the SBS TV newsroom at Artarmon on Sydney's North Shore. The most famous of them was living legend Lee Lin Chin, who presented weekends. She'd float around the office in her famously edgy outfits, including a padded red jumpsuit, and we chatted at the photocopier, printing off scripts. Other times, we'd have drinks after work, talking about poetry.

There were few other Asian journalists on TV across all the networks. Some of the networks would have had zero. In 2004, you could count us on your fingers. I would go on to develop a sixth sense for other Asian journalists in the Australian media – a kind of racial gaydar. You could echolocate another Asian journo from a mile away. Their faces stood out, and I would remember their names as they grew in number throughout my career.

The SBS cadetship took me far and wide, with postings at *Insight* and *Dateline*, back to the Melbourne bureau, and onwards to Canberra in an election year, John Howard vs Mark Latham. My short stint in the press gallery at Parliament House would fall outside the campaign, but it was an exciting foray into federal politics.

I was unaware of any other Asian journalist in the gallery – I may have been the only one at that point. Asian Australians were also underrepresented in Parliament, with only two that year, both senators: Liberal's Tsebin Tchen and Labor's Penny Wong.

Catapulted from my upbringing in the suburbs into Australia's seat of power, I walked the polished parquetry hallways in awe. At the same time, I felt disconnected from the place, and the gallery seemed too cosy with the politicians. This world seemed eons away from the one I grew up in, and out of touch with my dad's experiences.

Life-changing decisions were made on our behalf in the corridors of Parliament. The front lawns were designed so the Australian people could walk on top of their parliamentarians, a symbol of equality, but how could the politicians in this place speak for someone like me or Dad – or my Cambodian cousins, who weren't as politically aware as we were? Like many ordinary Australians, they lived in the wake of events rather than being able to shape them, and became engaged only at the ballot box every election cycle. Parliament needed to be more reflective of the people it stood up for, and to resonate with them more deeply, not just in terms of race but class too.

You could take the boy out of the suburbs but not the other way around. I couldn't escape my working-class roots. My folks were migrants who'd started out with factory jobs, then Dad had created opportunities and become a respected SBS broadcaster.

Sometimes in my job, as I rubbed shoulders with the political and cultural elite, I felt like I'd fallen out of a wormhole. Dazed, I would think, *Why am I here? How did I get here?* Some may have seen this attitude as a lack of confidence, but I saw it as humility – gratitude for what I had worked hard to achieve, and a recognition of all the obstacles I'd faced.

*

In 2005, I offered to film and produce a two-part feature on the preservation of Cambodia's ancient temples, which were threatened by neglect, mass tourism and the elements. I was twenty-four and visiting Cambodia for the first time on a part-holiday, part-assignment for SBS.

Dad came with me, helping to translate.

Cambodia revealed itself to be a nation of beauty and wonder, a land of sleeping stone faces and spectacular temples built by the ancients.

At Angkor Wat, the world's largest temple complex, I filmed with my video camera among the ancient stones of the famously magnificent Bayon temple. Monumental sleeping faces carved from stone loomed all around in timeless permanence, as if they were connected to the stars and the universe. This was a sacred site. At the small entrance to the main tower, my hosts from the heritage authority led me up a dusty metal scaffold. In the darkness, without harnesses, we clambered towards the bright light of the sky. Once outside, we perched at the top and looked about us. Like an adventurer, I was exploring what it meant to be Cambodian, and suddenly, I felt a connection to this beautiful landscape.

But this beauty was set against a backdrop of violent atrocities. As a Cambodian, how was it possible to hold your head high while knowing your country's past? How could you be proud of a culture that had turned on itself?

At the Choeung Ek memorial in the capital, Phnom Penh, the Khmer Rouge genocide was a dark feature of the tourist trail. Inside an elegant golden-roofed stupa, the dusty skulls of hundreds of individuals – their names unknown – were displayed in glass cabinets. A short walk away, old mass graves were marked with signs in Khmer and English:

86 mass graves. 8985 victims.

Mass grave of more than 100 victims. Children and women whose majority were naked [sic].

Mass grave of 166 victims without heads.

It went on and on in gruesome detail. I took snaps on my Sony Cybershot while wanting to throw up.

But the most disturbing place we visited was the Tuol Sleng Genocide Museum. Tuol Sleng had been a high school that the Khmer Rouge converted into a prison known as

S-21. At least twelve thousand people had been tortured and killed there.

Dad and I toured the light-brown chequerboard-tiled classrooms that had become torture chambers. Old bed frames and metal dishes were rearranged neatly in a tourist house of horrors. Haunting black-and-white photos of the victims stared back at us. Men and women of all ages wearing dark prison uniforms, and children, including toddlers, their eyes vacant, uncertain, their fear imperceptible behind blank expressions.

It was astonishing to think that my own living Cambodian relatives – my uncles, aunties and cousins – had avoided this fate, only to return to Cambodia decades later as tourists and take photos of their long-dead counterparts. Escape the genocide, return for a holiday selfie.

Walking around S-21, I felt chills bolt through my body. In one of the empty crumbling classrooms, I felt a presence, a creepy energy that made me dash into the corridor. I was a non-believer, but if spirits were real then they existed in that prison.

The visit reminded me of the Holocaust, of Rwanda, of the Balkans, and of the Stolen Generations. Each vile disgrace was different, but the intentions behind them were the same: people had wanted to wipe out others because they were different.

Everyone knew about the Holocaust, though. Everyone knew the number: six million Jews and countless others, including gays and lesbians. Two million was the official Cambodian number, but it was thought to be much higher. Bodies unaccounted for. People still missing.

Justice for the Cambodians was painfully slow. Nearly forty years after the Khmer Rouge took power, only three regime leaders had been jailed for life for their crimes. As for Pol Pot, he'd been put through a show trial in 1997 and sentenced to house arrest in his jungle home, only to die of heart failure – or so authorities claimed – less than a year later.

My childhood self-loathing of my heritage fell away, replaced by a solemn respect. Why didn't the whole world get up off its arse and shout for Cambodia? Why was there so much buck-passing? My mixed blood boiled at the treatment of my ancestors. The Cambodians' horror at the genocide should have been shared by everyone. We must never forget.

*

As a young journo, to get anywhere in the industry I needed to be on the road with my head out the window and the wind in my hair. That's where stories would be broken. I eyed the ABC with envy, a friend describing it as the holy grail of journalism. Certainly, a halo of prestige hovered over the national broadcaster. Right after I'd graduated from uni, the front door had been closed, but in 2005 a side entrance was pushed ajar. Whispering in a corridor, a colleague told me about a reporter's job going at the ABC in Adelaide, a city I had never visited and knew nothing about. Management was headhunting young talent from other newsrooms around Australia.

I applied and got the gig. I would again be uprooting my life.

Some thought I was crazy. Hell, *I* thought I was crazy. But when you're twenty-four, you can indulge a devil-may-care attitude.

At my farewell, a large crowd wished me well around a table in the centre of the newsroom, and I suddenly felt sad I would be leaving. They gave me a fancy pen and an oversized SBS-branded soccer jersey.

'There's still time to make a counter offer,' I joked.

In his office, my boss called it a sideways move. But I was hell-bent on breaking into the ABC – a mainstream broadcaster with a bigger audience and room to move. And I wanted to avoid becoming a stereotype at SBS.

From Adelaide, my plan was to return to Sydney and claw my way up the ladder. But I had swapped my life in the big smoke for an ageing and overwhelmingly white state, and as the plane descended in South Australian airspace, I thought, *What the hell have I done? Is it too late to withdraw my resignation?*

It'll be an adventure, I told myself firmly, the plane touching down with a skid. *Come what may.*

The ABC was housed in a tall brutalist building that stuck out in the middle of suburban Collinswood. 'The dream factory', as one presenter called it, satirically.

My desk was part of a bank of desks shared with the East Coasters, a bunch of other young journos – all women, some ethnically diverse – brought in from interstate. We sat in the centre of the newsroom. 'It's so they can watch us,' one of the others said, ominously. In front of me was the radio news desk; to my right, the glass booths of the small radio studios; behind me, the state political reporters.

What I hadn't realised when I'd signed up was that I was walking into a bloodbath. We'd been brought in off the back of a wave of redundancies, with losses of mainly long-time and much-loved staff.

'You came *from* Sydney?' one colleague said, eyebrows raised. 'It's usually the other way round.'

One of my first stories involved a food-poisoning outbreak, and on my twenty-fifth birthday I stood watching a truckload of spoiled smallgoods being dumped into a skip on a hot summer's day. The pile of slippery skins and processed meats glistened like The Blob. This was what reporting on the road meant.

I decided to make a go of South Australia – I would build enough experience for the return ticket to Sydney, break some stories and make a name for myself.

I bought a bright red Vespa and spent long afternoons waxing, polishing and caressing my ride's Italian-engineered curves. The maximum speed on the dash was eighty kilometres, but I could never push the engine past seventy, the needle on the speedometer struggling. In Adelaide, there were few major roads over sixty k, so it didn't really matter. I cruised the streets in sunnies and an armoured black jacket, feeling butch as I went wine tasting, foraging at the Central Market or shopping for vintage furniture.

Butch is a state of mind, and I soon discovered that the prospects for gay life in Adelaide were limited, especially for an Asian guy. I had swapped the smorgasbord of options in Sydney for a city with a paucity of gay bars, the most famous one being Mars Bar, a basement nightclub in a nondescript building on Gouger Street.

I'd generally avoided the meat market in Sydney, preferring to go out for the occasional drink, so it was Adelaide where I spent my prime rib years. Standing in bars, I became more aware of my Asian-ness, and the general indifference towards me where I would be the only Asian in the club. Later, when dating apps became popular, I would find that vague dissonance morph into the open hostility of 'not into Asians'.

In these hypermasculine spaces, I found myself making the same irrational comparisons I'd made when I was in high school, sizing up the bigness of Anglo and European guys against my smaller frame. While I was the fairly average height of five foot seven, I was lean, and taller and beefier guys would find ways of hiding me from the bartender when I stood behind them. My nose would sit at their armpit, their swagger taking up lots of space. Some men were built enough to generate their own centre of gravity, pulling in other guys like minor moons. All those meat and potatoes when they were young.

Like a scholar in a tweed jacket with patches on the elbows, a straight friend offered me his theory about the laws of male attraction. 'Women are small, and men are big,' he reckoned, while smoking an imaginary pipe. 'Gay men are attracted to men, so they are attracted to bigness. So Asians? Well.' In the gay economy, Asian men were effectively women who other gay men, apparently, had no use for. It was absurd.

I recalled a documentary I'd happened to see on TV in my final year of high school. *China Dolls*, a groundbreaking project about the gay Asian experience in Australia, had revealed to me a hidden world. The director, Tony Ayres, reflected on how racism in the gay community placed Asians at the bottom of a sexual hierarchy. That idea shook me up at a time when I was grappling with my own sexuality. As I watched in my darkened bedroom, I realised that if I came out, that was the world I'd be stepping into – a similar world to that of my high school, where a lower role was assigned to me, only more brutal. How could I possibly find a date?

As I went out and about, going to bars and parties and socialising with other gay guys, I found myself in the middle again – too assertive for the men who wanted submission and to fetishise me, too delicate for the men who wanted brawn. It took me ages to realise that I was my own person, and that I needed to seek out people who would desire me fully. But in that conformist world, it was bloody hard.

Eventually I too began to conform, using the chameleon superpower of accentuating my Eurasian-ness by growing a beard so I could be seen. My invisibility cloak disappeared, and other gay guys, and people in different contexts, stopped ignoring me.

'Asian with a beard, how did that happen?' guys would wonder.

'I can see the Portuguese in you,' they would say.

But I also came to realise that the *China Dolls* theory is unhelpful and outdated. It had reinforced my lack of self-worth in the period before I came out, and I'd carried it with me for too long. The theory was depressing, and only true if we accepted that role at the bottom of society. If we wanted to be treated equally, I figured we needed to be rid of the idea. It had been imposed on us by others: *That's where you belong.* We could choose either to keep our heads down – according to how others expected Asians to behave – or to stand up, speak out and support each other. There was no point in avoiding rocking the boat if there was nowhere for us to sit on the boat in the first place.

I had discovered that racism was the gay community's dirty little secret. While we banged on about inclusion, we couldn't ask others to accept us when we didn't accept our own. How could we let our own members feel belittled and derided in our bars and clubs and neighbourhoods?

Chapter Eleven

Infinite blackness. Then a faint sliver of light broke the gloom, gradually becoming brighter. It emanated from the centre and then outwards into a blur of colours and shapes. A phone was ringing, the type you hear in an office. There were voices, distant and garbled, of people giving orders and answering questions.

Suddenly a nurse appeared by my side. I'd been in an accident, he said. Concussion and a few bruises. I was lying in the Royal Adelaide Hospital with no memory of the events leading up to that moment. My brain felt like a flat battery, the synapses failing to fire. The bed began to move, and I was transferred from the centre of the ward to a more discreet area behind a curtain.

At least I remembered the year was 2006.

That morning I had left for work on my red Vespa as usual, a short ride up a hill. I wore a white shirt and grey suit pants, protected by my armoured black motorcycle jacket. I was just metres from home when, turning a corner, the scooter slipped. The right amount of grease on the road had conspired with a touch of rain on a hot dry day. What happened next was blank.

Adelaide was a small world, and by coincidence a connection of an ABC colleague was behind me and called the ambulance. My beautiful Italian was badly damaged and needed major repairs.

Outside the hospital window, it was already night. I'd been unconscious for about eight hours.

'Wonderful things, brains,' a friend would later say. 'Your head blocked out the trauma.'

Friendly faces arrived, many of them colleagues, and stood around the hospital bed. I vaguely remembered their names. I asked them for a copy of *The Advertiser* so I could catch up on the news, but as I started to read an article I felt an overwhelming sense of deja vu. 'Wait a minute, I've already read this!'

Only minutes earlier, my friends said, I had done just that. A few times.

I peered down at the article again. 'Wait a minute, I've already read this!'

They were horrified. To test my memory, they asked me who the prime minister was, and I answered correctly: John Howard. 'Still!' I hooted, back when prime ministers lasted longer than two minutes.

My brain was rebooting, much to their relief.

I was discharged on the same day, collecting my shredded suit pants and scratched helmet. My friends drove me out of the hospital as the ABC news came on the radio.

'Hey, I know that voice!' I said.

'Yes, that's Peter Wilson.'

'Oh. Peter. Wilson.'

'Yes, you work with him.'

'Oh! I work with him. Yes, I know. Peter. Wilson.'

Alone in Adelaide, I slept on my friends' couch. They came downstairs every hour or so to tap my hand, checking that I was still conscious. When I returned to work, I walked into a radio studio to read news bulletins. I stared at the panel of buttons, then the computer and back at the buttons. Nothing. My brain failed to register what to do. I panicked. Peter Wilson was nearby, and limped over. Slowly the rundown sharpened in my mind, and I presented the bulletins that day with my usual decorum.

As I explained what had happened to my memory, a colleague recalled a friend suffering concussion once: 'She was never the same again.'

Before I was discharged from the hospital, I was put through a scanner and the doctors gave me a clean bill of health, but I worried about whether the bump to my head would have a long-term effect. *What if my brain started bleeding? Had a few screws come loose? Or had some memories been wiped from the hard drive of my mind?*

Work called Dad to tell him his son had been in an accident. He decided to stay in Melbourne. It was yet another strange reaction from Dad, which I did not question.

'My parents would never do that,' the same colleague said, clutching her chest.

Dad would later shrug at me. Work said I would be fine, so I would be fine. Injured and admitted to hospital with temporary amnesia, but fine. Did not lose a limb and was not in a coma, so fine. Just the usual rough and tumble of life. Maybe if I were in a morgue, he'd bother to fly over.

'He did the same when I was in a car crash as a teenager,' I told my friends. 'No reaction.'

I'd learned not to fret over such things, but I couldn't help but feel that this time something else was going on. We'd made great strides in our relationship, bonding during our trip to Cambodia the year before, yet now we seemed to face another setback. His stony silence when I shared stories of being gay in a spirit of openness gnawed at me. I was forced to read Dad's mind again. In the vacuum of information, I speculated he didn't rush to my side because he was ashamed I was gay.

After coming out to him, I thought our relationship was ticking along. We carried on as father and son, but in truth we were going through the motions. As the years went by, his struggle with my sexuality revealed itself again and again.

'This is not a phase,' I repeated. 'It's like being Asian, that's how I am. You can't choose either. Who would? Why would anyone want a lifetime of marginalisation?'

*

As I grew apart from Dad, Sarah drew nearer, and Malaysia was calling me back. Sarah was now divorced from Hammad and was about to remarry. I didn't blink when she invited me to attend the wedding in sultry Kuala Lumpur. It would be my third trip to Malaysia. On a sunny afternoon, we gathered at my new brother-in-law's family home opposite an overpass and a yellow-domed mosque. Sarah was stunning in a traditional white gown and hijab, the tips of her fingers dipped in henna. A make-up artist had come to her house to transform her, and I'd watched her get ready. This was the first time I'd seen her in a headscarf.

The artist was a 'he/she', as Sarah described, a surprise to me in a Muslim-majority country.

'They're widely accepted in the bridal industry,' Sarah explained.

Away from the festivities, she'd pulled me into a bedroom and explained she would now wear a hijab permanently in her everyday life. To me, her earnest 'warning' felt overly dramatic and totally unnecessary, but I understood she felt the need to include me in a significant change that carried a lot of meaning for her.

The wedding was also the first time I was introduced to Islamic rituals. I was given a songkok hat and a baju melayu, a white loose-fitting silky suit partnered with a blue gingham cloth wrapped around my waist. 'Is this all okay?' I sheepishly asked Sarah, feeling self-conscious about being a non-believer in traditional Muslim clothes. She nodded solemnly and said she was grateful to have me as a representative of Mum's side, along with Aunty Madeleine, Aunty Anne, and a cousin. Sarah's father, Adel, had declined to attend.

The large living room was cleared for a small platform with fluoro-green and purple trim. In the centre, the bride and groom, the best man and the bridesmaid sat on golden chairs, laying their hands on a flat cushion on their laps and flipping their palms to the sky. The guests, in colourful silky attire, sat on the floor. The bride's family members stood to bless the wedding party with a sprinkle of rose water.

When it was my turn, I'd clasped Sarah's hands as tears ran down her face. 'Mum would be so proud,' I said, before pulling away to maintain my composure.

That joyful occasion was the closest I'd ever felt to Sarah, cemented by the sharing of new cultural rituals. She taught me Malay words and about the importance of arabesque shapes in Islam, and we ate wedges of soft durian in the garden at night. We listened to the call to prayer as it drifted across KL. Despite the wall that still stood in my mind, my trips to Malaysia reminded me of Mum, and Sarah seemed to embody her. A pilot light was burning deep inside me, behind all the bricks.

*

While the ABC called itself a national broadcaster, the Adelaide bureau was considered part of the BAPH states: Brisbane, Adelaide, Perth and Hobart, with Darwin unworthy of a mention. Apparently my career would be forever under 'the darkness of South Australia', as one person put it. Despite this, I believed that a journalist could find good stories anywhere. No matter how big or small your location, you simply needed to look for the right material, then relate it in a compelling way for a national audience.

I targeted stories that would receive Australia-wide attention, including those about immigration, remote Aboriginal communities, and the Murray–Darling Basin. Another concerned the plight of Guantanamo Bay detainee David Hicks. The three key people I harangued at all hours of the day were the foreign minister, Alexander Downer, Hicks's Australian lawyer, David McLeod, and Hicks's father, Terry Hicks. They must all have become sick to death of me over the several years I knew them.

Terry tirelessly fronted the cameras at his home in Adelaide's northern suburbs, day in, day out. I held out the mic as he stood on his dry front lawn, taking my questions without any sense of shame or embarrassment but instead an incredible stoicism. Terry loved his son because he was his son. 'Terry Hicks really is the Father of the Century,' I remarked to the crew as we drove back to base.

If I were in a foreign jail, I thought, my dad wouldn't fight as hard as Terry. I'd be disowned. If the Hicks family

All Mixed Up

were Asian, I speculated, they would have gone to ground, too overcome by the shame.

In Adelaide my stories proliferated on the network radio news wire, the scripts and audio arriving in Sydney with the slug and my surname: *hicks release – om, murray darling basin – om, holden jobs – om*. My stories also appeared on 7 pm TV news bulletins nationally.

'Who is this Om?' teased one Sydney newsreader, putting on a faux pompous voice the way Sydneysiders did when they spoke about the rest of the country.

Om was a strange-sounding name to some, probably the shortest surname in the entire Australian media industry, but my stories were good enough to run around the nation as lead items, making their way across the big cities, the suburbs, the farmlands, the bush, the outback and beyond.

Radio was about imagination – you could really get into people's heads. 'Don't underestimate the power of radio,' an older colleague once told me. When I read radio news bulletins, locally and nationally, I thought of how my name and voice were travelling into people's ears. An Asian Australian was being accepted into the most intimate spaces in people's lives: their homes, their cars, their bedrooms. My voice would ease them into bed at night and wake them up in the morning.

But despite my achievements, the big city lights across the desert had never felt so far away. I watched as my fellow East Coasters rolled out of town, one by one, for larger ponds and brighter opportunities. One ended up famous on *MasterChef*. 'You've got to be in it to win it,' she said cheerfully, her wheels spinning in a cloud of dust.

'We all thought you lot would get outta here,' a colleague told me. But it seemed my options were limited, and I feared that if I pulled up stumps, I'd never be able to get back into the industry. Even though my mind was screaming, *Quit! Quit! Quit!*, Dad's pragmatism weighed on me: 'Don't resign. Where will you go? It's a good job.'

For my father's generation, you held on to a job, and as a migrant worker in Australia with English as a second language, Dad had few choices. Having been treated as expendable, he looked at my steady work life with envy. I'd been working since I was fifteen and had pretty much never stopped. But in Adelaide I began to experience stagnation.

Perhaps naively, I sincerely believed in the process, and continued to apply for jobs internally. Work hard and you will be rewarded. Don't ask for favours. Do good stories and you will be seen. I applied for thirteen interstate jobs in total, but they proved elusive. Some of them were predetermined. I reached out to network contacts to no avail. A pat on the head missed the point about career progression: 'Keep doing what you're doing.'

When Labor leader Kevin Rudd won the federal election in 2007, I was posted for the night at the soon-to-be-former foreign minister Alexander Downer's electorate office in the Adelaide Hills. While I was watching Rudd's speech on a TV in the back of the ABC van, an older woman in glasses accosted me. 'Are you happy *he* won?' She was tipsy and holding a glass of booze. With venom, she asked, 'Can *you* even vote? Are you an Australian citizen?' I was speechless while one of the crew barked at her and she backed off. I did not report this incident to anyone; it was an example of the racism I'd learned to be silent about. When incidents like these happened, I didn't think, as an Asian person, I would be taken seriously by the white people around me. Keep quiet, as Dad would say.

Chapter Twelve

As the gulf between me and Dad widened, I felt alone and invisible. My visits back to Melbourne were tense. 'Why should I bother?' I snapped at Dad. Sarah felt far away in Malaysia. When east coast friends came to visit, I greeted them like an overexcited dog wagging its tail.

One Sydney friend tried to shake me out of it as we sat down for dinner at a restaurant. 'We cannot afford to be nihilistic,' she said, eyeing me sternly through her spectacles. She was right, but I still felt like I was headed towards oblivion, and that if I disappeared no one would notice.

Going to bars with the East Coasters, three straight women, I'd sit glumly with my drink, staring out at the straight men who gave me no attention. We attended Adelaide's famous festivals, which filled the city with colourful, flashing lights and crowds laughing and cheering along to comedians and burlesque performers. The smell of weed wafted among the trees. But once the festivals were done the city returned to its dark and dormant state.

I was approaching thirty, and Adelaide was the last place I wanted to be. Still single, I struggled to connect with guys. Several strange encounters ended with us lying under the covers in our undies. Waiting. Waiting. But nothing happened. One of them passed out fully dressed with his legs hanging over the edge of the bed. Perhaps, I decided, I was so flawed I was unlovable and undesirable with my black hair and my Asian body. I hit the gym and chugged muscle-building milkshakes to make myself bigger.

Back in Melbourne, my old uni friends were settling down with mortgages and marriages, and I eyed them with envy. Why couldn't I have what everyone else had?

Seeking validation, I became reckless with my heart and gave it to anyone. But this path I chose was my own. If there were anyone to blame, then it was me, and I smarted at my self-inflicted predicament. I'd used my career as a crutch, and now it was crumbling, and without success what was I? The confidence and devil-may-care attitude when I was twenty-four and living in Sydney had evaporated.

Key friendships sustained me through those years as I faced bumps in the road.

As I sped along the River Torrens on my Vespa, I breathed in the smell of earth rising from the banks. By 9 pm the Adelaide streets were dead. I revved the throttle harder and harder and pushed against the cold and the wind. 'Red goes faster,' the motorcycle salesman had told me. Suddenly the Vespa collapsed beneath me, the saddle stuck on the back wheel. What now? Pulling over, I realised the bike was kaput. I threw my helmet on the bitumen. 'Fuck!'

Tearfully, I called up my friend Simon, a veteran ABC political reporter and gay fairy godmother who liked to joke about dicks 'as big as a baby's arm'. He lived with his partner nearby.

After we'd lugged the scooter back to his old cottage, laughing all the way, Simon poured steaming Lady Grey tea into dainty floral cups on saucers, and in turn I poured my heart out. He wasn't old enough to be my father, but like Doug the lecturer, and a senior SBS producer before him, Simon seemed more like a father figure than Dad. I could never fail these men as a non-compliant son, perhaps because they too had failed their fathers.

Simon sometimes presented for *Stateline*, and on a secondment to the program I broke a huge scoop about plans by the state government to shake up the mental health system. 'Who did Jason have to sleep with to get that?' a green-with-envy political reporter remarked. I interviewed community advocates and people with mental health issues, but despite my extensive reporting on the topic, I never mentioned Mum's illness to my colleagues.

After her death, I'd told no one. Not even Kavindi or Dimitrios or any of my closest friends. Boyfriends were too fearful to ask. When a friend revealed their father was mentally ill, I froze, pretending to nod along as if I was a stranger to such issues. I feared that if people knew about Mum, they would think I was 'crazy' like her, and professionally I worried that people would question my judgement.

If anything, my reporting on mental health taught me to be more compassionate. But I hadn't yet realised that lived experience could make for even more powerful storytelling.

*

In the mid-to-late 2000s, when I was in Adelaide, 'diversity' had not yet become a buzzword, and discussions around the lack of representation in a representative democracy weren't part of the broader political discourse in Australia, let alone in the media industry. Back then, you couldn't talk about race without being viewed as a troublemaker, or playing the race card, or seeking special treatment – you were expected to be silent. Twitter wasn't yet a mainstream platform where a few fist-shaking sentences about what was wrong with Australia would garner attention – and in any case, I was averse to this kind of attention because I didn't see myself as an activist. It's recently become more acceptable to be an angry member of an ethnic minority on social media, but I believe that change is more than slogans. Being on air, and visible, makes my point: *I exist!*

I was one of a few pioneers in an unchartered media landscape, but it didn't feel like a brave new world. I sometimes felt alone. I'd realised I would have to yield to the system or make the system yield to me, and I quickly learned I would need to forge my own path through the bamboo *jungle*. It wasn't a bamboo ceiling, because you travelled across, not up.

Incrementally, the industry changed in complexion. By the 2010s, ethnic minority journos – or people of colour, as some prefer to say – had become more prominent, and some swiftly became trailblazers. They were soon winning Walkley and Logie awards. Because I'd started in the industry before them, they appeared to me as fast-moving objects. Despite my achievements, the pace of my career advancement had been glacial in comparison.

Generally speaking, there was a view in the media industry that cultural diversity was supposed to be the job of SBS, which had a legal mandate to foster it. Some thought that journos like me should be sequestered in the multicultural broadcaster under a kind of unofficial segregation policy. I'd often turn up to jobs where people immediately assumed I was from SBS.

The public had the same perception. The idea that I could work for the ABC or another channel was unfathomable to them. I once went to a GP – a fellow Asian – who responded in surprise when I revealed where I worked. 'Really?' he said as he inspected some moles on my torso. 'Really?!'

At the time, it seemed to me that the ABC saw little reason to represent migrant communities even though they paid their fair share of the national broadcaster's government funds. For many years, the official slogan was 'Everyone's ABC', but some people in the organisation appeared to forget that we had a duty to the public, all of them, whatever their race or class.

When I worked in radio, I sounded 'Aussie'. If you'd heard my voice on air and hadn't seen my face, you might have presumed I was white.

'Oh, you're that handsome man,' a woman said to me over the phone. She had seen me at a media conference earlier. 'I probably shouldn't say that,' she murmured.

'Um, that's very kind,' I replied.

'You know, you sound like you're tall and blond.'

'Some people might say that,' I replied gently, 'but I can tell you I'm not. I'm definitely Asian.'

Occasionally I would turn up to shoots where the interviewee immediately deferred to the white camera crew, making the assumption that one of them was the man who'd arranged the interview over the phone. Other times people's faces would turn grey when they saw me in person and realised I was the reporter – perhaps they expected a white laddish type after our friendly phone chat. *Yes! I am the reporter, and I will be directing the crew!* It was frustrating but also heartening because I'd changed their perceptions by smashing stereotypes. If I weren't a journalist, though, then how would they have treated me?

The news business is built on trust. That's our sales pitch, and the faces chosen to be in front of the camera are thought to be trustworthy. Would you trust a face like mine to read you the news? If not, why not? Would you rather have Brian tell you so, not an Om? Would you wonder if I could speak English properly, or believe I should go back to where I came from?

When I sent emails requesting interviews, I worried my messages would be treated as spam. Would my surname be overlooked when it popped up in the recipient's inbox? Would they trust a name like mine?

I chose not to anglicise it. Om had been warped into all sorts of nicknames: Omelette, Omster, Ommy, Om the Bomb, Little Om. But Om was my name.

'Where's Om from?' one man asked.

'My dad's side. Cambodian.'

'Oh, I thought it was Scandinavian.'

'Yes, an easy mistake – in fact, I believe "om" is an actual word in those countries,' I said, laughing along.

Most times these types of questions or misunderstandings came from a place of curiosity rather than malice, and the routine of dealing with them taught me how to be supremely patient with people. But I noticed these same questions were rarely asked of white people, who almost never had to consider their ethnicity because they wrongly thought they didn't have one. White Australians weren't asked every day, by people jumping up and down and pointing their fingers, 'What's your background?!'

A handy trick I used was to reflect the question back onto white people, evening things out. It meant we were all talking about race, not just mine, and I found that mutually sharing our heritage would open up the conversation.

'That's my background, what's yours?' I would ask them.

I could always see the strain on their faces, their eyes darting around for an answer because the question had never entered their heads.

I found out that another Asian journalist working in South Australia had been called 'a lesser Jason Om'. It sounded like a compliment but on closer inspection was an insult. The same journalist had been mistaken for me while on a shoot with a politician, and the comparison was silly – even babies had greater facial recognition. But it was no laughing matter: we were only as good as the next Asian journalist.

*

Racism makes you hyper-aware. It throws you into a constant state of paranoia and second-guessing. When you have race on your face, you can't wipe it off, and when you deal with some people, you question yourself over and over: *Was it racial?*

Was it racial when you were working as an editor of the student newspaper at uni and a woman from a high-profile charity said in a heated phone exchange, 'Oh come on, "Om Shanti",' and when you mentioned the conversation to your Anglo-Australian boyfriend, he minimised it?

Was it racial when you were praised for being 'eloquent and well-spoken' even though having these qualities was simply a requirement of your job as a journalist? Would a white colleague have been described in the same way?

Was it racial when your car was vandalised in your mostly white neighbourhood in the middle of the night by an anonymous person who keyed a thin line along the driver's side and scratched 'dog dog' into your windscreen? As a result, you started looking over your shoulder every time you parked your car, and from the street you peered into the neighbours' windows, thinking, *Was it you, or you, or you?* The police said it was probably a case of mistaken identity, but you felt you'd been targeted. Your friends were shocked but said your suburb was progressive, as if racism happened in some places and not others.

Was it racial when a person you thought was a mentor told you, 'You have competition,' when referring to another Asian journalist?

Was it racial when an older white man at the tyre shop refused to give you a roadworthiness certificate unless you bought two new tyres? You wondered whether he thought you were a chump and that he could exploit you because you were Asian. Would he have done that to a white customer, or were you going crazy?

Was it racial when someone said you were 'railing against white men' when you hadn't mentioned white people?

Was it racial when after you gave a class presentation at uni about the lack of minorities in the media, a white classmate you always found to be friendly tapped his shoulder and said, 'Mate, you've got a chip. A chip on your shoulder,' and walked off without a care? You fumed on the train ride home, thinking about how he lived in a rich suburb and owned an expensive MP3 player you couldn't afford.

Was it racial when a security guard scanned you with a wand at a commission hearing but your white colleague cruised into the building without having to go through the same process? And your colleague said, 'Don't take it personally, it was probably because of your big coat.'

All Mixed Up

Was it racial when you refused to play the game of 'Where are you really from?' during a speed-dating event, and a white guy reacted with faux outrage, saying, 'You see that? That's a real complex you've got there,' and you appealed to his Asian companion for some support but he chose to stay silent?

Of course it was all racial.

*

During my fifth year in Adelaide, a national radio role opened up when the Walkley Award-winning incumbent went on maternity leave. I gulped. At twenty-nine, I would step into her shoes as the sole correspondent for South Australia, filing stories for the daily ABC Radio current affairs programs *AM*, *PM* and *The World Today*.

Amid my persistent feeling of inertia, my confidence continued to take a dive, and I briefly worried about failure. I had to give myself a few slaps in the face like some boxer taking on the championship title holder – *You filed for the network before, and you'll do it again, come what may. You can do this.*

I would fly the flag for South Australia and show off my wares to the national network. Regardless of whether the role led anywhere, I would give it my all. But I vaguely knew that if I continued to be stuck, I would throw it all in and return to the east coast. Perhaps I'd settle for a better paid job – anything – where I felt valued.

*

Journalism can be a dicey job sometimes – often when we arrive with microphones and cameras we're not welcomed with open arms. Add racism to the mix and it can get pretty hairy. I'd never felt unsafe at work until I reported on a community gathering in the Adelaide Hills in late 2010.

Faced with a crisis over the record numbers of asylum seekers arriving in Australia by boat, the Gillard Labor Government had come up with a plan to build an immigration detention centre in Woodside, a small South Australian town in a federal Liberal electorate. Four hundred asylum seekers would be housed in repurposed defence accommodation. But the prime minister's execution of the plan was clumsy, with the announcement dropped on Woodside like a bomb. Many of the townspeople were apoplectic, and the fallout was ugly.

I packed my radio kit, jumped in the ABC's white Camry and drove about half an hour from Collinswood to the community gathering in Woodside. It was late afternoon by the time I arrived, and people were streaming into the venue, a cobblestone hall just up the road from the shops. Passing motorists honked their horns and jeered out their windows. At a pub across the road, a small group of drinkers were yelling, 'Fuck off, refugees!' It would make for great radio, so I crept towards them.

I'd always known that at some stage in my career I would have to face hostile interviewees, particularly people who might not like the look of me. But I also knew that when I carried an ABC-branded microphone, or when I was with a crew, I was safe. The ABC logo gave me protection: it was a trusted brand, and while it had its fair share of vociferous opponents, they would never have risked physically attacking a journo who worked for the national broadcaster. So I knew that as I went up to the group at the pub with my ABC mic like a magic wand, they would be neutralised. The law would come down hard on them if anything were to happen to me, an ABC employee.

I also wholeheartedly believed in providing balance and listening to different perspectives, and the opponents' view was fundamental in the telling of my story.

I sidled up to them and put on a smile as they smoked and drank beer. 'So what do you reckon about this detention centre?' I said casually.

'This is something that will wreck this beautiful little town,' one replied.

I extracted some decent grabs from them, then returned to the hall where I bumped into a friendly Channel Nine reporter, Virginia, who had Tanzanian and Swedish heritage. 'How funny is it that we're here?' she said with a laugh, and I chuckled. As far as we could tell, we were the only ethnic minorities there that night.

The hall overflowed with onlookers. Every chair was filled, and a small crowd stood at the back while others craned their necks near the doors. Frowning, with arms crossed, they'd come to listen to an official from the Immigration Department explain hastily drawn-up plans for the new detention centre.

The crowd erupted, jeering at the stage. I kept my recorder rolling and glanced over at Virginia, who was focused on her notebook. My face burned. I felt conspicuous. *Are you one of them? A refo?* I thought of my migrant parents and my cousins and their families, who were plane refugees. And I thought of my half-sister, a Muslim.

Once proceedings at the Woodside Hall were over, the crowd got up to leave. I stood near the entrance as they swirled around me. A tall man with long skinny arms walked past holding a One Nation placard in the air. People like him probably wished people like me didn't exist. I stuck out my microphone, trying to vox pop a few townsfolk before I left, but I had enough audio for the next morning's story. It would be a cracker.

Stepping out of the hall into the night, I quickly walked to the Camry, got in, made sure the doors were locked and started the engine. I couldn't wait to get out of there.

While I drove, the image of the man with the One Nation placard stuck in my mind, even as I tried to run through my script in my head. I glanced at my rear-view mirror. Every glaring headlight was suspicious. I imagined that man, or someone else from the hall, running me off the road like in the movies. Was I being tailgated? I pressed the accelerator and hit the highway as fast as I could.

Once I was past the security roller gate at work, I felt safe. I strode to my desk and started scripting and editing the audio. It was an electric piece that captured the tensions I'd witnessed that night. I finished filing for the *AM* program in the early hours of the morning, not long before Sydney would wake up and go to air.

My story led the program. Colleagues emailed me: *That was powerful radio.*

When I came into work that day, sleepy-eyed, a senior producer rang up. 'Mate, are you okay? We were worried about you.'

*

That national role would be the heyday of my Adelaide experiment. I received praise from heavyweight ABC personalities in Sydney, and I bought a new car and found a new boyfriend, a lawyer whom I met at a house party. He came six years after my last. Third time lucky, I thought. I accomplished some of the proudest work of my career, winning a top state media award for Best Radio Broadcaster in 2011.

But the role was temporary, and for a while it seemed I'd soon go back to the general newsroom. My frustration returned. No matter how many accolades I won – seven awards in South Australia – it didn't seem to be enough for me to progress. I wasn't enough for Dad or my career. As Asian Australians, were we expected to overachieve without fail and accept nothing in return from both our parents and society? As Asian Australians, were we supposed to walk through life undervalued, underappreciated and underestimated? My wheels spun round and round in a burnout, but it was no fun when you couldn't get away. 'Circles' by Birds of Tokyo became my anthem.

An emergency exit, though, was in the offing. It was another temporary gig, this time as a presenter on the rolling ABC News channel in Sydney, News 24, which had been up and running for a bit over a year. I'd applied before but the network had seemed unpersuaded. Now it was make or break. 'Be sure to have your blinkers on when you get there,' a veteran producer advised me, flicking out his fingers like flashing lights.

My boss in his glass office asked, 'Are you sure this is what you really want to do? Sometimes these things don't work out.'

'No, I'm going,' I replied. *Are you kidding me?*

Just as I was on the cusp of heading for News 24, my boyfriend broke my heart. The break-up strengthened my resolve to say goodbye to Adelaide. I was also glad I hadn't told Dad about him.

After my short stint at News 24 in late 2011, I secured a permanent position, and I again packed my bags for Sydney, this time about to turn thirty-one. I decided to leave quietly, after thanking friends and colleagues who'd stuck by me.

I was spent. After the break-up I felt as though the entire six-year experience was a nuclear disaster. Like a spaceman entering a new orbit, I rocketed along the highway at light speed towards the big smoke, leaving the drag of Adelaide in my wake, 'Midnight City' by M83 blaring, through Mildura, then Wagga Wagga, then I hit the outskirts of Sydney and knew I could start afresh.

The bright lights of the News 24 studio put a face to my name, and finally I felt I was seen, presenting rolling bulletins and reporting live from the field for *News Breakfast*. Sydney felt like a home away from home after six years in the wilderness.

I had hacked my way into the bamboo jungle and found myself in a clearing. I realised I'd never been the problem; it was the system.

Chapter Thirteen

Since the night Mum collapsed in bed, I'd kept track of the years. It was a kind of game, a way of pinching myself. Each anniversary was a milestone I'd never expected to reach, but I'd made it to one year later, then five years, then ten, then fifteen. The twentieth anniversary was in 2013. At the age of thirty-two, I realised I had survived.

That year, I was drawn back to long-form reporting when I moved to the ABC's *Lateline* program. With its catchy theme tune and hard-hitting investigations, the show had been a fixture on my TV during uni and beyond, and I loved how host Tony Jones would pick apart interview subjects. The program often broke big stories and set the national agenda, winning a truck-ton of Walkley Awards. At *Lateline*, I would be the only regular on-air Asian reporter in the ABC's prestigious current affairs stable: *7.30*, *Australian Story*, *Four Corners* and *Foreign Correspondent*. 'It means they're paying attention to you,' a senior boss remarked.

In the same year, the news came from Melbourne that Nan Ruby was gravely ill. The 91-year-old matriarch was dying. Although I felt uneasy about her, I wept over the idea of her life draining from her frail little body. Uncle Johnny and Aunty Madeleine were taking care of her.

After Mum's death Nan had disappeared, and we'd been out of touch for years. But from about 2010 I'd started calling in on her again, dropping by her place whenever I visited Melbourne from interstate. I grew curious about her. She still dyed her curly hair brown and could have been mistaken for an old European woman. Her accent was an odd combination of Malaysian, British and Australian. In my family, we all sounded different from each other.

Nan would hassle me about praying to baby Jesus – as opposed to the *adult* Jesus. 'At least go to church and say thank you to baby Jesus for looking after you,' she would insist, and I would mumble an answer. By then, I was a non-believer.

Over the next couple of years, she became increasingly paranoid. 'Why waste your money on relatives? Some relatives are quacks! They come, they eat, and leave. If they gave me a million dollars, then I would accept them. Put your money in the bank. Don't spend your money on friends. Give them money on their birthdays, but look after yourself.' She often lamented that no one came to see her, which was false. Then she would complain about having to see her doctor and how some doctors were quacks. She said she was lonely but that she didn't seek out her children for company. 'Why would I bother them? They have their own lives.'

On my last visit before she fell ill, I watched her frail body shuffle towards a shelf and come back with a plastic bag. It reeked of mothballs, stinking out the room. Inside was a framed photo of me and Nan, and several other loose photos of us. 'Here, take these, Jason.'

'Um, I don't want these – they were for you.'

'No, no, take. You never know what will happen to them after I'm gone. Somebody might take them.'

Her response puzzled me, but I thanked her anyway.

Before I left, I gave Nan a hug, her body all pointy bones in my arms.

'Come and see me when you're back in Melbourne!' she said eagerly.

'Sure,' I replied with a warm smile.

*

Nan Ruby died in October 2013. The funeral in Melbourne coincided with a pre-booked holiday, so I couldn't attend, but Dad went to film and take photos. The recording of the speeches showed my Malaysian cousins lining up to share joyous anecdotes, none of which I could relate to. As Dad stood outside the funeral parlour to film Mum's family releasing colourful balloons, I wondered what he was thinking. He hadn't spoken to Nan for twenty years – was he making sure she was gone? I watched the footage on a beach in Byron Bay, feeling empty and numb, my eyes desert dry.

Aunty Madeleine texted me while she and Uncle Johnny were packing up Nan's stuff. 'Is there anything you want to take?' she asked.

'Yes – a silver crucifix Blu-Tacked to the wall in her room.'

On the day Nan had returned the mothballed photos to me, she'd hovered towards a makeshift shrine to Jesus by her bedside, craned her neck up at the shiny crucifix, and explained she had taken it from Mum's coffin before it was buried.

Why waste a good crucifix, huh? But I'd held my tongue.

After my aunty retrieved the crucifix, I took it back to Dad. Beneath his confused smile, I could see an eternity of hurt. He shook his head, a small breath leaving his mouth. 'Swooh, jeez.'

'I'm giving this crucifix back to you because it's ours,' I said. 'It was meant for Mum, and this is where it belongs.'

I still had a lot of questions about Nan's frosty relationship with my parents. The unexplained tensions. The long absence after Mum died. And what had Nan said in those phone calls to make Mum cry? I'd refrained from speaking up, because who was I to bother an old woman? Now it seemed her answers were gone with her.

*

The convergence of Nan's death and the twentieth anniversary of Mum's death brought all my long-suppressed feelings crashing through the wall I'd built in my mind. It had already been riddled with hairline cracks I'd been papering over for two decades.

When I was about sixteen, I was at a friend's house getting ready for a party. My favourite red Adidas top was creased, and my friend's mum offered to iron it for me. 'It must be so nice to have your mum do these things for you,' I remarked to my friend.

Almost every episode of *Six Feet Under* had me bawling, and when Buffy's mum died in *Buffy the Vampire Slayer*, it tore me apart.

Innocuous questions from strangers, colleagues and supermarket check-out workers felt like interrogations:

'Didn't your mum ever teach you how to –?'

'What would your mum think?'

'What are you doing for Mother's Day?'

My Cambodian grandparents. Grandpa Khin is presumed to have died in the Khmer Rouge genocide in the 1970s. Grandma Sieng died in 1954.

One of the earliest photos of Dad (right) upon arriving in Australia aged sixteen as a Colombo Plan scholarship student. This is the kitchen of the boarding house in Coogee, Sydney, which he shared with other international students.

A portrait of Dad, man of the world, when he studied at Manly Boys' High in Sydney.

Mum as a young woman in Malaysia.

My Malaysian grandfather, Leo, with Mum and Aunty Madeleine at Port Dickson, Malaysia, 1970. The passenger ship they're on would take the family to Melbourne, leaving Mum behind.

Mum in Malaysia in 1970. She would have been pregnant with Sarah in this photo.

Mum and Dad, on their first date, Melbourne, 1973.

My parents on their wedding day, Melbourne, 1974.

Mum and Dad in Oakleigh, Melbourne, dressed up to go out in the 1970s.

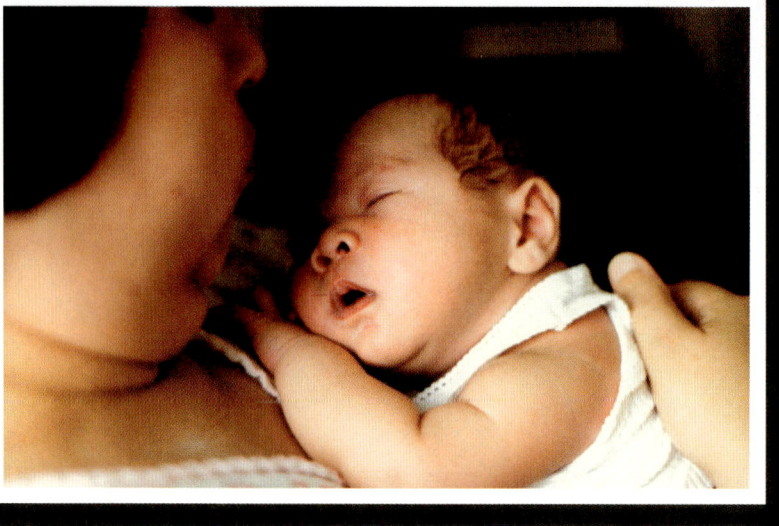

Mum holding me, 1980.

Dad and me at a party in the backyard of our Oakleigh house. You can see the thicket of bamboo in the background.

Mum and me in our front yard.

You can see Dad's radio contraptions behind me, as I listen to music in our house.

My Malaysian grandmother, Ruby, holding me at her house in Melbourne.

Me and my Cambodian cousin Dit riding bikes in his backyard in Oakleigh.

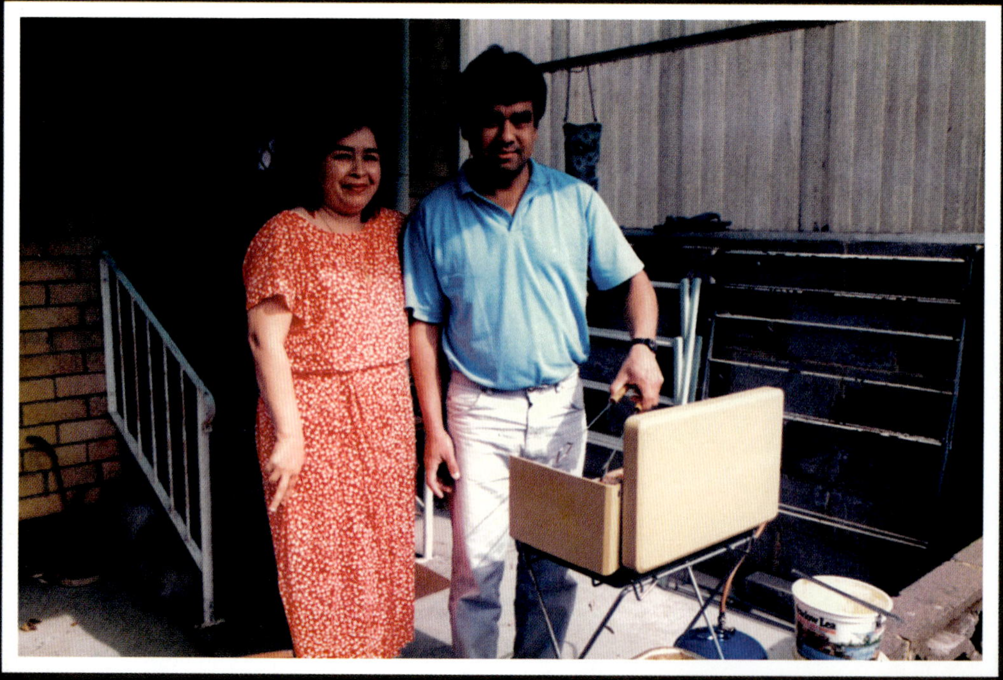

Mum and Uncle Johnny on our back porch.

Aunty Anne, Uncle Rod, Mum and me at Kuala Lumpur airport in 1984.

Me with Leon and Betty, our family's Jewish confidantes, during a party at our house in 1986.

Dad interviewing Cambodian Prince Norodom Ranariddh at 3EA (SBS) in Melbourne during a royal visit in the early 1980s.

Dad entertaining the locals in his hometown of Kralanh, Cambodia, during our trip there in 2005.

Me and Dad at the Royal Palace in Cambodia, 2005.

Me at the legendary Bayon temple at Angkor, Cambodia, filming scenes for an SBS TV story in 2005. I was twenty-four.

Me and Sarah outside the Islamic Arts Museum in Kuala Lumpur, 2006.

Sarah and me at her wedding, Kuala Lumpur, 2006.

I marched in the Sydney Mardi Gras for the first time in 2020, on the cusp of the coronavirus pandemic. It was also the first time the ABC took part with its own float. Dad watched the broadcast at home. *(Kevin Nguyen)*

Me and Aunty Madeleine, my mum's younger sister.

Uncle Chiv and his family at Khao-I-Dang refugee camp in Thailand, 1980.

Uncle Chiv and Dad, 2012.

Dad with his sisters, Touch and Chan, in 2021.

Me presenting live news bulletins in the studio at the ABC News Channel, Sydney. *(Glenn Chalk)*

In 2021, I won the Media Diversity Australia Award at the Mid-year Walkleys for *7.30* stories. *(Adam Hollingworth)*

Mum standing on the back verandah of Dad's share house in Caulfield, Melbourne, in the 1970s.

I poured myself into my career. No time for crying. No time to reflect on traumas.

But I'd be adjusting my tie in the mirror, or waiting at an intersection to let an ambulance pass by, when tears would well up. I'd be transported back to being that twelve-year-old boy on a darkened street, helpless as I waited for the paramedics, desperate for my mummy to wake up.

Would Mum be proud of who her little boy had become?

Now when I looked back on my childhood I would think, *What the hell was that all about?* I felt breathless. Ever since I'd bolted out the front door to seek help, I'd been running, ignoring the stitch in my side, because if I stopped to breathe I might collapse and never get up again. No one would be there to pick me up, or so I thought. I'd run to a point where I finally felt safe enough to turn my head.

When I did turn my head, I realised I didn't really know Mum or my Malaysian relatives. Who were these strange people who'd occupied my life and called themselves 'family'?

As the feelings I'd blocked out overtook me, I realised I couldn't ignore Mum any more. It was time to tear down the wall. I was filled with a new resolve. I would put my investigative skills to work and try to understand her sorrow. I'd join the dots to make sense of my confusing childhood, to interrogate any false assumptions and to ask the tough questions of my family and myself.

As Mum's son, I was owed an explanation. What had caused her to weep openly while waiting for my primary school bus outside our front gate? Why had she often muttered 'I'm so fed up' to herself? What did she mean when she said, 'Mum had a nervous breakdown?' What was Sarah's connection to Mum and how had her parallel life in Malaysia come to be? Once I answered these questions, perhaps I could breathe.

The following year I began putting together a plan of how to investigate Mum's life. The first step was to access my memories of her, good and bad, which required the task of abseiling deep into my mind, like the characters in the movie *Inception*. The good memories, it seemed, would be the most difficult to revive. Many of my recollections were nauseating, fragmented and disjointed, and renewed my feelings associated with the stigma of her mental illness. I recalled Mum as quiet and distant, sitting by herself on the couch, staring into space. She wept uncontrollably and was miserable for unexplained reasons. She said and did strange things that made me question whether she loved me, and I sometimes couldn't tell if what she told me was real or a fantasy.

One of my final clear memories of Mum took place on busy Warrigal Road near our house. Coming home from school on a cloudy afternoon, I jumped off the bus to find Mum standing on the footpath in her fawn-coloured coat with our little white dog, Spike. Her rosy cheeks glowed, and her smile was broad; she'd even put on make-up.

My instinctive reaction was embarrassment. It was my first year of high school, and there was no need for her to meet me at the bus stop in front of the other boys, who peered down through the windows, probably laughing at us. 'Was that your mum?' one of them asked me later, incredulous.

Stepping onto the nature strip, I pretended she was a stranger. I stared straight ahead and walked off as fast as I could with my heavy backpack on my shoulders.

'Jason!' She called out to me, but I don't remember what else she said.

Why was I so unhappy to see her?

Whenever I thought back to the night Mum collapsed, I felt guilty. I ran through all the things I could have done to save her. Maybe I could have been quicker up the hallway when I heard the terrifying grunts. Maybe I could have called triple zero straight away. Maybe I could have used the push-button phone on the desk in Dad's study rather than the rotary phone – that would have saved seconds. Why hadn't I just called my dad on his brick of a mobile phone?

I'd felt like the stupidest kid in the world. I would never be featured in a news report with over-the-top commentary: 'This is the brave young boy who rescued his mum.' I hadn't been able to save her.

*

Memories wouldn't be enough for a thorough investigation. At *Lateline* I'd learned the importance of documentation, as many a story relied on evidence from documents. What good journalist didn't get excited over one sentence in a freedom of information request or a leaked email that might reveal an injustice? I needed hard evidence: photos and recorded history, and corroborating recollections through interviews with family members and Mum's friends. I feared that if I didn't gather this evidence, Mum would eventually become unknowable like some of my other relatives, such as Dad's parents and Mum's father, Grandpa Leo.

Dad's parents, the Cambodian Buddhists, had died years before I was born. Dad kept framed black-and-white photos of them on a bookshelf in the lounge room. Grandma Sieng's face was smooth and round like the moon; Grandpa Khin's was weathered and narrow. They were ethnically

Chinese – Cantonese and Teochew – but Dad didn't know where they were born. 'Grandma Sieng? She was your real grandmother!' Dad would say. Their photos formed part of an improvised Buddhist shrine: a small glass vase filled with uncooked rice and crammed with incense sticks, surrounded by ash. Dad would light the incense and honour his parents' memory, bowing and praying as smoke wafted across the room. Their spirits, he said, were guardians over our family. I wondered whether I would be culturally obliged to carry on this tradition after Dad was gone, worshipping *his* memory.

Then there was my grandfather on Mum's side of the family. I met Grandpa Leo only once, when I was three, during a visit to his home in Kuala Lumpur. When I was fifteen, I learned of his sudden death when Nan Ruby sent me a rare birthday card. Next to the printed message wishing me a happy birthday, she had written, *By the way, Grandpa Leo has died after being hit by a car in Penang, Malaysia.* The circumstances were unclear, and I wasn't invited to the funeral or even told where he was buried.

Whenever I asked Dad about Grandpa Leo, who'd lived in Melbourne for a time before I was born, his face would screw up. Grandpa Leo was a pest, he said. 'Every time he came, bang on the door, and wouldn't go away.'

'Are you sure, Dad?' I countered. 'Maybe he was just being friendly?'

'*Nawwwww*,' Dad replied, a resounding 'no' in his Khmer accent.

My mixed-race, mixed-faith family was brimming with maddening mysteries. We were divided by countries, cultures and religions, and on the Cambodian side I had a language barrier with some relatives. Scattered around Australia and the world, we only caught up once a year at Christmas in Melbourne, if at all.

My family were a reticent bunch. I grew up without context, not knowing my parents' or grandparents' histories. I didn't hear any fond tales about the old homelands of Cambodia and Malaysia. What happened 'before Australia' was left blank, and maybe that was intentional. The past was a tender place to tread in a family prone to hiding their true feelings. Speaking back and speaking up were viewed as insolence. Keep quiet. Do not question authority. And yet, in my job, I was expected to do that every day. I told ripping yarns, yet in my family we often sat in silence.

As they say in journalism, what isn't said can be as significant as what is. Growing up in my family taught me to read between the lines, but while this is a useful skill in my profession, it doesn't help you get close to your loved ones. The guessing games were exhausting and pointless, and I ruminated on what wasn't on the record.

Secrecy is anathema to journalists. After ten years in the news business, I was attuned to dealing with defensiveness, denial, stonewalling, avoidance, evasion, deflection, weasel words, non-answers, minimising and plain old lying. The more I came up against a barrier, the more I grew obsessed with pushing it. Journalists pride ourselves on shining a light into the darkest corners of society and harnessing our powers of persuasion to force out the truth. For the most stubborn cases, I would use the 'We'll send a TV crew to your address' line, followed by 'We'll camp outside if we have to' – this often made people get back to me.

My family members were another matter. I cared for them. They weren't politicians who were forced, quite rightly, to take questions while reporters chased after them with camera crews. How far could I push my relatives before they got upset? Their silence likely involved shame, pain and even fear. But while I felt protective of my family, I came to realise I didn't have to shield them from whatever I found out, as long as I revealed it in a sensitive way.

Little did I know that my investigation would end up taking me to Malaysia. I would uncover harsh truths about Mum and her family, and confront the stigma surrounding her mental illness. The breaking of silences was long overdue.

Chapter Fourteen

The first step in my investigation into Mum's life was to pay a visit to Dad, sit him down, and ask him about Mum and what he knew about her life before they met.

Dad was a man of few words, and since I left Melbourne our contact had been intermittent. I was always the one to call him, and when I tried to continue our phone conversations he seemed to find me strange.

It was always me flying to Melbourne rather than Dad coming to Sydney.

'I hate Sydney, too much traffic,' his excuse would be, even though he'd made the effort to endure a long-haul flight to the US to visit his older brother, Uncle Chiv.

'Why should I come back to Melbourne?' I would snap back at Dad.

He maintained an interest in my work, but he was passive in his expression of it. I imagined that a white dad would ring up his son, now working on one of Australia's top TV shows, and say, 'Hey, mate, I saw that story about the prime minister, what an outrage!' Or text them, 'Mate, great job! Bloody proud of you.' Those dads were like the crews I worked with: affable, knockabout blokes who could spend hours chewing your ear off. Out on the road, I basked in their conventional maleness and the comfort of the fraternity; in the privacy of the crew car we could share war stories.

With Dad, there was no feedback loop. Being an Asian son, I felt my efforts were taken for granted. Since Mum's death, Dad had expected me to learn about life the hard way, like the rugby team shivering on the Andes in the movie *Alive*.

Every time I returned to my family home in Oakleigh, Dad appeared frailer. His hair seemed greyer, his stoop a little stoopier, his movements that bit slower. At sixty-nine, he lived alone. Officially retired, he was still doing the odd job interpreting Khmer. He continued to shuffle around the house in socks and thongs and oversized baggy jeans, which he found 'com-fuh-tuh-bul'. *Shuffle, shuffle, shuffle.* His square spectacles, which took up half his face, had never changed in style. He maintained his collection of clocks, including the one in the toilet.

A scientific man, Dad was excellent at fixing things, so whenever something broke down I called him up for practical help. One summer I'd driven to Melbourne and hit a swarm of locusts on the way, their mashed bodies becoming trapped in my car's grille. Not to fear: Dad had an answer. He emerged from the garage with a claw-armed contraption. Bending down, he picked out every little critter one by one.

But his inability to reciprocate verbally was as infuriating as ever. 'Sorry', 'thank you', 'proud' and 'love' were rarely part of his vocabulary, and sometimes he didn't even wish me a happy birthday. Despite this, at least on the surface, our relationship carried on.

Over the years, I'd continued to casually initiate conversations about my personal life. After the disastrous break-up in Adelaide, I'd confided in him while we drove to Melbourne airport to catch my flight back to Sydney. 'I'm so wrecked,' I said as we crossed the Bolte Bridge. 'Probably worse than after Mum died.'

'Wow,' he said. 'Even worse than your mother dying.' He continued to steer, steady at the speed limit. 'That's like my Vietnamese girlfriend.'

'Sorry, what?!'

'My Vietnamese girlfriend,' he said, as if I were deaf.

'What do you mean, *now*?' I said, alarmed.

'No, during the war.'

'Oh! Thank Christ for that.'

I sometimes found Dad hard to follow. We did not share the oneness of speaking Khmer, which may have brought us closer. My consternation would cause my voice to rise, leading to arguments and either one of us ending the conversation in a huff.

This time I was confused because I thought Dad despised the Vietnamese, who had occupied Cambodia from 1979. In the past, just the mention of them had triggered furious outbursts from him: 'The bloody Vietnamese!' If it wasn't the Vietnamese he raged against, then it was the Communists. 'The bloody Communists! Never trust the people with the black hair. You know, the Asians? They will slaughter you.'

'But, Dad, we're Asian!'

The romance Dad was talking about had taken place well before the invasion. He revealed that, when he was a teenager, his Vietnamese sweetheart lived next door to him. After he moved to Australia, she went off with a Cambodian soldier, and both were believed to have perished in the civil war. Dad couldn't express it in words, but I could tell he still felt gutted as he remembered opening her break-up letter in 1970.

This story would have remained a secret had I not told him of my own heartbreak. Dad was like a hermit crab who came out of his shell only to shoot back inside.

In mid-2014 I interviewed Dad in the lounge room, the largest space in the house, which had been part of a renovation in the early 1990s not long before Mum died. For her, the reno had been a destabilising experience; she'd described the house as 'upside down'.

On the honey-coloured floorboards sat a hard-wearing rug, a comfy charcoal sofa and matching armchair, a plasma TV and old stereo, and a small wooden coffee table overflowing with magazines Dad couldn't bear to throw out. Above the TV hung a large painting of Angkor Wat. The ceiling had exposed wooden beams that Dad stained himself – he did all the painting around the house.

Dad shuffled over to the armchair while I sat on the sofa. His voice was husky like crumpled pieces of paper rubbing together, his words emerging slowly, sometimes soft as a whisper but cracking like a whip when he became incensed.

We began with the day he first met Mum at Flinders Street Station in 1973. I asked him why they'd gone back to his share house in Caulfield, something I thought was strange for a first date.

'The landlady wasn't happy about it,' Dad said with a chuckle.

'Why didn't you go to a cafe or something?' I asked, not that Melbourne was then known for its cafe culture.

'Well, Mummy said, "Alright, I come and see how you live."'

'What was her personality like around that time?'

'She's kind. She's not a fancy girl, you know? She has a genuine, simple life. That's all. She doesn't put make-up and this and that. Other girls maybe put a lot of make-up, but she's just a simple person.' That matched up with what I knew of Mum growing up.

'What did you like about Mum?'

'Is pretty, she's like a beautiful person. She always wear something nicely, like, decent, to go out. And she mentioned, "I am looking for a partner," and we agreed we'd liked to get married and have a family.'

Good stock, on the face of it. In my parents' wedding photos on the bookshelf, Mum was lithe and luminous, but I knew her as chubby, which Dad said had been caused by medications for her mental illness.

'Straight away she mentioned she's not a single person, she's divorced and had a baby,' Dad recalled. 'Mummy told me the truth, other girls maybe hiding.'

Mum had lifted up her shirt, proudly and innocently, to reveal the stretch marks on her belly. Dad had never heard of such a thing before, but that was what having a baby meant. I recalled Mum talking about her stretch marks as I sat next to her on the couch.

After the blind date, Dad's landlady discovered he had broken the rules, and she promptly threw him out. With nowhere else to go, within a week he moved in with Mum. She was living in a two-bedroom rented flat in central Oakleigh with Nan Ruby and her two brothers, Johnny and Alex. By the end of the following year, 1974, my parents had moved into a small studio a short drive away, become engaged and got married – Dad, twenty-nine; Mum, twenty-five.

According to Dad, Mum's internal struggles began to present themselves in 1975, the year the Khmer Rouge seized power in Cambodia while Dad was cocooned in Australia. I asked him whether this was when Mum's famous nervous breakdown happened, but he was vague and couldn't recall the precise details of what that meant.

He was sure about the cause of her ill health, though. 'At the time I didn't know much about the symptoms,' he said, squinting. 'Suddenly she just – I forget the symptoms that she had. It's like too much in her mind. The worrying, because she left a daughter in Malaysia. In her mind she want to get Sarah to Australia at any cost. She just fell sick.'

With little knowledge of mental illness at that time, Dad sought help from a GP who referred him to a psychiatrist in Melbourne's outer-eastern suburbs. But Dad believed this first psychiatrist had overdosed Mum with medication, turning her into a dribbling zombie. For three days she slept in hospital, and when she awakened she was 'all saliva'. 'When she woke up, she said, "What day is it?" She stayed in that hospital for some time. When I finish work I drive my old Corolla to Ringwood. And then I come back and go to work, so that's very hard for me to go back and forth, back and forth, on weekends and all this.' His voice began to rise, the whip about to crack, and he shuffled in his seat. 'I could have sued him. You're stupid to overdose a person. She's not mad!'

'This was the 1970s,' I jumped in, 'so the first response was to put her in hospital?'

'Yeah, just put her in hospital. But she's not that mad, she's not going to kill anyone.'

It was difficult to tell precisely what had happened, but while I was no medical expert, it seemed to have been an over-the-top move by the doctor to sedate Mum when she'd probably first needed therapy before being prescribed any medications.

Dad sighed softly. 'Why put overdose, you know, two or three days.'

'You mention she fell sick, but what was she doing at the time? How did you know she was ill?' I was unable to picture the moment Mum had 'broken down'. Where had she been? At home? At work?

All Dad recalled was that she'd been babbling nonsense. 'I wish I had the knowledge like now, but I didn't then. Just a doctor said we should send her to a psychiatrist.'

It seemed as though Mum's nervous breakdown had happened all of a sudden. 'You weren't aware of the mental health problems until the breakdown?'

'Until the breakdown.'

'Around that time, then, before the breakdown, what kind of stress was she under?'

'The stress is she left Sarah,' Dad said adamantly. 'As a mother, she want the child, but because Adel took the child under Muslim law or whatever, she's upset. Sarah was the number one in her life, to get her.'

Mum had been working for General Electric and went on sick leave. Dad, too trusting for his own good, dutifully informed the company about her breakdown, thinking they would be sympathetic to their loyal employee of more than two years. Instead, upon her return to work, she was instantly let go without an explanation. In a letter that Dad found in his files, the company was dripping with praise for her and claimed she'd left of her own accord.

After Mum's experience in hospital, Dad found a new psychiatrist: a slim, bespectacled Chinese-Malaysian man called Dr Chong. I knew about him from childhood, and I decided to see if I could get some details about Mum from him. After a bit of googling, I found a Melbourne address and phone number for a Dr Chong, but I was uncertain if he was the right one – Chong was a common name, and the address of his office was different to the one I recalled.

Dad fossicked through the files he meticulously maintained in his study. His 'keep, still good' policy of hoarding meant he retained almost every scrap of paper from his life. A whole folder in his filing cabinet was dedicated to receipts should he need to return damaged goods. 'You never know,' he would warn me, 'you might need in the future.'

Dad pulled out a familiar mustard address book. Inside was Mum's handwriting in blue and red pen, along with multiple entries blotted out by white liquid paper. 'She covered them,' Dad said, shaking his head.

'Yeah, when she got angry.'

In a haze of tears, Mum would furiously white out the names of people who troubled her. If they ended up reconciling, she rewrote their contact details over the liquid paper.

I scanned through the names of my parents' friends and relatives from long ago. 'Who are all these people?'

'Probably all dead,' Dad replied dryly.

As I went through the pages, I recognised an address. Bingo – the same as the one from my Google search. It had to be him.

Back in Sydney, I wrote him a letter to which he replied by phone. Dr Chong, now in his seventies, was surprised to hear from me after more than twenty-five years. I kept the tone friendly to dispel any concerns that the son of a former patient might be wanting to sue him.

'She was Filipino, right?' Dr Chong said.

'No, Malaysian.'

'Oh yes, I remember.'

My heart skipped a beat when he revealed he still possessed her medical records.

'I can't believe you kept them after all this time,' I said incredulously.

'Yes, I did. They're somewhere.' I imagined they were sitting in a box covered in dust in his garage. 'It will take some time, but I will look for them.'

I hung up and jumped in the air with excitement. I had my first tangible lead.

Chapter Fifteen

Anyone who watched late-night commercial TV in 1990s Melbourne would remember a particular series of ads for whitegoods and home appliances with a screaming male voiceover: 'Ken Bruce has gone mad, Ken Bruce has gone mad, Ken Bruce has gone mad ... KEN BRUCE HAS GONE COM-PLETELY MAAAAAAAD!'

The said Ken Bruce appeared in a straightjacket, rocking back and forth with a stuffed parrot on his shoulder. Such a stigmatising image would never be aired today.

I'm not crazy, I used to tell myself. *I'm not COM-PLETELY MAAAAAAAD! like Mum*.

In the twenty years since her death, I'd thought about three ways I was not and would never be like her.

1. I loved driving. Mum never learned to drive because she was shit-scared of being on the road, with too many things going on for her to cope. I would hunch over the handlebars of my red Vespa and pretend to drag race with the cars at the traffic lights. When I upgraded to a car, I drove more

than 1300 kilometres from Adelaide to Sydney without a hitch.
2. I loved flying. Mum got so nervous during take-off that her arms shook. Dad said, 'I thought I'd bring her on a round-the-world trip. To enjoy. But she was really scared.' I had no such problems, though I loathed turbulence; I imagined the plane meeting the same fate as Malaysia Airlines Flight 370.
3. I could hold down a job.

This is what stigma around a parent's mental illness does to you: you keep tabs on your own sanity. And being in such a high-risk category – childhood trauma, history in the family, young, male and gay – I knew I had to do everything in my power to avoid becoming another casualty.

*

A few times I tagged along with Mum on her visits to Dr Chong. The trip to his consulting rooms meant a forty-minute bus journey from our place, travelling north along Warrigal Road through Melbourne's outer east. On the way back, we'd stop by the Oakleigh mall for a long john bun filled with jam and cream. Mum would watch me tenderly as I scooped the cream down the middle with my tongue and left the pastry uneaten. 'Tsk, Jason.' She'd shake her head.

When she disappeared behind Dr Chong's door, I'd be left in the waiting room by myself, swinging my legs on a chair as I stared at the grey carpet and grey walls. One time I stepped inside Dr Chong's room as we were about to leave. I sat in front of his wooden desk next to Mum and licked cake crumbs off a small white plate like a dog, much to their amusement.

Of course, I'd never been privy to what Mum said to Dr Chong in that room, because her sessions were confidential. I now hoped her medical records would prise open her mind, revealing its logic and chaos.

Three months after I first contacted Dr Chong, I received a second call from him. My deadline for *Lateline* that night was upon me, but I immediately took the call.

He'd found the records, he told me. He needed a formal letter from Mum's executor, Dad, in order to release them, and a small charge for copies on his 'lousy photocopier'.

I ended the call with a huge grin on my face. Finally, some answers.

Another two months passed before the records arrived. They came on the day the ABC announced four hundred jobs would be axed because of the Abbott Government's $254 million budget cut to the national public broadcaster. It looked like *Lateline* might be on the chopping block, and as I trudged back home after work that night, I spotted, in the darkness, the yellow A4 envelope from Dr Chong poking through my mailbox.

'Not tonight.' I sighed, feeling drained, and tossed the envelope on my desk, where it sat unopened for a month.

I decided to take it to Melbourne and open it with Dad at Christmas.

*

Now I had a lead with the records, I started thinking about what other documents might help with my research. From the depths of my mind, I recalled the letters Mum had written to

Sarah in the 1980s. I wasn't sure whether they still existed but knew it would be easy to find out, just a matter of asking Sarah. I hoped her record-keeping habits were as meticulous as Dad's.

My sister and I hadn't spoken for a while – we kept in touch with the occasional message – and the last time I'd seen her was on a visit to Malaysia in 2008. I hadn't been back since, while she'd remained in Kuala Lumpur, working as a university lecturer, and now had two sons.

I called her on WhatsApp, but after a few words the line became scratchy and dropped out, so I emailed her instead. A few days passed before she replied.

> Dear Jason,
> Thanks for the email. I am happy to know of your plans. I think it's a great idea and I am happy to help in any way I can.
>   I will look for the letters this weekend and will scan and email to you. I have Mum's wedding album and some photos of me and her.

I told Sarah not to bother with scanning the letters. I'd come to Kuala Lumpur in the new year, January 2015, and pick them up from her.

Feeling confident about the investigation, I decided that before heading overseas I'd conduct interviews with Mum's siblings: Aunty Madeleine, Aunty Anne and Uncle Johnny. I planned to question them separately in order to prevent collusion. Like a cross-examiner, I'd treat each of them as if they were a witness in a dock – in the most empathetic way, of course. Dad had already been a surprisingly cooperative witness.

*

In the lead-up to my trip to Melbourne in late 2014, I steeled myself for what might be inside Mum's medical records. Could there be something awful about Dad? Were there cruel words about me? What if she'd told Dr Chong she didn't love me? The records might confirm my worst fears.

I rang Dad. 'Do you know if there will be anything distressing or *explosive* in the documents?' I asked in journalese.

'No, just normal medical treatment,' he replied matter-of-factly.

That was how I should treat these documents, I figured. Matter-of-factly.

In my career I was used to examining reams of stomach-churning information while remaining detached. I would focus on the importance of the story and the mechanics of how I'd get it to air. What was the best angle? What were the most impactful grabs that might hold a viewer's attention for a couple of minutes? This was a kind of journalistic armour I'd learned to hide behind, and with Mum's medical records I decided to do the same. I'd shine a light into the blackness of her torment, whatever that may have been, and slay it once and for all.

I flew down to Melbourne with the yellow envelope. On Christmas Day, when Dad and I were seated at the dining table, I tore the envelope open and pulled out a manila folder of papers. Turning to Dad, I addressed him as if he were a small child. 'Before we go on, are you prepared for what's inside?' Once Pandora's box was open, there would be no turning back.

'Yeah, that's the facts,' he replied calmly. 'Just see what happens.' Dad was so game; there could have been anthrax inside the envelope and he would have answered the same way.

I put on my armour and opened the folder.

The documents were arranged in reverse chronological order, starting in the 1990s and going back to the 1970s. There were records from several different physicians and typed letters interspersed with illegible and faded notes in doctors' scribbles. I decided to concentrate on the letters, which were a printed summary of the scrawl. I read the contents out loud, looking up at Dad now and then to make sure he understood.

The incident with Monty the kitten was explained by Dr Chong:

> I reviewed Mrs Om on the 16th of June 1992 and 7th of July 1992. Her psychosis remained stabilised. However, she has problems at home with her husband. Her son Jason wanted a cat and she was not in favour of it. Her husband said she was too fussy about cleanliness at home.
> – 8 July 1992

'Not in favour of a cat' was putting it mildly.

As I continued to read, a disturbing picture emerged. While my parents had always referred to one nervous breakdown, it turned out that Mum had suffered a series of episodes and mild relapses, what appeared to be several 'breakdowns': in 1975, three years after she'd left Sarah in Malaysia and about a year after she'd married Dad; in 1982, two years after my birth; and twice in the early 1990s, when according to the records it appeared she'd stopped taking her medication – that matched up with my recollection of her laughing on the front lawn.

She complained that her brain was very sick. She believed there was a tumour. She believed the Stelazine was making her brain sick. Her husband said that she had been talking strangely for three months and it was getting worse. She talked nonsense and she believed she knew everything.

– 21 May 1992

She felt unwell since July 1989. She had problems with her family. She felt that her husband and son made her feel like a servant. Her libido was high and unfulfilled. She experienced a bad odour in her head. This was probably a hallucination. She has problems with her thinking.

– 15 January 1992

On 30th November 1982, she had to be hospitalised because of a brief psychotic episode. She was very suspicious, had delusions of persecution and believed that there were 'ghosts' in her home.

– 9 December 1982

A magpie warbled in the garden, and a gust of air stirred the wind chimes on the porch. Dad sucked on a tooth. When I reached the last few pages, I found something that stunned us both. I paused and took a breath. 'Do you know what this is about?' I asked calmly.

'No, don't know that,' Dad said, inspecting the paper.

It was a letter from a general hospital dated December 1974, eight months after my parents' wedding. It explained that Mum had taken an overdose of pills after feeling depressed. In my first interview with Dad, he'd recalled her falling ill in 1975, but the event outlined in this letter preceded that.

'Is this a suicide attempt?' I asked, an obvious but necessary question. What else could it have been? An accident?

Dad struggled to remember what had happened forty years ago. 'I can't remember that we called an ambulance?' he said, his face scrunching up.

I slid the letter across to him, and he leaned over and mouthed the words as he read them. A clock on the mantelpiece began chiming the Westminster melody.

'Surely you would know?' I pleaded. 'Nineteen seventy-four, before Christmas? She took an overdose and ended up in hospital?'

'I can't remember that. I don't know, "take overdose".'

The clock chimed. *Ding ... ding ... ding ... ding.*

'No, I can't remember,' he said, shaking his head before heading to the toilet.

I stopped my recorder and took a break, my stomach heaving. Poor Mum, so fragile. Twenty-five years old and in Australia for only two years. Whatever had happened to her destroyed her.

When Dad shuffled back from the bathroom, his face was creased. He sat at the head of the table and swiped the surface with his finger as if sweeping grains of sand. I struggled to accept he'd forgotten such a life-shaking event.

'Does it surprise you?' I asked.

'Yes, it surprises me that she took overdose. I can't remember.'

'How can you not know?'

'I don't know.'

'Did she not tell you? How did she get to the hospital?'

'That's what I want to know. How?' After that, he went silent.

A memory came to me. Mum was in one of her fed-up moods as she sat in her favourite spot on the couch by the record player. 'I just want to die, Jeh-sun. I want to die.' Her voice sounded like a deflating bagpipe. I lay down beside her and put my head on her round belly, wishing she'd never leave.

*

While the medical records catalogued the obliteration of Mum's mind, explaining the what and the how, they failed to answer the why – the cause of her ill health – besides general references to marital and family problems. Dad maintained that the enormous weight on Mum at that time was being separated from Sarah in Malaysia. But the most striking thing about the records was that they made no mention of Mum's previous life in Malaysia, or Sarah, or Mum's ex-husband Adel, or Nan Ruby who I believed had given her perpetual grief over something that wasn't yet clear. The records focused mainly on the tensions in my parents' marriage in Australia, and our anxious suburban lives in the 1980s and 90s. Dad and I came across as the bad guys in Mum's black-and-white narrative, even for trivial things such as wanting a cat in the house.

The most critical event documented in the records was the 1974 suicide attempt, the cause of which was vaguely defined as Mum being under family pressure and feeling depressed. How could that have been enough to send her spiralling down a course of self-destruction? Had a series of traumas added up over time, eventually crushing her, or was there one cataclysmic trigger that I was yet to uncover?

There was at least some optimism in the records. While taking her medication Mum had been getting better, and there was no record of her overdosing again. It was sobering to think that if the overdose had been fatal, I would never have been born, and Dad would have been made a widower only months after getting married.

The records provided only a brief summary of what had happened with Mum during a limited time frame, mainly from one doctor's point of view. There had to be more, I thought. I felt that frustrating vagueness when a story doesn't add up, and had a journalist's instinct to keep pursuing it until there was clarity.

I grew more curious about Mum's divorce. I knew that Adel had taken custody of Sarah and that Mum had left her behind in Malaysia, but I didn't know the specifics. I'd never given it much thought because my relatives had always described the break-up blandly: 'They got divorced.' The details were buried, perhaps because the elders in my family carried a deep shame about divorce, a burden I didn't share. Australian marriages went off the rails all the time, and I'd always assumed that Adel and Mum had split in a generic way, while Sarah had been handed over in a routine custody battle through an orderly court process.

I had never heard Mum say a bad word about Adel, a man who lived overseas and had no contact with us yet was the third person in my parents' marriage. In fact, Mum had raved about him incessantly. I'd known about his heroic prowess in the bedroom when a child shouldn't have. Once during an argument between my parents, Mum had held my arm, bent down and whispered these things in my ear. *No, Mum, I don't care about whether you're feeling frisky or horny. Bit rude.*

But another memory didn't sit well with the narrative I'd come to accept about my mother's first marriage and divorce.

One night when I was eleven, in 1992, I was sitting on the couch with Dad when he erupted in indignation, his body tense. He was pointing at the television, apparently enraged by a news story about the Gillespie children.

The Gillespie saga was a sensational international custody battle. During an access visit in Melbourne, a Malaysian prince had abducted the son and daughter he'd had with an Australian woman and taken them back to his country, their birthplace. The mother's name was Jacqueline Gillespie.

Dad seemed incensed. 'That's what happened to Mummy!'

A photo of the nine-year-old son, Iddin, appeared on the screen, and I thought he sort of looked like me, a bit mixed. But the story was complicated, and I didn't know exactly how it related to my family.

*

A few days after Christmas, more of Dad's recollections came to the surface. One night, he brought them up unprompted as we shared jasmine tea at a Chinese restaurant, opposite the blaze of a servo on Princes Highway.

'The things just come up,' he said, referring to his feelings. The *things*.

'Let's do another interview,' I suggested as we finished our meal.

On the drive home, he announced, 'I remember now, we went to Warrnambool after she was ill.'

'Okay, stop talking, save it for the interview,' I said, familiar with the way people told stories at the most unpredictable times. Often the camera crew would still be setting up when the interviewee started sharing all their best material.

'In my Corolla,' Dad kept going.

'Stop, Dad, I need to take this down.' I hit the accelerator.

At home, back in the lounge room, Dad recounted that he and Mum had gone on a road trip after her suicide attempt, which he still couldn't recall. 'Maybe we never told anyone.'

It was the summer of 1974, when their factory workplaces closed for the holidays, and Dad had heard about a magical lake that changed colours throughout the year. It was in the town of Mount Gambier, about a five-hour drive away, just over the border in South Australia. They packed their bags into his white second-hand 1970 Corolla, along with his Petri camera and tripod, then travelled along the Great Ocean Road.

At the Twelve Apostles they stopped to take photos beneath a cloudy sky, Mum sitting on the bonnet with her hands in her lap as Dad leaned against the car and clasped her shoulder. The wind tousled their hair, and frosted waves crashed into the spectacular limestone cliffs in the distance.

Further down the road they stayed overnight at the coastal town of Warrnambool, and the next day travelled onwards to Mount Gambier where they visited the town's famous Blue Lake, located in the crater of an extinct volcano. Mum posed for a photo, barely managing a smile, her arms crossed over her red shirt with white polka dots.

'On the trip, what did Mum talk to you about?' I asked Dad.

'Nothing. Just look around, she doesn't talk much. You know the sick person. I don't think she enjoyed it.' He'd thought the trip would help cheer her up. In his own quiet way, he'd been trying to pull her back from the brink.

'As a couple, though,' I said, 'as a husband and wife, you share things, so surely she talked to you about things? What did she talk to you about? She never explained, "I'm upset about this"?'

'No.'

'"I have these concerns about something"?'

'No.'

'Then what did you talk about?'

'Nothing. We don't talk much.'

'Did you talk to her?'

'I can't remember. Maybe I talk and we just drove.'

Chapter Sixteen

The next witness to take the stand in my investigation would be Mum's younger sister. I hoped she'd give me details of Mum's life before she migrated to Australia, as well as information on her first husband, Adel, and their marriage and divorce.

Aunty Madeleine had an ethereal quality about her. She wore black mascara and blue eye shadow, and her voice was as light as air. When I was a boy she was largely absent from our life in Melbourne because she lived in Launceston, Tasmania, with her Vietnamese husband and two sons.

She once paid us a brief visit when I was in Year Eleven, appearing like an apparition at our house with her long auburn-tinted hair and baggy woollen jumper. Unlike Uncle Alex's surprise visit at Hungry Jack's, hers was welcome. I sat on the couch with her, basking in her warmth and the afternoon sunlight streaming in through the windows, as she asked me about school and told me about her life in Tassie. I felt she was someone who could hold a conversation and took an interest in the world around her, and I wondered why Dad hadn't married her instead of Mum.

Aunty Madeleine later sent me a letter filled with positivity. 'Take care and God bless,' she wrote. This made me feel less forgotten by Mum's family, and I was glad when my aunty moved back to Melbourne.

In the years after that she was in touch regularly with me and Dad. She often checked in with Sarah too, becoming a kind of de facto mother to us. Every now and then, Aunty Madeleine would visit Mum's grave and send me photos of the flowers she placed there. 'Love you,' she would say, to end her conversations, a phrase that felt alien to me.

Now sixty-three, she listened to motivational CDs in her car and believed in the healing power of crystals. While she was a practising Catholic, she kept figurines of Buddha and Ganesha next to the Virgin Mary on a shelf. She believed that Mum still existed somewhere. 'She's watching over you,' Aunty Madeleine liked to say in an attempt to comfort me.

The words were certainly kind, and I half-believed the reassuring superstition despite my non-believer status. I sometimes wondered whether the fortuitous events in my life were Mum's work. Perhaps she was the reason I got promoted, or perhaps she helped me find a nice date. At the same time, I was sceptical about the existence of an afterlife, feeling sure that there was only one fragile and finite life.

After a bit of cajoling, I convinced Aunty Madeleine to come over to Dad's house for an interview. A few days after Christmas, she arrived wearing oversized sunglasses that made her look like a celebrity. We sat in the scrappy backyard on green folding chairs, a blue folding table between us. One of Dad's analogue clocks, hanging on the outside of the brick garage, ticked loudly above us. After bringing my aunty a tall glass of water, I set up my smartphone to record the interview.

All Mixed Up

Aunty Madeleine was two years younger than Mum, and her recollections began in their 1950s childhood. In the early days money was scarce, and the family of eight moved around a lot. Nan Ruby and Grandpa Leo went wherever the jobs were, with Grandpa working as a car salesman at one stage. From their home town of Penang they shifted to Singapore for a few years before moving to Kuala Lumpur.

They lived in several different homes in the Malaysian capital, while Nan made sure there was one constant in their lives: the teachings of the Catholic Church. Grandpa held a looser authority over his children and was less didactic about morals, 'blowing his money on women', or so Aunty Madeleine believed.

Under Nan's rule, the children had to gather round a makeshift altar every night. Kneeling down, they recited ten Hail Marys while fingering their rosary beads.

On Sundays they were forced to attend Mass at 8.30 am, after bathing and then dressing up in light clothing, the girls in short-sleeve cotton dresses. They would walk to a local church where they observed Holy Communion and Confession in the stifling humidity. Aunty Madeleine loathed the routine and she 'mumbled prayers'. Sometimes they went to Mass in the evening as well. 'Sinners,' Nan labelled her children if any of them skipped these rituals.

Along with the fear of God, Nan wielded a bamboo stick fashioned into a cane, perhaps like Dad's. Any disobedience, even just speaking back, was greeted with an almighty whack. But sometimes the children worked out a way to hide the cane – usually behind a cupboard – to render their tormentor impotent. It was a surprising parallel to my own attempts to dispose of Dad's bamboo cane. Rather than teaching me to respect him, this form of corporal punishment bred fear and resentment in me.

The children were assigned chores. Aunty Madeleine, eleven, collected fresh food and groceries from the market and cooked meals, and Mum, thirteen, was an expert at keeping the household clean. The two sisters stuck together, walking to their Catholic primary school as a pair. When they were a bit older, they would talk to each other about boys.

I asked Aunty Madeleine what Mum had been like, and she recalled a stunning girl who had beautiful long black hair and wore Western-style shorts, skirts and dresses. 'She was very attractive. She used to mix it up with girls who smoked and gossiped.'

About the mid-1960s, the first boy on Mum's radar was an older Eurasian called Donald, but that secret romance didn't last long. Sparks flew later when Mum, sixteen, was introduced to a Muslim Malay, Adel, by another pair of Eurasian sisters who lived up the street.

The story went that Adel had eyes for one of these sisters, but when Mum appeared on the scene she enraptured him. He was apparently much older than her – no one in my family could, or would, tell me his age – and also lived nearby. With his dapper dress sense and neatly combed hair, he was a charmer. Fit and handsome, he came from a well-off, educated family.

On weekends Adel would pick Mum up in his car and bring her back to his parents' house. They went on dates to various shopping centres and eateries in the city, while Aunty Madeleine tagged along. Sometimes the three of them drove down the coast to Port Dickson, ninety kilometres south of the capital; Aunty Madeleine was left to play among the waves while the lovers chatted and cuddled on the beach.

'Adel was good-looking, he liked music,' Aunty Madeleine recalled. 'During that time, he was kind to her. He treated her well. His family spoke English and they welcomed Patsy as part of their family.'

All of this was kept secret from Nan Ruby and Grandpa Leo.

'How did you cover it up?' I asked Aunty Madeleine. 'How did Mum cover her tracks?'

'We would just say we went to a friend's house.'

'Did Mum have any issue with the fact Adel was Muslim?'

My aunty went quiet at the question. 'No,' she said softly, pausing. 'No.'

'It didn't occur to her?'

'It didn't occur to her.'

'She just really liked him?'

'Mmm.'

The invisible religious boundaries couldn't be breached, because in Mum's mind there were none.

*

As we sat outside in the warm summer air, chatting about Mum's secret romance, Aunty Madeleine apologised for the gaps in her memory, including key dates and details. She tittered. 'It's funny how my memory is so sketchy.'

She couldn't be precise about when Nan and Grandpa became aware of their Catholic teenage daughter's relationship with a Muslim man. But she vividly remembered the violence that took place after the truth was revealed.

Nan Ruby exploded. Instead of reaching for her reliable bamboo stick, she found a brick and lurched towards Mum, while young Aunty Madeleine stood there, powerless and horrified. 'I can still see Nan picking up that brick,' she told me mournfully. 'She was going to hit your mum.'

Nan raised her arm and held the brick in the air for a few seconds. Then, perhaps thinking of the consequences, she withdrew and set down the weapon.

Another time, during one of their many arguments over Adel, Nan pulled Mum by her hair. 'It was because Adel was a Muslim,' Aunty Madeleine said, referring to Nan's objections.

Grandpa Leo, on the other hand, apparently couldn't give a toss. Nothing could stand in the way of the happiness of his 'diamond daughter', who could do no wrong. Mum was Grandpa's cherished mat salleh, which means 'beautiful white lady', referring to her European looks. His carefree attitude towards Adel infuriated Nan, and his adoration of Mum apparently made his wife madly jealous.

Despite my grandmother's attempts to split up the Catholic and Muslim lovers – Mum was dispatched to live with a relative in a town north-west of KL – their relationship persisted, until Mum snapped and ran away to live with Adel's family.

In 1968, in an act of defiance that irrevocably deepened the divide between Mum and her Catholic family, she eloped with Adel. She was nineteen. Her family was invited to the reception, but Nan and Grandpa declined.

To marry Adel, Mum had to convert to Islam – a fact unknown to me until my interview with Aunty Madeleine. I felt silly for not joining the dots earlier, even though it had been yet another unspoken aspect of the past in my family.

I recalled seeing Mum in a headscarf in a colour photo of unknown origin from the family archives, dated August 1970. Standing in front of a waterfall, Mum wore a sleeveless batik dress that flattered her figure. She would have been about six months pregnant with Sarah, though it wasn't showing. Back when I'd discovered the photo, I had assumed the headscarf was simply a fashionable addition to her outfit.

*

One year later, a tragedy further entrenched the religious division between Mum and her family. On 13 May 1969, Malaysia's simmering racial tensions exploded into riots in Kuala Lumpur, with ethnic Malays and Chinese attacking each other. The catalyst was the outcome of the general election a few days earlier. A state of emergency was declared and a curfew ordered. The official death toll is about two hundred, but other estimates put it at more than six hundred.

While there were conflicting accounts of who had started the violence, one thing was for certain: Malaysia's racial tensions were out in the open, running red hot like the weather, and they had to be contained. The streets were dangerous as rioters torched buildings and cars.

The oldest son in Mum's family died in the violence. He'd been caught up in the chaos after missing the curfew, unable to get home in time. He was only in his twenties. According to family lore, his body was left lying in the street as Kuala Lumpur burned. After that some avoided uttering his name, referring to him only as 'my older brother'.

With a son slain and a daughter married to a Muslim, it seemed the Catholic Eurasians turned their backs on Malaysia. But even before my uncle's death they had already been preparing to leave. They'd finalised their passports and paperwork to migrate to Australia for what they described as better job prospects. The race riots had delayed their departure, and in 1970 they packed up and set a course for Melbourne.

Mum was pregnant with Sarah, about five-and-a-half months, when Nan Ruby, Grandpa Leo, Aunty Madeleine and her two brothers boarded a passenger ship bound for Australia. The eldest daughter, Aunty Anne, remained in KL with her Goan husband and three young children.

At twenty-one, Mum bade her parents and siblings farewell at the Port Dickson dock. But something was terribly wrong: Mum's face was bruised. She waved away the explanation along with her family. 'We asked her what the black eye was about, and she said, "Oh, they were playing cricket in the garden and the ball hit my eye,"' Aunty Madeleine recalled. 'We took her word for it that the ball hit her face.'

As the gang plank slid away, the water began to churn white, and the ship carrying the Catholic Eurasians sailed southwards to a new frontier. From the deck, Mum's figure appeared smaller and smaller until she was a dot, swallowed up by the blue horizon.

'After that I didn't have much contact with her,' Aunty Madeleine said.

As I sat with my aunty in Dad's backyard, my blood began to simmer. I clutched my phone as it kept recording, and resisted the urge to run away. The revelations about the brick and the black eye angered and sickened me.

I pressed on. Maintaining my composure, I went back to the journalism and realised I'd reached a gap in Mum's story. We'd covered the 1950s to 1970 in KL, but what had happened to Mum between 1970 and 1972 while she remained in Malaysia? At this point in Aunty Madeleine's recollections, Sarah hadn't been born yet, and Mum and Adel were still together. I was two years short.

'What do you know about their break-up?' I asked.

'Not much.' My aunty sighed. 'Not much.'

My mind raced, and my questions tumbled out. Aunty Madeleine's usually easy demeanour became tense as our sentences overlapped each other.

'So what was your knowledge about why she came to Australia?'

'My knowledge was that she had gone to Aunty Anne's place –'

'Fled?'

'– and that Adel had come and said that he wanted the baby. He wanted Sarah.'

I paused, trying to grasp the significance of these events. 'Okay, but you don't know much about that?'

'No.'

'So your understanding –'

Aunty Madeleine interrupted. 'Aunty Anne will be able to tell you and give you an exact description,' she said, adjusting herself in the chair.

Perhaps I should have probed further, but I decided there was nothing to gain from hammering Aunty Madeleine with questions, and that I should be gentle with her after she'd opened up. As she'd just reminded me, the direct source for information on those two years would be Mum's older sister, Aunty Anne, who happened to be in Melbourne that summer, visiting from KL. She was next on my witness list.

I glanced at Dad's noisy clock: an hour had passed. I moved on, turning to what Aunty Madeleine knew firsthand. She went on to describe her relationship with Mum from 1972, which, apart from the odd phone call or interstate visit, was disconnected, with Aunty Madeleine living in Tasmania. 'We lost touch really,' she said.

'What kind of conversations did you have and what did she tell you about missing her daughter, Sarah?'

'We never used to talk about it.'

'Ever? Why not?'

'She wouldn't discuss it with me. Mum was very private, wouldn't tell me anything that was making her unhappy. But looking back, I believe Mum grieved. Separation is grief. She ached in her heart to have Sarah come and live here, but I don't believe they would have had a chance. It would have been a no-no, meaning that Adel would have never let Sarah join Patsy in Australia.' Aunty Madeleine sighed, her expression hidden by her large sunglasses. 'Tsk. If your Mum was alive today, she'd be getting all the support from me, absolutely.'

Chapter Seventeen

'Look ugly!' Dad said, shaking his head in disgust as I drove his silver Corolla through the cemetery. He pointed to the cluttered rows of black marble headstones that resembled a small city. 'Look terrible!'

In the back seat, Aunty Anne didn't seem to be paying attention. She appeared enraptured by the immaculately maintained rows of rose bushes and the gently landscaped lawns. 'Oh, roses, so beautiful, lah!' she purred, putting emphasis on the 'ful' in the elongated Malaysian way.

Mum's eldest sister, now in her early seventies, was clucking again, her sentences full stopped by the flourish of that colloquial Malaysian word 'lah'.

Aunty Anne loved saying 'lah'. She clucked like a loving mother hen:

'Yes, lah.'

'No, lah.'

'Nonsense, lah!'

Lah. Lah. Lah.

Now she said, 'In Malaysia they don't look after the

cemeteries. They are scary, full of drunkards and drug addicts, lah.'

To me, the tranquil gardens, with botanical names such as Banksia and Gardenia, were certainly a welcome distraction. Going to the cemetery was a ritual I tried to avoid, partly because I lived interstate but also because it brought up awkward feelings.

When I was a teenager, Dad would bundle our little dog, Spike, along for the trip. At Mum's bronze plaque, we'd stand uncomfortably, two lone figures not meeting eyes, wordless except for Dad talking to Spike. It was much the same in my adulthood, minus the pet, so at least this time we had company.

With her straight black bob, Aunty Anne was a contrast to free-spirited Aunty Madeleine. Her feet were firmly planted on the ground, and she was more practical and earnest. While Aunty Madeleine had travelled the world, Aunty Anne had committed to her life in Malaysia and raised three children with her husband, Uncle Rod. She had a warm smile and could be funny with her blatant honesty. She often urged me to visit her in KL with the promise of a free room and daily cooked meals, and I was about to take her up on that offer; in the new year, I would travel to visit Sarah in Malaysia.

Ahead of our interview in the afternoon, Aunty Anne, Dad and I had decided to take some flowers to Mum, a small bunch of brilliant red and white dahlias wrapped in brown paper. As clouds began to march overhead, we parked at Mum's row and walked across the manicured lawn to her spot at the end. Dad was in his baggy jeans and a black *National Geographic*-branded fleece jacket, and Aunty Anne was in billowing chinos and a black-and-white striped cardigan.

As we approached the grave, I noticed that an ill-fitting plastic vase had been slotted into the plaque; it was supposed to sit neatly in the ground but was poking out.

'Wait a minute, I fix,' Dad said. He wandered back to the car.

My aunty held the bouquet as I stared at the weathered lettering in desperate need of a good polish. When I was twelve, Dad had appointed me to choose the plaque's image and words, and I remembered flicking through the catalogue in the cemetery office. The best picture, I'd thought, was of the Sacred Heart, an iconic image of Jesus with a halo and a glowing heart in his chest.

Although I hadn't met my sister then, I'd decided to include her name. Whatever ambivalence I may have had about her up to that point, reason prevailed. She was Mum's daughter and deserved to be acknowledged. The plaque read: *Beloved wife of Narong, dear mother of Jason and Sarah.*

'It was raining cats and dogs that day,' Aunty Anne recalled of the burial. 'The Chinese believe that when there's rain on the day of the funeral it means the dead don't want to go.'

It had been more like a flood. With the angry sky emptying on us, I'd stood in a forest of umbrellas in my wet school uniform, a whirlpool of orange clay mud gathering around my polished black shoes. As Mum's coffin had been lowered into the ground, I'd pictured her body in her fine clothes, rotting along with the other bodies under our feet. 'Worm food, that's what happens!' Dit had cried out in the background.

Dad returned from the car, carrying a small crowbar. On his knees, he began attacking the dirt in the slot. Soil flew everywhere. The wind picked up, red and white petals floating away. As Dad's actions became more furious, the plaque, seemingly steadfast, flipped over on the grass. We'd come to pay our respects, and my father was desecrating my mother's grave.

'Oh my god, Dad. Oh my god.'

'Aiyah, lah,' Aunty Anne muttered.

He kept digging with the crowbar like a madman.

'Dad, that's enough!' I said, but I couldn't stop him.

Once he was done, he patted the plaque back into place and replaced the vase, which slotted in neatly. 'There. Yeh.'

'We'd better get that fixed, Dad.'

After arranging the bouquet we stood around aimlessly, Dad chatting with Aunty Anne while I took some photos. That summer was fickle, and it started to drizzle.

'Let's get outta here,' I said, hands in my short pockets. 'It's gonna piss down.'

We cantered back to the car, the sky turning grey-blue.

'Never mind, lah,' Aunty Anne said. 'I say my prayers later.'

*

In the afternoon, back at Dad's house, Aunty Anne sat on the charcoal sofa while I took the armchair. Out of earshot, Dad clattered around with the dishes in the kitchen.

I wanted Aunty Anne to fill in the blanks left by Aunty Madeleine. Why had Mum left Sarah behind, and how had Adel come to have custody of her?

As a witness in my inquiry, Aunty Anne was a little reluctant, sometimes frustrating, and tended towards self-censorship. A few times she struggled to understand my Aussie accent.

'What did you see?' I asked.

'I didn't *say* anything.'

'No, I mean *see*. See.'

I pushed her gently and brought her back to the questions.

'Not a nice story, lah,' she said. 'A lot of bad things.'

This kind of diversion happens occasionally in interviews when the subject presumes a journalist is seeking a particular narrative of an event – but that wasn't what I was after. 'I'm just looking for the truth,' I insisted.

'Yah, there's the truth, but there are a lot of sad things not worth telling you sometimes because it might affect you. You will get upset.'

'No, I'm not going to get upset. I'm just trying to understand the truth of the matter. I don't want you to be holding back.'

Aunty Anne's lips pursed, her right elbow twitching.

'Are you okay?' I asked.

She looked away. 'Certain things very hard to bring it out,' she explained, gazing into the distance. 'A lot of hurt ... and sadness ... and disappointment.'

Was I being overly eager? I wondered if I should slow down. 'Are you okay?'

'No, no, I'm alright,' she said quickly.

*

In 1970 Aunty Anne was living with her husband, their two young boys and toddler daughter in a predominantly Chinese neighbourhood of Kuala Lumpur. Their rented two-storey terrace had a sparse garden where she grew lace ferns in pots. A white rendered wall and a metal gate surrounded the corner property.

That year, Mum was pregnant with Sarah. As her two-year marriage to Adel began to disintegrate, she turned up distraught on Aunty Anne's doorstep at least twice. The first time, Mum came in the night, her face wet with tears. Her older sister quickly pulled her into the house, where she took refuge for several months.

The second time was in early 1972. While Adel was at work, Mum packed her belongings and brought Sarah, about fifteen months old, to Aunty Anne's place.

Another swollen eye – this time Mum had 'fallen down'.

She slept in an upstairs bedroom with baby Sarah. But as Aunty Anne recalled, the young woman taking shelter in her home wasn't the bubbly person she'd known as a girl. Instead of being her usual jokey and joyful self, Mum was distant and detached. The light inside her was beginning to dim. 'She was slightly off.'

Aunty Anne was deeply worried about her sister as warning signs became more apparent. One day Mum absentmindedly tried to plop little Sarah into a bath full of scalding water, and Aunty Anne grabbed the child before she was burned.

One evening, long after pitch-blackness had fallen on the neighbourhood's narrow streets and back alleys, Aunty Anne and Mum settled with the four children in the downstairs living room. Uncle Rod was out.

It was almost bedtime when they heard the toot of a car horn and the slow rolling of tyres. A car door opened and slammed shut. Through the window they saw Adel stroll into the front courtyard – Aunty Anne had forgotten to lock the gate.

My aunty tensed. She went to the door immediately and asked Adel what he wanted. He demanded to speak to his wife. Aunty Anne ordered her children to stay inside while she and Mum went outside.

Clutched to Mum's bosom was little Sarah, wearing a smocked dress of pink checks with cute buttons. In the dim light, Mum faced her husband.

With few words, Adel reached for the girl and wrested her from Mum's arms.

The women were blindsided.

'I divorce you,' Adel said before sauntering out the gate with Sarah and driving off into the night. As a Muslim husband, that was all he had to do to divorce his wife.

Inside the house, my cousins had been playing with toys and listening to music. Oblivious to the goings-on in the courtyard, they suddenly sat upright, terrified by Mum's uncontrollable sobbing and wailing.

*

The family quickly closed ranks and prepared to dispatch Mum to Australia for her safety. Nan Ruby would sponsor her. Letters were written up. Permission was sought.

Uncle Rod was a well-connected businessman who worked in the motor industry. In March 1972, he sought advice from a contact in the Australian Trade Commission in KL, explaining his sister-in-law's predicament. In a typewritten letter I found in Dad's files, Uncle Rod informed one R.W. Holberton that Mum wanted to join her family and 'forget the past'.

By May, Mum had applied through the Australian High Commission in KL: *I shall be much obliged if you could consider my case owing to the fact that my parents, brothers and sister and relatives have settled down permanently in*

Australia. I will assure you that I will not be a burden to the Australian Government as I have been assured of a job.

The wheels of bureaucracy between the two countries turned quickly. In early June, Mum had an interview with the High Commission, and within two weeks she received approval to migrate to Australia. The divorce was settled, and the immigration papers were stamped, signed and delivered.

In Melbourne, Uncle Johnny dipped into his savings and paid to fly his sister to her new home. By the time Mum found herself standing by the departure gate at KL's international airport, the plans for her future were neatly tied up. With her long black hair flowing down her back, she wore a pristine dress and clasped a new handbag. A suitcase with all her belongings was on its way along a conveyor belt to a Malaysian Airline System plane. There would be no fond farewells, and no chance to pop by a souvenir shop to buy a trinket as a reminder of her country of birth. She was leaving Malaysia with the image of little Sarah fading into the night, and a hole in her heart. Her arrival in Australia would defy the neat migrant narrative of someone seeking out a more fortunate life in another country.

Aunty Anne and Uncle Rod said goodbye to her at the airport.

'It is for your own good,' Aunty Anne recalled saying.

Mum began to cry.

Uncle Rod took hold of his sister-in-law and wished her well, saying he hoped she'd find a new husband in Australia. The vicar of a Catholic church in KL had even signed a note certifying that Mum was 'free to marry', officially bringing her back into the fold of Christianity.

As Mum stepped onto the plane, Uncle Rod turned to Aunty Anne. 'Poor thing. It's for the best.'

At the other end of Mum's journey was a foreign city. Waiting for her was Nan Ruby, who would never let her daughter forget her decision to run away from her Catholic family to marry a Muslim man. At the same time, Mum was a pariah in Islam, as leaving the religion was a grave sin. She was an apostate.

'Patsy did it all on the quiet,' Aunty Anne recalled. 'She left our house, she defied my mother, went to stay with Adel and got married. Then she came and told us she was married. She really broke my parents' hearts.'

*

As I sat in Dad's lounge room listening to Aunty Anne's version of events, I struggled to understand how Mum had let go of Sarah so easily. The way my aunty explained it, Mum hadn't screamed for help or yelled at Adel, or chased him into the street, or thrown herself in front of his car, banging on the bonnet and windows.

'I can still see the picture in my mind, how he grabbed the child from her,' Aunty Anne said with a sigh, the r's trilling on her tongue, her face as taut as a drum. *Grrreb*. 'I will never forget that day for the rest of my life until I go to my grave. The way he grabbed the child, lah. Terrible.'

'Why didn't Mum leave Sarah inside the house before she went out to see Adel?'

'I had no maid at the time. He just went towards her and grabbed the child.'

'Was there any warning?'

'No warning, just grabbed the child.'

'Did you scream?'

'No, no, I didn't scream.'

'Did Mum scream or shout?'

'No, she just cried.'

'But –' I paused, my mind ticking over. 'Did Mum try to pull away?'

'No, she didn't pull away.'

'Why not?'

'How to pull away?' My aunty's voice began rising in pitch. 'He's got a grip of Sarah already. She didn't want to hurt the baby, lah.'

'Did he run away?'

'No. Just walked away, calmly turned and walked away. Like nothing. Took the child and put her in the car.'

I also found it difficult to believe that Mum had left Malaysia without her baby so willingly. It appeared Nan Ruby had forced Mum to come to Australia, wielding so much power that her daughter had simply obeyed – as an Asian, you did not defy your parents, otherwise you were out on your arse.

I thought of how Uncle Rod had written in his immigration letter that Mum wanted to 'forget the past', which certainly wasn't a legal prerequisite to come to Australia. How could Mum have wanted to simply forget about her daughter, my sister, who had been very much alive in the present?

'Why didn't Mum stay and try to fight?' I asked Aunty Anne.

'No point, lah. Adel already showed his hand and said, "Divorce."'

'Could Mum have fought for custody of Sarah?'

'No, she had no money to take to court.'

It seemed Mum could do nothing to get Sarah back. Adel would never have allowed his daughter to grow up in another faith. Even if Mum had mounted a legal fight, Aunty Anne said she would have had no chance of winning.

'That is why Sarah became a Muslim and still today she is a Muslim.'

After baby Sarah was snatched, Aunty Anne went to Mum's bedroom and cleared out her wardrobe, throwing her Malaysian-style sarongs and baju kurung into a suitcase. The next day she bought Mum new dresses, new shoes, a new handbag and a new set of cosmetics. Any reminder of Mum's Muslim life was purged, and the suitcase full of her old clothes was donated to charity. 'I gave it to some poor people,' Aunty Anne told me.

'Did Mum agree to that?'

'Yes, she agreed. She didn't want the clothes. She was very grateful for what I did for her.'

'She asked you to get rid of her stuff?' I said, my eyebrows raised.

'Yes.'

'She asked you?' I had to be sure: there was a distinction between Mum desiring to do this and being pressured by her Catholic family.

'She told me to get rid of everything. If she's going to Australia she doesn't want any remembrance of her old life. So I got everything, lah. I being the eldest looked after her very well. I told her to forget about the past and go and live with Nan.' Aunty Anne added proudly, 'I'm the devil that got your mother to Australia.'

Chapter Eighteen

I took Dad's car five minutes up the road, past a shopping centre where the quarry used to be. At least it hadn't been turned into a tip.

I parked up a side street and walked around to the house where Nan Ruby used to live with Uncle Johnny, the closest sibling to Mum in the 1980s, and the most present member of her family during my childhood. He still lived there by himself.

A year older than Mum, Uncle Johnny was now sixty-six. He'd never married, and he'd lived with Nan Ruby until he was forty-seven, when he declared independence and bought out her portion of the mortgage; she moved to a unit across the road. He was a workaholic, rarely taking a break from his hospital assistant job. Once when he had a few weeks off, he chose to stay at home and tidy up the place, which he said had 'gotten out of control' – looking around his fastidiously neat house, I couldn't imagine what he meant. He didn't own a car, preferring to brave the busy suburban roads on his trusty bike.

Today his small dining table was covered with a clean white tablecloth. It was cluttered at one end with Christmas chocolates and bottles of vitamins. His once full head of thick black hair now retreated in wisps of white.

'Can I put some music on?' Uncle Johnny asked. 'It helps me relax.'

He went to find a CD and put some piano music on his stereo.

I reminded Uncle Johnny how, when he dropped by our house, he and Mum would greet each other in Malay.

To my surprise, Uncle Johnny revealed that he and his sister had actually been taking the piss. 'I really didn't like Bahasa Melayu. I was no good at it, and I wanted to forget about it.'

Throughout the interview I had to slow him down several times as he jumped from event to event.

He recalled Malaysia's race riots of 13 May 1969. A Chinese acquaintance had advised him to seek shelter. '"Don't hang around the city. Go home. They are expecting trouble,"' Uncle Johnny recalled her saying. 'She knew something was going to happen, so I listened to her. That night they went berserk, and the Chinese and the Malays started massacring each other.' Uncle Johnny's dark features could have put him in peril. 'She practically saved my life because I would have been mistaken for a Malay. A Chinese person would have killed me. That was my luck.'

He pulled out an old photo album and showed me pictures of Mum when she first arrived in Australia. They were taken somewhere in the Victorian Alps, in the depths of winter. Having swapped tropical Malaysia for bone-chilling snow fields, Mum was underdressed in white slacks, a bright red short-sleeved knit and white mittens. Her long black hair stood out against the snow. She wore a pair of shaded sunglasses, posing like a glamorous model. She was stunning.

These images jarred with what had been hidden in Mum's mind.

'I think your mother was very heartbroken,' Uncle Johnny reflected, 'having to deal with her first marriage and, most importantly, not having access to her daughter. When she came to Australia, she was always distant, always thinking of Sarah. It was mental torture for her to think that her daughter was there in Malaysia.'

Mum had confided in him about her difficulties adjusting to her conversion to Islam. 'She was not terribly keen on the Qur'an,' Uncle Johnny said. 'She said she was false to learn the Qur'an. Coming from a Catholic background and then going to learn the Qur'an is not easy. But her mother-in-law was determined for her to do it.' Mum had known nothing about her new religion, he said. 'You're born and baptised Catholic, and all of a sudden someone puts the Qur'an in front of you and asks you to learn it. And it's not even written in English!'

I found it hard to believe Mum hadn't seen all of this coming. Surely she'd gone into the marriage with open eyes about Adel being a Muslim?

When I put this to Uncle Johnny, he nodded but added, 'When you're in love, religion has nothing to do with anything, really. They say love is blind, and, to her, I don't think she thought about the religion. Religion was not even in her mind. She was in love with Adel and that's it.'

Uncle Johnny confirmed that the family had boycotted Mum and Adel's wedding. 'We were a bit fanatic ourselves because we were Catholics and we disagreed with her marrying a Muslim. My only objection back then was religion, really. I look back now and think it was unfair.'

After being brought up under Nan's dogmatic regime – 'As a kid, I had religion shoved down my throat' – he became fed up with Catholicism, much to her bafflement. Well into his adulthood, she continued to pester her son about why he'd stopped going to church.

*

Trips to the beach typified Mum and Uncle Johnny's early childhood in Penang. During the holidays, Grandpa Leo would take the whole family, in two round trips of his car, to a bungalow by the ocean. The six children would wander down to a beach lined with fishing boats, where they'd collect seashells and watch the local fishermen pull in their long nets laden with fluttering fish. The men were generous enough to throw the kids a few spare ones to take home for dinner.

Back then, according to Uncle Johnny, Mum was a sensitive, pretty girl who was full of heart. But by the time she was living in Oakleigh, she'd become a different woman.

She would ring him up, insistent. 'Johnny, are you coming over?'

After he arrived on his bike, she would offer him a soft drink and a bowl of canned lychees with vanilla ice cream. As the round white fruit swam around in the sugary water, they sat on the couch and passed the time listening to a Brenda Lee record spinning on the turntable. It was often the song 'All Alone Am I' – a melancholic tune I later recognised as one Mum had hummed in the shower.

'Do you think Mum could have got better?' I asked Uncle Johnny.

His eyes searched the space in front of him. 'I don't know. She was alright on her medications. She had her moments. Sometimes she would feel bad, and other times she would feel happy. She was a bit up and down.'

Up and down, just like Mum used to say.

Nan Ruby had wanted nothing to do with Mum's treatment. 'To her, mental illness was very taboo,' Uncle Johnny explained. 'Nan didn't want to talk about it. She didn't want to address the situation. To her, it was a shameful thing, which of course it is not.' Something was bound to happen to Mum after all she'd suffered, Uncle Johnny reasoned. 'It was a pressure cooker.'

While he was unaware of Mum's suicide attempt in 1974, he recalled a phone call from Dad on the night she'd collapsed in bed in 1993. From the hospital, Dad had asked Uncle Johnny to inspect the mirrored bathroom cabinet and check all the bottles of medicine. As he twisted their lids open, he discovered the bottles were full or near full, meaning Mum hadn't swigged them down. The doctors had flushed her stomach with charcoal, wrongly thinking she had tried to end her life.

The next morning, Uncle Johnny was on autopilot and clocked in for work without considering taking the day off.

Later, after the funeral, he bought a bunch of flowers and jumped on his bike. For ten kilometres he rode along the dangerous four-lane roads out past the industrial estates and arterial junctions of the south-east, where the trucks rumbled perilously close to cars, let alone cyclists. Once he'd found the lawn he was searching for, he walked with his bike towards Mum's fresh grave, a mound of dirt like a gash in the grass. He rang his bell, saying hello to his sister.

As I sat with him at his dining table, his face creased and grew wet with tears, so I quickly asked a different question to lighten the mood.

*

When we said goodbye, Uncle Johnny cheerfully encouraged me to come back if I needed anything else. But as I walked to Dad's car, I thought about how he'd wept, and I worried I'd pushed him too far. My uncle had been the first to crack; my aunties hadn't wavered. Dad, as usual, had been impervious.

In my work as a journalist, without blinking I stretch people's boundaries every day, asking them to pour out their hearts in the name of a story. I am always surprised by how open some interviewees are, no matter how painful their loss. Just like my family members, I was not one to open up easily.

In 2011, a woman approached me as I stood outside a bushfire evacuation centre. I hit the record button and held up the mic as she calmly told me that she and her fourteen-year-old son would be returning home to ashes. She wanted nothing from me except to tell her story, to be listened to, on national radio.

Another time, later that year, I sat under gum trees in country South Australia with a woman who had lost her brother to suicide. I teared up with her.

As for Uncle Johnny, I reassured myself that he probably needed to let out his feelings. After all, this was the first time we'd spoken in more than twenty years about what had happened to Mum.

I'd asked him why he disappeared during the three years following Mum's death, leaving me and Dad in the cold. I remembered the day he came over after his long absence, like a soldier returning from a war. I stood awkwardly, with few conversation topics. He torpedoed to the backyard, said a few words to Spike, then left. The visit lasted minutes.

'I don't know,' Uncle Johnny said softly. 'I went a bit blank too.'

*

The next day with Dad, I expressed my surprise at everyone's sudden openness despite years of painful silence, their religious sensitivities and the difficulties in breaking down their own walls.

Dad was quick with his answer. 'Because you asked.'

Uncle Johnny's interview would be the last in Melbourne. I was heading home to Sydney and then off to spend a week in Malaysia. Aunty Anne would return to KL too, and I would stay at her place for a night with the promise of a home-cooked meal. The remainder of my time would be spent cocooned in a fancy hotel downtown between visits with Sarah and other relatives.

Dad continued to pull out prehistoric documents from his filing cabinet. 'Painful,' he said, shuffling into the lounge room. His face was puffed out like an inflated paper bag as he dumped some files on the floor.

'What?' I asked.

'It is painful. Painful to read.'

I went over to the small pile. Alongside a condolence book and an old pink notebook filled with more of Mum's liquid paper mess were a few odds and ends: a dot matrix printout of an invitation I'd designed for Mum's funeral, a pink hospital card labelled with her personal details, and a leaflet about helping children cope with grief, which had an illustration of an Amanda Vanstone lookalike reading a book to a couple of kids. I smirked at a note from a counsellor offering support. Counselling? I hadn't received any. A Coroner's letter confirmed Mum had died of myocarditis and that we had the option of requesting an inquest. There was none. Curious about myocarditis, I began googling, and discovered that some medications could cause it. Mum was in her forties, seemingly young to have heart problems. Dad said she'd been receiving injections every three months for her depression. Had her medication interfered with her heart?

Then I sighed. This meagre pile of paper had become what was left of Mum's life: bureaucratic detritus.

But on New Year's Eve, Dad uncovered something more interesting: old letters that revealed my parents' efforts to bring Sarah to Australia in the late 1970s, with the help of family confidante and Jewish librarian Betty.

The first letter, handwritten by Betty, was addressed to Australia's Commissioner for Community Relations, Al Grassby. A former Whitlam Government immigration minister, he was a multiculturalism advocate known for his colourful dress sense.

Betty wrote:

From photographs I have seen of Sarah, the child is beautiful, healthy and happy.

My friend's wife now wishes to bring her daughter who is now eight-years-old to this country.

The question is, how could she go about doing this, supposing of course that the father will give his permission, or would that permission not be necessary?

Would the Malaysian government allow the child to leave? Would the Australian government let the child in? Is there a consulting service to discuss the problems involved in this move?

The young couple are very insistent on doing something about the child and have asked me to write to you on their behalf.

– 13 August 1978

About two weeks later, a reply came from Commissioner Grassby's office. But he mistakenly thought Dad rather than Mum was seeking custody of Sarah:

> The position is that custody would have to be granted to him, and then there would be no difficulty about bringing his child to Australia.
> My recommendation is that he seek legal custody of his child, and then it is simply a matter of arranging for him to come and a visa would be automatically granted for a dependent child of an Australian citizen to come here.
> Once he has secured custody in accordance to the law of his birth and residence then you could contact me and I will be happy to help further.
> Kind regards,
> Yours sincerely,
> (The Hon) A J Grassby
> Commissioner for Community Relations
> – 29 August 1978

Even though the commissioner had muddled up the details, it seemed that Mum, as an Australian citizen, could seek legal custody of Sarah. I read the letter back to Dad and pointed this out, but he couldn't explain why they hadn't hired a lawyer to beef up their case. Perhaps it had been the cost.

Three years after Grassby's letter, my parents again tried to bring Sarah to Australia, this time by writing to a family friend of Adel's. In Dad's files, a typewritten letter dated 1981 proposed an adoption. While it was signed by Mum, its style was so formal that surely someone else had written it, probably Betty on Mum's behalf.

All Mixed Up

The contents were startling and profound. A desperate last-ditch appeal.

I took the adoption letter back with me to Sydney and saved it for my trip to KL. I knew that Sarah needed to see the words for herself.

Chapter Nineteen

In preparation for my week-long trip to KL, I went all out and updated my ancient gear with new equipment: the latest smartphone, a laptop, a digital SLR camera and a digital audio recorder. With all these gadgets, I had become my dad.

I also packed the adoption letter Sarah needed to see, and a hundred dollars Dad had chipped in to spend on gifts for my nephews.

Concerned about flying with Malaysia Airlines after the two disasters the previous year, I booked with Qantas. My flight took me to KL via Singapore, a familiar route, and I welcomed the soupy humidity that hugged me on the night of my arrival in that chaotic metropolis. KL's roads were designed as if the town planners had spilled a bowl of noodles on the ground.

My fondness for Malaysia helped keep the pilot light of Mum's memory flickering. Here, there were only two seasons, dry and wet, and it was perpetually hot and muggy. Everything sweated; even cold drinks were coated in beads of perspiration.

This was my fifth trip to Malaysia, and I was excited at the prospect of long tropical nights eating out with my relatives at colourful open-air markets. I salivated at the thought of flaky roti and rich chicken curry, and a cold glass of teh ais, a traditional iced tea copiously sweetened with condensed milk. On menus it was listed alongside mugs of Milo, an Australian drink that Malaysians adored.

I also looked forward to using 'can' as a slang word, meaning 'can do', and adding 'lah' to the end of every sentence like Aunty Anne did.

'Shall we go out for some roti canai, lah?'

'Can, lah!' in the affirmative.

In the darkness I arrived at Aunty Anne's house, her warm face greeting me at the door as fragrant aromas wafted from the kitchen. 'Come, come, come.'

These days my aunty lived alone with a speckled Dalmatian mongrel at her feet. Uncle Rod had succumbed to cancer in 2006; he'd been a heavy drinker but a light smoker, and the disease had attacked his lungs.

The two-storey terrace had a small courtyard with a car space and a patch of lawn. It was typical of the homes around KL, crammed up against each other for blocks and blocks. Most properties had spiked metal gates and bars on the ground-floor windows to stop unwelcome intruders. Discreet but deep open gutters ran along the streets below the front fences, large enough for small children to fall into – I knew this well, having stumbled into a gutter on a previous trip.

Aunty Anne's tiled living room was unchanged since my last visit, the walls panelled in dark wood.

'I cooked for you,' she cooed, then winced from the pain in her legs caused by a recent fall. Apologising for being out of it, she sat down at the dining table.

I went round to the kitchen and approached the stove with anticipation.

'Take on the pot there, lah,' she called from the living room. *Lah. Lah. Lah.*

My mouth watered as I scooped out a generous serve of fragrant yellow curry, kari ayam, onto a plate. It was a dish Mum used to make, a spicy concoction of chicken pieces on the bone with chunks of soft potato in a thin, rich gravy. I sought it out at Malaysian restaurants in Sydney, and it never failed to bead my forehead with sweat.

After I finished the last delicious morsels, I went to bed with a headache caused by my long flight. In the featureless upstairs room with parquetry floors, I slept soundly in my jocks under a thin white sheet.

*

The first time I went to Malaysia was also my first overseas trip. It was 1984, and I was three. We visited Mum's birthplace, Penang, in the north-west, to see family and the sights.

We flew from Melbourne via Singapore, landing in steaming KL to be greeted by Uncle Rod and Aunty Anne at the airport. 'Aiyah, such a handsome boy, lah,' she clucked, and handed me a new white monkey soft toy, a furry friend for my beloved Monkey. Later I met Grandpa Leo for the first and only time, as well as my Goan-Malaysian cousins.

Outside a Buddhist temple in Penang, I stood on a bridge over a pond where half-submerged turtles moved around languidly. I reached into a plastic bag, pulled out a handful of shredded leaves and sprinkled them like confetti over the bannister, feeding the turtles. I was wearing a T-shirt printed with R2-D2 and C-3PO, and Mum stood next to me in a pink singlet and red slacks. Dad, the amateur photographer, flitted around capturing the event from different angles: action shots of me dropping the leaves; perspective shots looking down on the dozens of slimy turtles; wide shots of me and Mum on the walkway; and a super-wide angle of just me on the bridge.

At a Penang beach, Mum stripped down to a swimsuit and we frolicked in the shallow waves. We took a train up a steep hill and had tea amid lush gardens, a blanket of mist hanging over the city below. We visited a relative's house where we sat on an outdoor swing chair; Mum laid her arm on the back of the seat, and I imitated her. I was wearing my favourite Vegemite T-shirt.

Decades later, I discovered that trip to Malaysia had been more than just a holiday. 'Mummy wanted to see Sarah,' Dad told me.

In 1984, Sarah was thirteen and remained unknown to me. Twelve years had passed since Mum had seen her baby daughter.

'Aunty Anne,' Dad said. 'She was the one who arranged a meeting between Mummy and Sarah.'

It had taken place at Sarah's high school in KL and was all done in secret.

*

I woke to the sound of a running tap and the clatter of dishes in a sink. A dog barked in the distance, and a motorbike purred outside. The red curtain over the glass-slat window was glowing, the Malaysian sun beating behind it.

Downstairs I noticed that the rest of the house was sweltering, and Aunty Anne told me that my room was the only one with air conditioning.

After using the basic hose shower in the downstairs dunny, I stickybeaked out the back of the house. There wasn't much: a concrete courtyard faced an empty laneway and the rear of neighbouring houses. But next to the back door was a junk room filled with sunlight that fell softly through its window. Something about that room made me linger for a while in the doorway.

Aunty Anne had prepared a breakfast of toasted white bread and boiled eggs, and after eating I sat down with her on the couch for our second interview. The Dalmatian-cross sat quietly by her feet.

On the monitor of my DSLR camera, I showed her a photo of my visit to Malaysia in 1984. It was a photo of a photo from one of Dad's albums, taken at KL airport on our way back to Melbourne. A youthful Aunty Anne appeared in a blue floral dress. Next to her was Uncle Rod, his hands clasped on his knee. Mum wore a white dress with blue-and-yellow diagonal stripes, her face melancholy. Unknown to me at the time, she had just secretly reunited with Sarah. And then there was me, three years old, wearing a tartan shirt and clutching the white plush monkey.

'That's you, is it?' My aunty inspected the monitor, smiling. 'Spoilt brat!'

We laughed.

'You pushed your mother and father around,' she said of me as a little boy. 'Yah, pushy from young!' She chuckled, but I suspected she also found me pushy as I probed her memory about Mum's secret meeting with Sarah.

Aunty Anne recalled that Mum, Dad and I had stayed in the upstairs room where I was a guest now, and that at one point Dad had gone dead quiet when Mum threatened to ring up Adel 'just to annoy him'. 'He took it seriously – he got grumpy,' my aunty said of Dad. 'Otherwise your dad, bottom line, he loved your mother very much.'

I realised that Dad had made a tremendous gesture in paying for the flights and bringing us over so Mum could visit a girl who wasn't his flesh and blood. And although twelve years had passed since the night of the snatching, it must have been nerve-racking for Mum and Aunty Anne to arrange the meeting.

I wiped my brow. 'At the time, were you scared?'

'I was not scared of anything. I was doing the right thing to take her to go and see her daughter.'

Aunty Anne had gone to Sarah's school with Mum in one of Uncle Rod's chauffeur-driven work cars. My aunty recalled briefly seeing Mum 'manja manja with Sarah', a Malay expression meaning to pamper and fuss. The pair then disappeared from her line of sight. When Mum returned to the car she seemed delighted to have seen Sarah but was upset at the same time. Aunty Anne provided few other details, and I expected that Sarah would tell me a lot more.

The conversation turned to a topic I hadn't planned to bring up: Nan's tense relationship with my parents. As a boy I'd never understood the frost between them, but now I knew what had happened with Mum. How about Dad, though?

A few weeks earlier in Melbourne, Aunty Madeleine had revealed to me that Nan was 'very nasty' to him in 1993 when Mum was comatose in the hospital. 'Nan Ruby wouldn't let me have dialogue with your dad,' Aunty Madeleine had told me. 'I was the bringer of news to Nan every time I came back from the hospital. I used to have telephone conversations with your dad in the evening, and I can remember Nan coming out of the bedroom and being angry because I was talking with him.'

Sitting on the couch in KL, Aunty Anne revealed more. 'My mother was always against your father. Now she's dead, I can say, lah.'

Nan had wanted Mum to marry a white Australian man. A puteh.

'A white man wouldn't have tolerated your mum as much as your father tolerated her,' Aunty Anne declared. 'Your dad tolerated her a lot, and he loved her.'

In the case of Aunty Anne's marriage, Nan had disapproved of Uncle Rod because he was Goan, calling him 'black fellow'. That was consistent with what Dad recalled of Nan when they'd first met. He had found out through Mum that Nan called him an 'ah-chong' behind his back. 'How is the ah-chong?' she would say.

Nan's Islamophobia and racism made no sense to me, given our family was all mixed up. She'd had mixed blood too.

*

In my aunty's stifling living room, I kept listening to the mother hen as she clucked. *Lah. Lah. Lah.* Eventually, a staggering revelation popped out like an egg.

Aunty Anne's eyes widened. She halted. Her words emerged slowly, as if she thought they might tear a hole in the universe. Unrelenting heat radiated through the walls. 'Nan felt your father took your mum's life. Did something to her. Nan told me he took her life. They had a fight. He pushed her, and she had a heart attack. Nan thought he got rid of her, lah.'

My brow furrowed. My breath escaped me. Nothing came out.

Dad wasn't even there to see Mum collapse. I was.
Nan Ruby wasn't there either. I was.
I was there. Called the ambulance. Did CPR.

Nan's belief had been absurd and false, a toxic lie.

'What was your reaction?' I asked Aunty Anne casually, hiding behind my journalist's armour to maintain my composure.

'I didn't believe her.'

A memory came to me from the night I'd called the ambulance. Uncle Johnny was speaking to Nan on one of the phones in Dad's study, a sliver of light beneath the door. Crouched down on the polished floorboards, I eavesdropped.

'Murder her?' Uncle Johnny exclaimed. 'He did not murder her!'

I absorbed those words and held them tight. Most of the time they'd lain dormant in my mind. I'd thought Nan was referring to me, an assumption that tortured me whenever it entered my thoughts.

More than twenty years after Mum's death, Nan's grudge against Dad was finally explained. She'd decided he'd murdered her. But why had Nan's lie been allowed to remain unchallenged for so many years, especially while Dad and I had been plunged into the deep freeze?

Nan Ruby's authority over her adult children had been so potent that they'd held on to this secret until after her death. Now I understood why Uncle Alex had said there was 'confusion', during that visit he and my cousin Daniel had paid me at Hungry Jack's. It had been confusion on their part – Dad and I were owed an apology.

The events of the past were immutable. I thanked Aunty Anne for her frankness, even though it was tardy. I finally knew the truth, and that was enough for me.

*

That afternoon I visited the house where Sarah had been taken from Mum's arms. It was a short drive away, so Aunty Anne's eldest son, my cousin Sam, and his wife, Elise, picked me up in their white Mazda hatchback.

With his light brown skin and short stature, you couldn't tell that Sam and I were related. At fifty-one he still had a youthful exuberance and an easygoing nature. He and Elise were practising Catholics, Elise the more superstitious of the two. A Portuguese-Eurasian originally from the city of Malacca, she was a gentle woman with a broad smile, black square glasses and a mid-length dark brown bob.

When we pulled up at the two-storey house, which stood on a corner near some shops, I jumped out of the car and knocked off a few shots on my DSLR camera. The property was larger than Aunty Anne's current home, an open gutter running like a moat around the white rendered fence. Red Chinese lanterns hung along the eaves of the ground floor, and the top floor was smaller and set back. On the balcony, the current occupants had laid out white sheets on a clothes horse in the hot sun.

This was Mum's ground zero, the fault lines rippling outwards from Kuala Lumpur to Melbourne, traversing time and space.

I hopped across the street in the heat and stared back at the house, trying to picture the snatching as I mentally retouched the image before me. I replaced the cloudless blue sky with pitch-black darkness, got rid of the cars lining the street, the satellite dishes and the clothes horse, and shone a dim spotlight over the salmon-tiled front courtyard, unlocking the light brown metal gate so that Adel could enter and then slink out to his car with baby Sarah. Mum's cries in the night followed.

I filled in what had happened to Mum in the days after. The upstairs windows had tinted glass, but I imagined her immobilised in one of those rooms. She was lying on the bed as the walls and ceiling slowly closed in, the meaning of the incident only beginning to dawn on her. Uncertainty heaved in her gut over whether Sarah would be returned. Mum's sense of self was being chipped away, her world spinning out of control.

My cousin Sam was about nine at the time, and on the night of the snatching, his mother ordered him to stay inside with his younger brother and sister. '"Stay in the house! Quiet!"' Sam recalled her saying. 'My mum was like Saddam Hussein.' He laughed. 'We'd played with Sarah, and for us, to have a little baby like that was thrilling. Sarah meant a lot to us.'

He remembered being terrified by Mum's sobbing, and then seeing her sitting in a chair as she wept and wiped her eyes with a handkerchief.

A few days later, while having breakfast downstairs, he heard an almighty crash in the upstairs bedroom. Aunty Anne rushed up to find her sister collapsed on the floor. Afterwards, Mum was quiet and 'in her own world'.

For the children, Sarah's sudden disappearance was a shock. A curious young Sam asked his aunty why her baby had been taken in such a way. 'We were sad that Sarah was gone just like that, but your mum never answered me,' Sam said. 'She kept staring through a wall. She was miles away, so far away.'

*

While having dinner with Sam and Elise at their home, I learned that, spookily, the downstairs junk room at Aunty Anne's had belonged to Grandpa Leo for a time.

In the 1990s he was marooned in KL with no money or job prospects. He'd returned to Malaysia after getting divorced from Nan Ruby, a short time after their arrival in Melbourne in 1970. He was said to have become a layabout in Melbourne while his children worked in factories to bring in the money, and at the breakdown of their marriage, Nan had banished him to Malaysia.

The daughters of the family would never forgive Grandpa's violent outbursts towards Nan during their childhoods. 'He was quite cruel to my mother,' Aunty Anne recalled. 'Once he hit her and was throttling her. I took a broom to hit his hand so he would let go.' And Grandpa had enjoyed the comfort of other women's beds. As my aunty put it, 'If you wrapped a skirt around a coconut tree, he would go for it.'

Grandpa never recovered from losing his favourite daughter, his beautiful mat salleh, but had no means to attend the funeral. A day after Mum's life support was turned off, he sat quietly on a chair in Aunty Anne's concrete courtyard, smoking like a chimney. The word had come from Nan Ruby in Melbourne: 'Not today, not tomorrow. The day after tomorrow, they will off the machine.' 'Off' used as a verb in the Malaysian lingo.

A puff of smoke went up. Then another, and another, as Grandpa took a drag and exhaled. He stared at the sky, a gold packet of 555s next to him. He didn't eat for days, only consuming coffee and cigarettes, tears dripping down his face.

'Why God take Patsy?' Grandpa wondered, his hands raised to the sky. 'Why not take me?'

He went to the cupboard in his room and opened the door. On the inside were old photos of his children. Staring at their faces, he lamented the loss of a son in the race riots and a daughter far away in Australia. Every night he made the sign of the cross and prayed for his two dead children.

Elise had taken pity on the old man and visited him often. After his death, she would walk past his room and feel his presence. 'I'm telling you,' she said to me, 'sometimes he's sitting there.'

Chapter Twenty

After staying with Aunty Anne, I shifted to a hotel in the heart of the Malaysian capital. Checking in at the front desk on an upper level, I waited patiently for the clerk to finish up on the computer. The hotel bustled with Arab tourists wandering the carpeted corridors, the men walking alongside women in black burqas. In the mirrored wall I spied another couple of women in burqas on a plush circular lounge.

'Thank you, sir,' said the clerk. 'Here's your key. The lifts are right behind you.'

In Malaysia I liked to indulge in my heritage on Mum's side, jumping in and out of the culture as I pleased even if I was only 'half'. I tried out my rudimentary Bahasa Melayu. 'Terima kasih,' I replied in my best Malaysian accent, stretching out the last syllables to sound authentic.

I had never been taught the language, but 'thank you' was one of the few Malay words I'd learned later in life. Another well-known expression I was familiar with was 'selamat datang', meaning 'welcome'. These words had been famous in our house because they'd featured in a tacky Malaysian tourism ad on TV. 'Selamat datang,' I used to tease Mum, and she'd giggle.

Up in my room, the translucent bathroom basin glowed yellow. Large windows provided a commanding view of the lush manicured gardens and water fountains of KL's city park below, and the gleaming Petronas Towers opposite. I pushed back the golden sheer curtains and pressed my hand against the hot glass, feeling the humidity emanate from outside. I was grateful to be in a luxurious air-conditioned cocoon.

Curious, I flicked on a gay dating app on my phone, square tiles lighting up. But then I swiped it off. No time for playing around – and I didn't feel safe.

*

The next day at breakfast, in the hotel lounge overlooking the Petronas Towers, a white British man was complaining loudly to a very patient staff member. 'Why is there no bacon?'

To me, the answer was obvious: bacon was not halal and therefore off the menu for Muslims. I resisted the urge to stride over and admonish him: 'Why are you so ignorant?' It was the same urge I felt when people spoke dimly of Muslims without realising I had a Muslim half-sister.

'It is a policy of the hotel,' the attendant tried to explain.

'I don't understand – I want bacon,' the man said in a spoilt-brat tone.

Today I was meeting up with Sarah, who had taken time off work and was driving in from her home on the outskirts of the city. In the past month she'd been upending her house, searching for the letters Mum had written to her when she was a girl.

Seven years had passed since I'd seen Sarah in person, during my fourth visit to KL in 2008. Since then, we'd only been in touch through intermittent messages and phone calls over WhatsApp. In our adult lives, she and I were like the protagonists in the novel *The Time Traveler's Wife*, who jump in and out of each other's timelines. I could count the number of years on one hand when the two of us had been together in the same time and space.

'We came from the same womb!' Sarah liked to say with an extra flourish on 'womb', which for me conjured up imagery of cells dividing in Mum's body. Same womb, sure, but my dad was a Cambodian migrant, and Sarah's dad, Adel, a Malay. We were born in different countries, ten years apart. We had different faiths and different cultures with different values. Over the years, she'd become ever more faithful, while I'd become more faithless. It made me wonder whether I fit into her world view.

No matter what, despite our differences in culture, beliefs and outlook, we were always little brother and big sister, adik and kakak. We were our mother's children: in Sarah's words, 'Blood is thicker than water.' And as different as we were, we shared the same curiosity about our mother and her unfinished story. However, we'd continued to avoid the tougher questions and had never broached the past in detail. 'What was she like?' Sarah would continue to pester, but I withdrew, offering her one-word answers. 'She was crazy,' I sometimes wanted to say. This trip would be the first time we would interrogate what little we knew about Mum.

I was nervous – it had been a long time between crossover episodes. Would I like the new Sarah? She had foreshadowed she'd be wearing a headscarf today, perhaps hinting at anxieties about being accepted by her foreign half-brother. 'I am a sinner! We are all sinners!' was her new catchcry, but I failed to see any evidence of sin in her life. I saw my sister as a successful person, a loving mother raising two beautiful boys. I wished she were kinder to herself after all she'd been through.

I met Sarah in the gleaming white lobby. Carrying a small backpack, she wore a tight black hijab that framed her shiny face and a dark outfit that went down to her toes. With my hipster quiff, casual T-shirt and colourful shorts screaming 'tourist', we resumed our roles as the odd couple.

Sarah appeared well, but her demeanour was strangely reserved. I smiled and refrained from hugging her, in line with Muslim custom. Any touching between men and women in public was frowned upon; I'd become more familiar with this through mingling with Muslim communities as part of my job. Still, it felt funny not to hug my own sister.

'How was the flight over?' she asked.

'Pretty good, I caught up on movies. Did you bring the letters?'

'Of course.'

We went up to the hotel lounge and took a table near the back, Sarah ordering a cup of peppermint tea. After we'd reacquainted ourselves, she pulled a purple folder and two battered photo albums from her backpack and placed them on the table. I reached over to the folder and snuck a quick sideways glance at the photocopied sheets of typewritten letters inside, suppressing the urge to tear through them right away. I decided to read them in the privacy of my hotel room, the objective journalist in me determining that I should view the letters independently.

Sarah nursed her cup of tea. 'I don't know why Mum asked me to keep them together, but I kept,' she said of the letters. 'Maybe this is why.'

I was sceptical. Mum couldn't have known her son would one day fossick through her writings. She'd probably meant 'just keep the letters together' in a perfunctory way, telling her daughter to store old papers tidily.

Or was Mum drawing us together from the other side, as Sarah suggested?

Our meeting was certainly a giant leap for me and Sarah. Together with the information I'd gathered in my investigation, the old letters might be able to join up our understandings and memories of our mother, and perhaps help Sarah finally answer the question she'd often asked me: 'What was Mum like?'

'I sometimes wonder why Mum left me,' Sarah reflected. 'I felt abandoned, but I never hated her nor felt any love for her. I just didn't know her well enough. All my life there were always questions. So many unanswered questions,' she added, shaking her head. 'The truth will come out, God willing.' She held her tea and continued to eye the folder, her face unusually austere. I wondered what was running through her head, but she was inscrutable. 'You're my closest connection to Mum, you know that?'

As we contemplated what the letters meant, Sarah began weeping into her cup. She pulled out a tissue to wipe her nose.

My sister always cried at the very hint of Mum. During some of our phone conversations she'd cracked easily while I quietly stifled tears at the other end of the line, where thankfully I remained hidden.

In the hotel lounge, I felt exposed. I vowed that I wouldn't cry in public. Restraint was my reflex, and I wanted to avoid the attention of the busy staff. I was trying to keep it together as I had for more than twenty years. Such feelings were like an insurrection inside me that I pushed down brutally.

Sarah's old photo albums were filled with fading images in black-and-white and colour, cataloguing Mum's life with Adel before their marriage imploded. Several newer photos showed Sarah as a little girl at various ages, seemingly unharmed, presumably after she'd been taken from Mum.

Mum's romance with Adel appeared to be intoxicating, with lazy days spent at the beach. A black-and-white scene showed the pair sitting against a jagged rock that rose out of the sand. Mum, perhaps in her late teens, wore a patterned short-sleeved dress while Adel was shirtless in a pair of dark trunks, a big leg hitched up against the rock. Another shot had Mum sitting on top of a different rock. She wore a checked flannel shirt, perhaps Adel's, and a pair of revealing white shorts. Elbows on her knees, she cocked her head to the side suggestively. Her chin rested on one hand, her pinky finger in her mouth, a cheeky smile on her face. The camera ate her up.

'These photos are amazing,' I told Sarah, awed.

I stopped in my tracks when I came across a startling picture of Mum wearing a white lace veil that went down to her waist. She was sitting in a cane armchair, staring at her finger as Adel bent down to slide a ring on it. The next shot showed her then clasping his hands, her face bowing to almost kiss them. Sarah explained that the two photos had been taken in 1968, on the day Mum married Adel in a traditional Islamic wedding ceremony, the nikah.

I would later learn more of the story behind these photos through a Malaysian source who will remain unnamed.

The nikah took place in an upstairs room in a white mansion not far from the centre of Ipoh, a tin-mining town about a two-hour drive north-west of Kuala Lumpur. A small crowd of family members and close friends gathered for the occasion. The men sat cross-legged on floral rugs while the women sat opposite. Adel, perched on a cushion, wore a white baju melayu and a songkok hat. Mum wore a dark dress and the long white lace headscarf.

An imam officiated the proceedings. He began with prayers and the men joined him, their palms facing upwards to the sky. After a few words about the dowry and the witnesses, the paperwork was signed. The room was promptly cleared for the festivities, and long white sheets were laid out on the floor. A meal of rice, spicy chicken and rose syrup cordial was served. The guests, all in traditional Malaysian dress, sat on the carpet and busily tucked in, their fingers pressed together, swirling food into their mouths. Tall metal teapots that resembled genie bottles were nearby so guests could wash their hands.

I wondered what had been running through Mum's mind that day. In the nikah photos she appeared nervous and tense, her face unsmiling and solemn. But according to my source, she was elated.

Her conversion to Islam, I learned, would have involved some red tape, but it was seemingly as simple as filling out a form. People who wanted to convert were asked to sign papers at a government office and adopt a Muslim name. They then had to recite the Shahada creed in Arabic: 'There is no god but Allah, and Muhammad is his messenger.' Converts were issued with a grey booklet with red writing on the cover: *Certificate of Conversion to Islam*. And inside: *This is to certify that (Name) has embraced the Muslim Religion of his/her own free will with effect from (Date). He/She has duly registered with the Religious Department Selangor and has chosen his/her name in Islam as (Name). May Allah help him/her in this sacred cause, AMEN.* A passport-size photo of the new Muslim was attached.

The booklet might have seemed like Mum's ticket to Islam, but as it turned out, true commitment to the religion required more than signing on a dotted line.

Mum's booklet wasn't in Dad's filing cabinet. Perhaps it had been among the belongings that Aunty Anne threw out in the purge before Mum migrated to Australia.

As I continued scanning through Sarah's albums, I found another astonishing image. It was in a black-and-white newspaper clipping of the wedding reception held after the nikah. The photo showed a wildly ecstatic bride in a Western white dress, her mouth wide open with joy. She was cutting an extravagant three-tiered wedding cake – almost as tall as her – in a pretty garden setting; Adel, in a tuxedo, stood close by her side, his expression impassive. Both gazed down at the knife as it sliced into the cake.

The Patricia in this newspaper article was again a stranger to me: lithe, glamorous and full of vigour. The smile that shone through in the wedding cake photo was unlike anything I'd seen growing up in the shadow of her breakdowns in Melbourne.

The reception had been held in the lush grounds of the Ipoh mansion on a Saturday afternoon, with an elite group of around a hundred guests gathering for the lavish tea party. Malaysia had declared independence from Britain back in 1957, but there were many signs of Western sensibilities aside from the outfits worn by the bride and groom. The men wore white short-sleeved shirts, thin black ties and thick-rimmed spectacles; the women wore dresses that showed off their bare arms and legs, their hair coiffed in neat black bobs.

Malay, Chinese and Indian guests rubbed shoulders with white British families.

Tall trees and neatly trimmed hedges framed the stately mansion in the background. The building's foundation was concrete, with square columns flanking its entrance. The top floor was clad in weatherboards, and wooden slats allowed for the tropical air to circulate.

The bride and groom sat at a long table in the centre of a manicured lawn. Mum looked gorgeous in her body-hugging white wedding gown.

As it was a high society event, members of the local press attended. It seemed the couple were minor celebrities. But as I'd learned from Mum's siblings, her family were absent despite being invited. I remembered what Aunty Anne had said about this: 'We didn't go to the wedding because Patsy was now a Muslim. My mother discarded her.'

I was planning to visit the Ipoh mansion in a few days.

*

Mum's letter writing had usually taken place at the kitchen table or at our blue folding table in the middle of the lounge room. Looking thoughtful and serious, she would plunge her fingers onto the typewriter, each strike of the keys punctuating the air, every line heralded by a *PING!* and followed by the cranking of the carriage return lever. Her words were precious, conveying our life in Melbourne to teenage Sarah.

Mum used aerograms: thin, almost see-through sheets of paper that folded back on themselves into an envelope. They were easily spooled through the manual typewriter, and a cheap form of international airmail. The aerograms Mum bought from the post office usually had touristy images on them such as Uluru or kangaroos.

Dad recalled how immensely proud Mum had been of her typing skills. Among the old documents he'd unearthed from his files was a 1966 Pitman Examinations Institute certificate for elementary typing from Malaysia. It declared that at seventeen, Mum could type twenty-five words a minute.

Mum never let me read her letters before she licked the seal and sent them on their way. When we walked to the milk bar for lollies, she would slip the aerograms into the mouth of a red mailbox at the end of the shopping strip.

The arrival of a reply from Sarah was always a cause of celebration for Mum. She'd wander down the driveway to check the mailbox, sometimes numerous times, even though she knew the postie came once a day. She would linger at the gate, looking up and down the street for something or someone to arrive.

*

In my hotel room, I was about to crack the old letters open. I'd let a whole day pass before I read them, allowing myself to enjoy the sights and sounds of Malaysia. After the sun went down and the Petronas Towers lit up, I sat on the crisp white linen of the bed in my luxury cocoon and placed the purple folder in front of me.

My heart thumped. I dreaded the possibility of nasty surprises, yet more dark secrets or a torrent of invective aimed at me or Dad. I imagined Mum telling Sarah about all the bad things I'd done.

'You're a real handful, you know?' Mum used to say before she lobbed her thong at me. 'Get out of my sight! You were a mistake.'

Was she going to be as cruel to me in the afterlife as she sometimes had been in my childhood?

Steeling myself, I lifted the flap on the folder and spread the papers across the bedcover. The letters were out of order, some with missing dates. I rearranged them consecutively, counting roughly eighty letters. They began in 1987 and ended in 1993, the year Mum died in Melbourne.

The first tentative letter didn't have a month and was littered with spelling and grammatical mistakes, which mildly annoyed me. Handwritten corrections were scribbled over the typewritten words. Mum's voice was light and sweet as she urged Sarah to connect with my Malaysian cousins living in KL.

6th, Monday 1987 [sic]
Dear Sarah,
To start with your typeing [sic] is very good. Thanks for your nice letter. I hope all is well with you. Pet, I would like to enclose this quiet [sic] expensive little two piece pants and shirt for Uncle's 2-year-old son because as you told me, he gave you $200 Malaysian ringgit. Just tell him straight it's from Aunty Patsy. And darling, the two earrings and one lip stick is for you, pet.
    Mum is still doing part-time work. Narong goes to work as usual. Jason is on school holidays. Don't forget to let mum know should you change your address.
Mum is also glad you will get your pay next week. Would you like to ring Jarrod or Claire up? There [sic] telephone No: is ——. Just ring them and have a chat.

Well dear, Mum has to end now with love to you.
Bye bye.
Love, Mummy. Xx

Straight after reading this letter, I panicked. What if the rest of them were just as basic? I quickly turned to the next one, lapping up every detail. Mum's words were direct and simple, perhaps reflecting the brevity needed for aerograms – there wasn't much space on them to elaborate. Folded out, they were about as tall as A4 sheets but narrower.

Vivid descriptions of our home life flowed off the pages. They were almost poetic, as if she were singing.

> Sarah, summer is coming to the end. Sarah, autumn will be here soon. Mum's garden is very beautiful. Sarah, our apple tree is full of good apples. Sarah, Jason planted tomato plant and we have lots of tomatoes to eat. Sarah, our orange tree have a few orange fruit. Sarah, our lemon tree has a lot of green, small lemons. I would say there are some hundreds of lemons when the lemons are ripe. Our peach tree gave us a lot of sweet peaches this year.
>
> – 20 February 1992

Back then, Dad usually had his head and gloved hands stuck in the dirt, tending to our plants, weeding, or mowing the lawn and spreading the clippings as mulch. I sometimes joined him. I added daffodils and jonquils alongside his gladioli, Dame Edna Everage's favourite flower; Mum would snip the sword-like blooms and arrange them in a vase in the hall. Dad also taught me about grafting – the act of binding a cutting to a different plant so they would grow as one – and transplanting, which involved uprooting a plant and putting it in another part of the garden. If it wasn't given enough love it might struggle in its new home.

At other times, Dad attacked trees:

Sarah, Narong cut down the apple tree.
– 1 March 1993

I remembered when it had come down as part of Dad's war on trees. First to go was the sweet peach tree at the back fence: 'It's too big. Get rid of it.' Then the bitter apple tree went: 'I will get someone to come dig up the roots.' Then the sweet-smelling cherry blossom tree in the corner of the front yard, which Mum loved to stand under, its petals falling like snowflakes.

After Mum died, my beloved banksia tree at the front gate was next. I was fifteen.

'It will ruin the fence,' Dad proclaimed.

I'd grown the banksia from a seedling until it was five metres high.

'It will wreck the foundations,' Dad declared, pointing to the base of the brick fence, which barely protruded. What was he on about? He saw a future calamity, real or imagined. Everything wild in the garden had to be cut back. Everything chaotic had to be contained.

*

Mum's letters were overflowing with tenderness for Sarah, and there were touching passages about the many thoughtful gifts Mum had posted to her.

I am glad that you are happy with the eyeliner and the money. Mum just feels, I miss you. Darling, would you like some more lipstick now that you're working? Try to put light make up when you go to work. Mum is so glad for you.

– 23 June 1987

Mum bought you three pairs of earrings, a nice purse to put your shillings and a blush for your cheeks. And the nightie is from Mummy's mother.

– 11 August 1987

Thank you for your nice letter. Pet, Mum is very happy for you. I think you're great, darling. So pet, you're clever to make cakes. You're a clever girl. You are also attending sewing class. You are busy, sweetheart.

– 21 February 1989

Mum used terms of endearment profusely in her letters to my sister. When I strained my memory, I remembered her saying them to me too, like a stroke on the head. Those days of being nurtured felt like a lifetime ago, and remembering them was difficult. Eventually my mind coughed up some disjointed snippets: Mum holding my arms up as we danced in the lounge room, my tiptoes on top of her feet; Mum letting me lick the vanilla batter from a spoon as I helped her bake a cake; Mum drying me off after a warm bubble bath of lurid blue Mr Matey. She used to sit by our pink tub, minding me as I splashed around with a fleet of floating toys.

Mum was a smell too, I remembered: her curry puffs filled with spicy minced meat and diced potato cooling on the kitchen table; the rose-scented pink floral paper she lined her drawers with; the musk of her favourite soft brown leather jacket; the heady fragrance of the hibiscus, magnolia and jasmine flowers she picked from our garden.

When I was in the wrong, Mum backed me up. One time in primary school, while we were waiting for the rundown school bus to arrive in our street, I thought it would be hilarious to place a large branch on the road as a car approached. A woman driving with her kid slowed down and hurled abuse at Mum for being an irresponsible parent, but she simply waved the woman away, replying with a polite, 'Fuck off!'

I recalled the quiet smile on her face one summer night as we stood in the front yard watching an enormous swirling swarm of golden scarabs – friendly Christmas beetles – that had invaded the large gum tree on our kerb. The hot dry air was electric with their soft buzzing and the flickering of their wings. On their drunken flight paths, they bumped into our faces like gentle pieces of hail. Mum was lost in her own world, mesmerised, while I hooted and leapt around to catch them.

As I read her letters, Mum the woman slowly rose to the forefront of my mind. I was starting to see her true self, not just her illness. The only thing I couldn't recall clearly was her voice.

But how could I have so easily forgotten her effusive love? Why had I been so quick to dispense with that in my urgent need to survive? Her affection was like the giant yellow Big Bird cake at one of my birthdays, a crowd of school friends around me, hot party pies and sausage rolls warming in the oven. She was the gentle embrace I'd missed when there was none during my teenage years living alone with my father.

All Mixed Up

*

There were several surprising lines about Mum keeping the Muslim faith. She'd married Dad as a Catholic and been laid out in a casket in a Catholic church, and Dad and I had never seen her practising Islam. We'd eaten bacon and Aeroplane Jelly, and lived with a pet dog in our house. But thinking back, I realised I hadn't seen her pray to any particular god, and we hadn't gone to church. It seemed to me her ideas around faith had been a bit mixed up.

> As I told you Sarah, Mum will keep the Muslim faith in my heart.
> We are going to Washington DC for four weeks. Mum is going to be Buddhist when I get to Washington, sort of Buddhist faith, because Buddhist faith is only food, no money involved. And a safe child birth.
> As I told you, don't take anything too serious.
> — 27 January 1988

Was Mum joking, or had she been in a muddle? The rest of her writing revealed that her basic knowledge of Islam was poor. For instance, she asked Sarah what a hajji was; Sarah explained it was a Muslim who went to Mecca as a pilgrim.

Mum's references to religion were inconsistent. She told Sarah she went to Catholic church once a year for Christmas – something I'd never seen her do – but also said she wanted to become a Buddhist.

'When she got worked up, she wanted to change to a Buddhist,' Dad would later explain. 'Then she burned incense and prayed.'

*

In the letters from the final couple of years of her life, Mum's words were more urgent and incoherent. There was a desperation that spoke of her despair at losing Sarah.

And then, a revelation: unbeknown to me, for some reason Mum had been expecting Sarah to visit her in Australia.

Dear Sarah,
Sarah, Mum is very, very sorry about everything.
Sarah, please excuse Mum about everything. Sarah, Mum is very, very sorry.

Sarah, Mum will wait to see you soon.

Sarah, this May, Mum will be six years not working. Sarah, Mum went to the job centre, there is no job for Mum, the lady at the job centre said to Mum.

How is everybody Sarah? Sarah, Mum wish to be there with you and everybody.

Sarah, Mum has very expensive things in this house. Sarah, very, very expensive things. Sarah, which I take them to my grave.

Sarah, I love you very much. I have to end here with love and kisses to you. Do write to Mum. Bye bye. All my love to you, dear daughter.

Love,
Mum XXX.

– 7 April 1992

Mum never met up with Sarah after this letter. She died waiting for her to arrive.

And what did Mum mean when she said she was 'very, very sorry'?

The pain emanating from the letters seemed to seep into the plush hotel room. I felt Mum's loneliness and sense of isolation from being stuck in a suburban house, and her helplessness at being separated from her daughter. She was stranded, her love snagged on her circumstances: *Mum wish to be there with you and everybody. All my love to you, dear daughter.*

I swept up the papers, put them back in the folder and curled up in bed. Then I wept. Not over the loss of Mum, but at my newfound comprehension of the struggle she and Sarah had endured.

My eyes stung. It was a type of mourning I hadn't experienced before. I was grieving for *her* loss, not mine: *Mummy*, how *you* suffered.

As memories flowed back to me, I yearned to hold Mum and comfort her. I wished I could give her a hug for all the times I'd treated her badly because of the stigma of her illness. I would probably have been gentler had I known of the hardships she was grappling with. I would have been kinder, as much as a twelve-year-old boy could try to be. But how could I have done that when nothing had been explained?

I spooned a pillow and fell asleep, exhausted.

Chapter Twenty-One

On day four of my Malaysia trip, I bought some small cakes from the glossy department store-style food hall at the hotel. They were an offering for my anonymous source, who would speak to me and Sarah that afternoon. I tucked the adoption letter I'd brought from Dad's files in Melbourne, the one my sister needed to see, into my backpack.

Sarah arrived in her small red hatchback, wearing a dark brown headscarf and a black jubah with a muted brown pinstripe trim. A gold fern-leaf brooch was pinned to her chest. I jumped in the front seat with the box of cakes on my lap, and we slid along the city's arterials of spilt noodles. When we came to a tunnel, I mentioned our mother's letters, keeping it light and brief. 'Mum really loved you,' I said. 'Whatever anyone says about her, don't forget that.'

Sarah continued driving, her eyes on the road, listening quietly.

'And I'm so glad there weren't any nasty things said about me. That's what I'd feared. Mum used to call me a real handful.'

My sister laughed.

'She also talked about Nan Ruby being unhelpful.'

'Really?' Sarah sat up.

'Yeah, I think Nan always gave Mum a hard time. They always used to have tense phone calls that made Mum cry.'

'Huh.'

'Nan was Islamophobic,' I said.

Sarah's eyes popped out of her head, the car veering slightly. My uncouth Australian ways shocked her. I was the youngest on the Malaysian side of the family, and you weren't supposed to speak about your Asian elders with such bluntness.

Or maybe I was wrong about that – maybe Sarah had already suspected something and had been looking for confirmation.

I told her about one of the times I'd visited Nan Ruby's house in the years before she died. As Nan prepared some food in the kitchen, the collection of family photos on a lounge-room shelf caught my eye. There were shots of me, my mongrel collection of Malaysian cousins, and a sepia-toned picture of my mostly European great-grandparents who were said to be Portuguese-Burmese and English-French. I knew even less about them, only that their children would produce a multi-ethnic multi-faith clan, and in turn their children's children would do the same thing. Mum and her sisters would have kids with Goan, Cambodian and Vietnamese men. My wonderful mixed-up family.

But something was amiss.

'Where's the photo of me and Sarah?' I asked Nan.

The photo in question was from my third trip to Malaysia in 2006, the year Sarah got married to her second husband. The day after the wedding we visited the impressive Islamic Arts Museum in KL. Outside, we posed for a picture in front of a stunning teal mosaic wall of swirling curls and flowers. Sarah wore sunglasses, her long wavy black hair flowing down her back; she hadn't yet started wearing a daily hijab. I put my arm around her, holding her close, and we both smiled for the camera.

Sneakily, I'd given the photo to Nan in the spirit of inclusion and common humanity. It turned out this had been a mistake.

Nan rambled, avoiding my question about the photo's whereabouts. She wandered around the kitchen. 'I loved your mother,' she said. 'I used to look after you when you were a baby.' True, once or twice. *And you asked for money.* And then: 'Muslims. Why would I mix with them?' She gave me a sideways glance, a smirk on her face.

I said nothing. Where did that leave Sarah?

When Nan Ruby died, forty-five years had passed since Mum ran off to marry a Muslim man and convert into 'one of them'. It saddened me that Nan had never made space for Sarah in her heart, her Catholic pride unmoved.

But as I sat next to Sarah in the car, speeding along the road in KL, I realised my sister and I chose to be in each other's lives. We were not our grandmother.

*

At the home of my anonymous source, Sarah and I were sitting alone on a bench in a stuffy living room when I decided it was time for me to reveal the adoption letter.

I'd given my sister no warning, and I casually pulled it out for inspection. Sarah put on her reading glasses and leaned forward, holding the paper in front of her, her elbows on her thighs. She read the words out loud, starting off confidently, but as she went on her voice began to tremble, pausing at times.

The letter was dated 1981. In it, Mum wrote to a family friend of Adel's. Sarah had turned eleven that year.

> How are you and your family keeping? I am sure you will be surprised to receive this letter from me after all these years. You must be aware by now that I am in Australia. Since you are a good friend of Adel's family, I am appealing to you to help me.
>
> I do not like to go back to everything in detail, but this I would like you to know, that Adel refused to hand over my daughter to me when we separated in KL. He took Sarah by force away from me and did not give me any support prior to me leaving KL. I had no alternative but to turn to my elder sister and my mother for help.
>
> After my divorce, I decided to migrate to Australia to be with my mother. My relatives had nothing whatsoever to do with my divorce. My mother accepted me home, and I got a job and started working till I met my present husband. We have been married for seven years and have got a son. No matter how long time has passed, I have never forgotten my daughter, and I have always sent her parcels and presents for her birthdays.
>
> In 1975, my mother made a trip to KL to visit my elder sister and her other grandchildren. She even visited Adel's mother so that she could see Sarah and be with her for a short visit, as she had not seen my daughter before she left for Australia as Sarah was not born yet.
>
> She had a conversation with Adel's mother who was very nervous about allowing Sarah to spend a day with

my mother at my sister's home, although my mother assured her that we could not take Sarah out of the country without Adel's permission, and that it is not that easy to comply with the immigration laws.

Now, to cut the story short, I have written several letters to Adel asking him to let me have Sarah since he is happily married and has got a son, but I have not received a single line from him. I have come to understand that Sarah is seldom living with him, and she is in his sister's care.

As a parent I am sure that you too will be aware how much it means to me to be separated from my daughter. I am appealing to you and your wife to try to talk it over with Adel since you are our good friend.

My husband and I have got our own house, and we are financially able to give her a sound education, and maybe send her to a university in later years. If Adel consents to give Sarah to me, we will have to make proper arrangements for her to come to Australia.

According to Australia's divorce laws, each of the parents concerned is granted access to the child or children, whenever it is permissible to be with them during the school holidays, but here again Adel must not be selfish and keep Sarah for himself alone.

I have written this letter with my husband's consent as he is in a position to adopt Sarah as his child. I trust that with your help and guidance you will be able to settle our problem amicably.

'A mother's love will only cease when the sun leaves the sky, and when the clouds stop rolling by'.

With this in mind, with your sound education and humanity, I am sure that you will not fail me.

I am looking forward to a favourable reply from you.
Yours sincerely,
Patsy Om.
P.S. All my letters are kept in my file for further reference.

— 23 September 1981

I'd found no reply to this letter in Dad's files.

When Sarah reached the end of the page, I was unprepared for her reaction. Her words petered out and turned into a wave of sobs that struck her body. Her face was swollen and flushed, her hijab tightening around her head. As her tears fell, she let out a wail, wondering why her father had taken her from Mum as a baby.

'Why did he take me if he didn't want me?' Sarah cried, appealing to the sky.

For a few moments I froze, unsure if I should move in to comfort her. I remembered having to hold back on the day we'd met up at the hotel – no touching allowed. But in this private setting, as I watched her cry, Sarah morphed into a little girl, abandoned on a bench and desperately alone. A little girl crying for her mother.

I felt helpless.

Fuck it. In that moment, my sister needed her brother. Just this once, I was going to break the rules. I slid along the bench and put my arm around her. Her head fell into my chest, and I put my chin on her shoulder.

She couldn't see my face or my tears. I was going to be strong for her.

'Don't worry about your dad,' I said gently, as she sobbed into my T-shirt. 'What matters most is that Mum never let go of you. She never forgot you.'

I held my sister for a few minutes, until her wailing subsided. As we got up to leave, she made light of it, beaming through her wet face. 'Did you expect me to cry?' she teased.

'The people who helped you and Mum stay connected are bloody heroes in my books,' I said as we walked back to the car.

*

That night I went bar hopping with Sam and Elise. I'd heard about a hip speakeasy in a hard-to-find location in the nightlife district Bangsar – my kind of bar. We lurked around in the darkened streets in Sam's white Mazda, a little lost, until we found a large warehouse with a welcoming sign of glowing white letters: *All that matters is that drink in your hand*, followed by another in green neon: *You look fine*.

I drank a witchy concoction and let the heaviness of the day's emotions swish around in the big round wine glass, ice cubes clinking. A bartender with a tattoo sleeve, dressed in black, had conjured up an elaborate gin and tonic for me, adding a tea strainer that contained dried lavender and other pungent herbs. It bobbed around on a chain in the glass, in a too-cool-for-school way, hitting my lips as I sipped. Sam and Elise chose similar brews, and we laughed the night away, our conversation forgotten by the time we reached another trendy bar, this one with cane chairs and vintage furniture.

I let the sweet alcohol swim around my veins and put a grin on my face, my body becoming slack. In Malaysia, alcohol is considered haram, forbidden, to believers, but there are still foreign tourists and other non-Muslims to serve.

Sometimes everything in my life felt tense and heavy. Dealing with Mum's illness and loss. Dad's foreignness and silence about my sexuality. The cultural and emotional complexities of my relationship with Sarah – even as I'd comforted her, her body had felt leaden as she sobbed into my chest. Sometimes I felt like I was walking through wet cement as I held the dead weight of tragedy. Mum was the most exhausting one to carry. All of it required energy from an internal engine that combusted its little heart out. *Keep moving.* But how much more could I carry? And how much longer would family dramas continue to shape my life? I wished I could swan through the world with a loose heart and a feather-like lightness of being. I wished to be untroubled, and free of the sour memories. To move forward with sweetness and simplicity. Why couldn't my family be orderly and neat, unified and the same? When could we choose to stop marinating in our trauma?

Slowly I got tipsy, the drinks providing me with succour. Flowers and quinine.

The next morning I woke up in the hotel surprisingly refreshed, one of those cleansing hangovers. Maybe it was the herbs.

I was about to enjoy a leisure day with Sarah and her two sons. Our plan was to hit the shops and treat my nephews with the money Dad had given me and some of my own. This day together would be a much-needed reprieve from the investigation, and I regretted not scheduling more time off.

I wandered downstairs and found the three of them sitting at an outdoor table near the hotel's side entrance, which opened onto the city park. My younger nephew, Danny, was in primary school, while Ayman was now sixteen. He'd grown taller than me and Sarah, which we speculated came from Grandpa Leo, who had been a beanpole. Orange was the colour of the day, with Sarah and Danny wearing matching

T-shirts, Sarah in an orange batik headscarf. Ayman wore a light grey hoodie and donned round black spectacles I hadn't seen before, giving him a scholarly air.

Over a quick coffee, I peered at Danny, who was doodling on a piece of paper. His perspective drawing consisted of a few black lines disappearing into the distance.

'What is it?' Sarah said in Malay to help me along.

'Train! Train in a tunnel.' He smiled.

Ingenious.

'Wow,' I said, 'that's very perceptive.'

We strolled through the city park, past the lush gardens and fountains, to a luxurious mall where families in colourful loose-fitting clothing idled away their time among the big international brands in air-conditioned comfort. We made a beeline for the Japanese mega-bookstore Kinokuniya, where we could indulge in our mutual love of reading.

Putting on a mock-stern voice, I ordered my nephews to choose books wisely, giving them an undisclosed budget. Dad's money plus mine worked out to be a hefty sum when converted from the modest amount of Australian dollars to Malaysian ringgit – about three times as much. I found it such a delight to play the cool Australian uncle to my sister's children: all the fun and no responsibility. Like the role of brother, it still felt new to me.

As Danny and Ayman ran off among the shelves, Sarah came forward with a curly, unprompted question. 'Do you feel awkward standing next to me, with me in a hijab?' She liked to test me.

'No,' I said after a pause, 'because you prepared me for it. And I do a lot of news stories with the Muslim community back home.' I was trying to impress Sarah with my familiarity with Muslim Australians, and I had made contacts in the

Sydney community where Australia's largest population of half a million lived. Each story I did reminded me of my sister. 'I've even interviewed the Grand Mufti of Australia,' I bragged.

What Sarah decided to wear wasn't my concern, and I'd accepted her as a Muslim a long time ago. I considered her my family, even if only by 'half', and nothing could change that.

'Did I tell you my favourite colour is green, the colour of Islam?' I joked, bringing a smile to her face.

We were deep among the bookshelves when Ayman, in his round spectacles, scooted back to us, a thick book in his hands.

'What's this?' I asked curiously.

'It's a book on graffiti,' he said with a smile.

He was wonderfully artistic like his mother. Both of the boys were.

'That looks pretty cool. You know, Melbourne has a big graffiti scene. Even Banksy's been there.' The book was cheap by Australian standards, and I waved my hand upwards to signal he still had many more ringgits left in the kitty. 'Keep going.'

Ayman's eyes widened.

After collecting more books and toys from a variety of shops, we left the mall with a handsome loot.

'Say, "Thank you, Uncle Jason,"' Sarah said to the boys, eyebrows raised.

'Thank you, Uncle Jason!' they singsonged.

Chapter Twenty-Two

In Sarah's old photo albums I'd found an address for the grand white mansion in Ipoh where Mum and Adel got married: it was on the invitation to their 1968 garden party reception. The newlyweds had lived in the mansion for a time. Wanting to get a sense of the location and what life might have been like there for Mum, I asked Sam if he could drive me there. He agreed, Elise decided to join us, and we chartered a course for Ipoh the day after the shopping expedition with my nephews.

Before we left KL, we stopped for breakfast at a small cafe near a bustling food market in the suburbs. The street was crammed with cars. At the cafe entrance, a man was spinning thin sheets of roti on a round hotplate. At another stall, women were busy arranging fresh young coconuts ready to be scalped and drunk by thirsty customers.

We took a seat at a laminated table. I wasn't feeling hungry, but Sam and Elise chose to wolf down hot flat rice noodles in chilli sauce from foam containers. In keeping with the theme of our road trip, Sam introduced me to Ipoh white coffee, which by tradition came in a white cup emblazoned with a green floral design. The coffee tasted smooth and sweet; the key ingredients were margarine and condensed milk.

I took another sip of the sticky brown drink and glanced at Sam. 'Thanks again for doing this.'

'Okay, lah.' He smiled. 'We are family.'

After our pit stop, we drove to Mum's old Catholic boarding school. On the outskirts of the city, its grounds were set in the side of an overgrown green hill. The security guard at the gate waved us in after Elise whispered a magic password. Sam zigzagged the white Mazda up the road in the shadows of tall trees, parking at the top. The city appeared far away except for the conspicuous Petronas Towers.

Apparently alone, we wandered around the peaceful gardens near the chapel and nuns' quarters, which were in the same nondescript building. Meandering back down the road, we came across a white statue of the Virgin Mary standing on a plinth with her palms facing out by her sides. Someone had left a candle burning in a glass at her feet. Elise stretched out her arms, palms up, and began whispering to the statue, nodding at times, as if she were chatting to an old friend.

We hit the road again along a smooth highway out of KL, passing large tracts of jungle. I sat in the front passenger seat, leaning into the vent that blasted out cold air.

'You know, Jason, you are the lucky one,' Sam said while driving.

'I'm not sure what you mean.' I hadn't considered my luck. 'I don't think "lucky" is the right word. I saw Mum die, and Sarah was separated from her. I don't think either of us are lucky in that sense.'

While our lives had taken very different trajectories, we both had our own traumas. When it came to loss, we were the same.

'Well,' Sam said, 'what I mean is, you ended up in Australia with a better life. Better off compared to Malaysia. Australia is a free country.'

The jungle landscape out the window was a blur. As we approached Ipoh, monolithic limestone hills emerged, their hunched shapes resembling giant slumbering beasts. Along the main road into the city we drove past large government buildings, fortified barracks and the main hospital. In the centre of town, we took a break at a crowded restaurant where a ring of food carts served hot noodles and custard tarts. Sweaty young men in caps bellowed out the orders while a man poured liquid custard from a teapot into little cups of yellow pastry. After the long drive, we greedily dug into plates of char kway teow and a piquant dish of flat egg noodles topped with minced meat and chilli.

Once-vibrant shophouses stood on the main street, sapped of their colour by a lifetime of tropical humidity. One yellow building was marred by broken wooden shutters and boarded-up shops, the grandness of its arched walkways and cornices now a distant echo of a more prosperous era.

I tried to imagine Mum going about her daily life in Ipoh as a newlywed, with the expectations of her marriage and new religion weighing down on her. Perhaps she had strolled through the town, window-shopping in the muggy heat, pausing occasionally to size up a colourful batik dress or hijab. Perhaps on this very street she had stopped for a white coffee at a cafe, and gazed upon the bustle, thinking of the baby girl forming in her womb. In Melbourne, Mum's daily pick-me-up had been a mug of instant International Roast with milk.

After we scoffed our food, Sam punched the address of the mansion into the car's GPS. We went around the block and got lost after he missed a turn. I pulled out my smartphone to track our movements, and a pulsing blue dot appeared on the screen, showing we were getting closer to our final destination.

We pulled up on a verge and tumbled out of the car. Elise opened a large black-and-gold umbrella to shade herself. On one side of the road there was a fenced-off vacant lot behind a billboard boasting about a multistorey development of luxury suites: *Best location, best price.* On the other side there was a thicket of overgrown trees where the mansion should have been.

The estate I'd seen in the wedding photos was long gone. I scanned the trees from the road; dead vines hung off the branches like spaghetti. Most of the dense greenery was in spooky shadow, but I could see the outline of an abandoned building behind a thick wall of shrubbery. The roof had collapsed. The windows were just empty frames.

Was this the mansion where Mum had celebrated what should have been one of the happiest days of her life? It had to be. There were no buildings beside it, and the location corresponded with the lot number. I could see columns, still standing despite the years of neglect, that looked like those in the photos.

*

My anonymous source told me Mum's Muslim life in the Ipoh mansion had been privileged and luxurious by the standards of the time. She lived in the house with Adel and an extended family of in-laws and children. It was staffed by servants and gardeners. But even though Mum could have been pampered, she apparently busied herself by helping out with the cleaning. Known to be fastidious, she made sure the house was spick and span, paying particular attention to tidying up her parents-in-laws' room.

In Islam, cleanliness is next to godliness. I was unsure whether that tenet had inspired Mum's cleanliness at our house in Oakleigh, which had sometimes reached the level of obsession. Taking long and frequent showers throughout the day. Wiping down the kitchen bench repeatedly. Putting our heavy gold curtains in the washing machine regularly, even though they appeared clean. Parts of Mum's brain may have been a shambles, but she'd liked to bring order to our house.

Eventually Mum and Adel had moved out of the mansion to a more modest house on the other side of town, where they lived simply with a menagerie of pets. Adel kept an aviary of colourful parrots, some of which could talk. In Sarah's black-and-white photos, Mum stood on the lawn in a floral dress, a large white bird perched on her arm. In another, Adel had one hand on his hip and a white bird on his other hand, its wings outstretched. He appeared to be very much in control. Exuding confidence, he looked regal in his polo top and shorts.

We left the old ruins and drove around the Ipoh suburbs, trying to find the second house. With no address, we cruised through the cramped neighbourhoods, passing tall dour apartment blocks and terraced rows of small homes. On the side of the road was another vine-covered building with burnt-out shutters.

'There were hills in the background of the photos,' I said. 'Let's look for some hills.' But the whole town was surrounded by hills. Our search was in vain.

We stopped by a brown creek opposite some houses in a side street. Thick bush and a tangle of vines overran the banks. Sitting lazily on one of the tentacle-shaped branches of an old tree, a fat lizard stared at us. It turned its head but was too indifferent to run away.

As I took a few photos, Elise peered over my shoulder at the camera. 'Can you see the face in the photo?'

What was she talking about?

'Can you see it?' she repeated.

'Um, I can only see the lizard. Do you mean the lizard?'

'There is a face there,' she said quietly before wandering off. She muttered something to Sam then got back in the car.

'Elise wants to go,' he told me. 'Something not right.'

My skin crawled. The sun disappeared under a cloud. The jungle was giving off a weird energy, and I was glad to head back into town for drinks and dinner.

*

Driving out of Ipoh at twilight, we coasted past the limestone cliffs and the Buddhist temples set in stone. I felt flat, wishing I'd been able to visit the mansion, but I took some comfort in having discovered a place where Mum once lived. It made me feel closer to her.

I realised that the rise and fall of the mansion could be seen as an analogy for Mum's first marriage. The grand facade was full of promise, but the marriage was flimsy, and Mum became an empty shell just like the decaying building.

In her letters to Sarah, I found this:

> About me and Dad, it's a closed Allah book. Yes, Dad hit me about four times, but you know something, towards the end he was good to me. He even wanted a baby boy from me.
> — 5 January 1988

I read that letter several times, initially bewildered and then indignant at Mum's naivety and her casual appeasement of Adel. At first I could not accept it.

But later I forgave her. When someone you love has you under their thumb, such a reaction is natural.

Chapter Twenty-Three

Just wondering whether I can wear shorts? I texted Sarah from my hotel room.

Today we were visiting her old high school, where Mum had met her for a secret rendezvous in 1984.

Sarah replied: *Hmm. Usually they have a dress code for parents and visitors to most schools. I think it's safer to wear pants.*

Despite the stifling heat, I took the demure option of trousers. A man required a high degree of respectability when visiting a prestigious all-girls college in Malaysia.

Sarah picked me up from the hotel. She was wearing a tightly done dark brown hijab and an embroidered baju kurung in a contrasting shade of brown.

We drove a short distance through the bendy streets of the inner city and up a hill to the campus. It sat opposite a dense forest reserve that long ago had been sectioned off by KL's forefathers as an island of peace amid the urban sprawl. The school was housed in an old Christian convent. The main building was three storeys high and lined with rows of brown arches, the rooftops at either end topped with conspicuous Christian crosses. But while the school had Christian origins, it opened its gates to students from all different faiths, allowing Malaysia's distinct ethnic groups – Malays, Chinese, Indians and Eurasians – to study side by side.

After checking in with security, we walked up some stairs with our lanyards to a covered walkway overlooking a large grass courtyard. In the background, tall glass skyscrapers stood out against a cloudless blue sky, juxtaposed with the brown heritage archways. A group of schoolgirls in navy-and-white uniforms, some wearing white hijabs, bowed politely as they filed past.

'Is that what you used to wear?' I asked Sarah.

'Yes, pretty much the same, though the skirt was a bit longer.'

She took me to a nearby empty classroom. The pink door was open, and inside were wooden desks grouped together, pencil cases and water bottles sitting neatly on top of them. This was the classroom where Sarah had been sitting at her desk one morning when an unexpected visitor came calling – Mum.

'I would have turned fourteen that year,' Sarah recalled. 'If I'm not mistaken, I was having history class. I remember the teacher was talking about the chronology of things happening.'

The principal from the adjoining primary school had knocked on the classroom door. Mrs O'Brien, a kindly Eurasian woman, looked directly at Sarah and addressed her by her Muslim name, then asked the teacher, 'Could she be excused for a moment, please? Someone is here to see her.' At her teacher's nod, Sarah rose from her chair and followed Mrs O'Brien along the narrow walkway to the main office.

All Mixed Up

'You are going to be very surprised about who is here to see you,' Mrs O'Brien said as they walked. 'It's someone who is going to make you very happy.'

When they reached the waiting room, a rotund lady was sitting there in a summery floral dress. Her face was round and rosy, her features Eurasian, her thick black hair in a neat bob with a part slightly to the side. She was beaming like she had just won a million Malaysian ringgits.

The lady got up and approached Sarah, who stood frozen.

'Sarah, I'm your mother. I'm Patsy, your mother.' The lady kept smiling as she reached out and embraced Sarah, who felt the lady's soft body tightening around her. For a moment they stood in an awkward hug.

If this lady was indeed Sarah's mother, it seemed she had risen from the grave. Growing up, Sarah had been taught to believe her biological mother was dead.

'Do you remember me?' the lady asked.

Sarah blinked.

The lady pulled away and glanced at Sarah's ponytail. She inspected the girl's baju kurung, a uniform of a white top and a sky-blue skirt flowing down to her heels. 'I'm surprised you're not wearing a headscarf. I thought you might be?'

Sarah was speechless.

Mrs O'Brien left as the pair acquainted themselves. Sarah took the lady past the history classroom and down a flight of stairs to the canteen, which opened out onto a concrete courtyard. The girl was floating along the path in a dreamlike state, her eyes transfixed by the lady's face.

They didn't talk for long. The lady said she was surprised that Sarah spoke good English. But Sarah could find little else to say, fumbling for the right answers, while the lady's melodic voice rose and fell as if she were a bird. The sounds around them faded. The faint hubbub of a hundred girls, even the cicadas in the nearby forest, fell away. All Sarah could hear was the lady's voice.

The lady explained she had come all the way from Australia – she lived in Melbourne and was visiting Malaysia with her husband and a son, Sarah's half-brother. She then explained that Sarah had maternal relatives living in KL: Aunty Anne, Uncle Rod and their three children.

And then, as quickly as it had started, the short but precious meeting was over.

Before the lady rose to leave, she slipped Sarah her Melbourne address and a phone number. *Please write*, she insisted. It was the only way they could stay connected across the seas.

Mrs O'Brien returned and ushered the lady away. Sarah stared at the back of her head as she became a flowery blur in the distance.

*

As I wandered with Sarah around the school, a chill went up my spine at the thought of taking the very same steps as Mum, thirty-one years ago. I imagined her anticipation, then her nervous excitement at being close to Sarah. Finally she was able to hold her daughter again, twelve years after Adel had ripped Sarah away from her.

Mum must also have been assailed by an enormous sense of powerlessness. The circumstances were against her: her former husband had custody and control of her daughter, and as a child Sarah was even more powerless than Mum.

Among the brown archways something stirred inside me. I sensed Mum's presence. I could feel her. Free-spirited Aunty

All Mixed Up

Madeleine's comforting words came to me: *She is watching over you*. Perhaps my aunty was right – perhaps Mum was standing with me in her summer dress, helping me to uncover her truth and find some clarity.

A narrow walkway, just wide enough to fit two people comfortably, led me and my sister to another part of the school. More pink classroom doors. Signs that said, *Keep right in single file*. The temporal residue rubbed off on us.

'And this leads to the canteen,' Sarah said, ushering me down some stairs to the place where she and Mum had spoken briefly: a cracked concrete courtyard surrounded by flowering bougainvillea and small pots of palms. Outside the canteen dozens of schoolgirls milled about, gathering for lunch at rows of long benches.

We stood for a moment in the hot sun, my pants chafing against my legs and my carefully coiffed hipster quiff wilting in the heat, beads of sweat gathering on my brow. I wished I could have worn shorts.

Sarah looked wistful as she scanned the buildings. She was lost in the 1980s.

I pulled out my camera and snapped some shots of the school grounds. A striking mural of the Petronas Towers on a wall. A sign conveying words of wisdom: *Talk less, listen more. Less insults, more results.*

When I swung around, Sarah's face was flushed and wet with tears.

'Are you alright?'

She needed a gentle pat on the back, but I couldn't do that in public.

'It just reminds me of every day coming to school, you know? With puffy eyes.'

'What do you mean?'

'I used to come to school in the morning with swollen red eyes. From the crying.'

The sun beat down on us. The concrete seemed like it was on fire, and Sarah was too hot to touch. I decided against probing further. 'Okay, let's go then.'

On the way out, Sarah went to say goodbye to the principal. As I waited, I took a seat under the brown archways overlooking the street. From that peaceful spot on the balcony, the tall trees in the nearby forest reserve felt close enough to touch. I closed my eyes and listened to the hypnotic high-pitched tune of the cicadas, rising and falling like ocean waves, the whispers of schoolgirls in the background.

'Those trees?' Sarah said as we were leaving. 'They're meranti. There are monkeys and other animals in them.'

I suggested we take a look. 'Do you want to go up there? Maybe we could find a seat, a place to talk?'

Sarah's brow furrowed under her dark brown hijab. 'It might look a bit funny.'

Funny? I screwed up my face, puzzled, then realised it might appear suggestive if a single man and a woman in a hijab skipped into the forest together. Not that anyone was watching. And we were related.

'Can we go back to the hotel where there's air conditioning?' Sarah asked urgently.

I glanced at the shady trees up the path. Wind in the leaves and moving shadows.

'Okay, we'll go back. Get something to eat.'

*

'At the back of my mind, I sort of instinctively knew that the person who was coming to see me was Mum,' Sarah recalled. 'It was like an instant instinct, but I wasn't sure.'

We were back in the cool cocoon of my hotel, sitting at a booth in the shiny food hall, our plates heaped with items from the buffet. Malaysian curry on mine, sushi on Sarah's. 'I rarely get to eat it,' she explained.

I put on my journalist's armour and threw questions at her, starting by asking about the moment she'd set eyes on Mum.

'I recall the lady standing up, greeting me,' my sister said. 'That's very sharp in my mind. In my heart, I was saying, *This is Mum.*'

'Even before she opened her mouth?'

'Yes. I was amazed.'

'Spellbound?'

'Yes. I was like, *Is this really happening? Is this really real?* It never occurred to me that she would come.' Sarah took a deep breath and looked away as she gave me more details of the meeting. Speaking about the hug, she said, 'I felt awkward because there was no bond. There wasn't any bonding. I think on her part it was a tighter hug. She was holding me closer. It's not that I resisted her, it's just that the moment was awkward because she suddenly appeared. I was in shock. Later I felt proud because I knew I was of mixed blood. I know from my features, I know that I am. I look different from my other siblings in Malaysia. I know that I'm a mixture, so when my mum came it confirmed to me that my mum's Eurasian. I have a proud feeling.'

'Up until that time, you knew you had a mum, right?' I asked.

'Growing up, there was confusion.'

When she was little, Sarah received unexplained gifts in the mail, which were passed on by a person who acted as intermediary. The parcels were filled with dresses, pyjamas, towels, dolls and chocolates. One day, the intermediary let slip that the gifts were from her real mother in Australia. They believed Sarah had the right to know.

'My grandmother denied it, saying, "Your mother's dead."'

'Did you believe her?'

'At the back of my mind, I didn't believe that Mum was dead. I thought, *Why is this issue such a secret? Why are they keeping it away from me?* It was always on my mind.'

'You were onto them?'

'Yes.'

Mum became part of Sarah's family folklore, a mythological creature to be spoken about in anger or not at all. But the secret meeting at the school provided Sarah with proof that Mum was alive and real.

'My dad kept denying it. One day he pointed to my stepmother and said, "This is your mother,"' Sarah recalled. '"She is the one who gave birth to you. She is your mother. There is no other mother." And I got so angry.'

After the shock of meeting with Mum, Sarah clambered onto a school bus, bas sekolah, for the 45-minute journey home. The bus groaned down the hill, making its way past schoolgirls streaming out the gate, then past a man selling icy cendol treats from a cart. Sarah stared out the window as she replayed the unexpected encounter with the woman in the summer dress, her mother, Patsy from Australia. 'I was flashing back to the experience of Mum.'

'What happened when you got home?'

'I acted like normal, like nothing happened. I was worried my family would find out because prior to that meeting, I would always get a scolding if I asked too many questions about Mum. We had family fights over this issue. I was anxious. What if Dad found out? What would he do to me?'

'That's pretty scary?'

'Yeah. How would I contain this information?'

'Did you run scenarios in your head about what would happen if your dad found out?'

'He would scold me – he would beat me up,' Sarah said firmly. 'That's the assumption. He would get onto me and really work me up. He was really strict. You go to school and you come back, and that was the routine every day. The other girls were more advanced than me. They already had boyfriends. They call it tea parties, going with boys to tea parties after school.

'When Mum said she wanted to correspond with me and that we should write to each other, I was afraid because my dad would kill me. I was fearful. What should I do? Should I or shouldn't I? I had mixed feelings. Being Asian, or being taught not to say things that might hurt the other party, I said, "Okay we'll do that," but deep down I was scared.'

*

It was a while before Sarah spoke to Mum again.

As we sat together in the food hall, Sarah told me that in 1986 her dad and stepmum had hatched a plan to move from Malaysia to Australia. They sold their belongings and travelled to Perth, where they stayed with family friends.

This was the first time I'd heard that Sarah had been in Australia at that time, and I was astonished to discover yet another point where our lives could have intersected. Another opportunity missed.

Sarah had skipped a year of school for the trip. Her parents, she reckoned, had gone crazy, but the stint in Australia gave her a sense of what life there could be like.

She'd grown curious about Patsy, and she had the landline number with her.

On a trip to a mall with her family friends the following year, Sarah found a Telecom payphone and dialled the number. She looked over her shoulder, checking to see if anyone else was around; the call had to be quick lest the adults became suspicious. One of her friends covered for her.

Although Perth was on the opposite side of the continent from Melbourne, Sarah suddenly felt within reach of Patsy. 'I was very excited to know I was there, and that she was there in the same country. At the back of my mind, I was thinking, *I wish I could go see her.* I was already *near* her.'

Sarah pressed the receiver to her ear, hearing a tone as the interstate STD call connected to Melbourne.

'Hello?' It was Patsy.

They spoke briefly. 'It was maybe a few minutes, five minutes or less. I just told her I was in Perth, and she was surprised, asking, "Why are you here?" So I explained to her about our trip and then told her that "Daddy doesn't know I'm calling you".'

They spoke a little more before Sarah had to rush off. She looked over her shoulder again, said goodbye and hung up the receiver.

'I do remember her voice,' Sarah told me.

'See, I can't remember. Tell me about her voice.'

'Her voice was high-pitched. Going up at the end.' Sarah paused, looking into the distance, before imitating Mum's voice with a funny sound. 'Like *eeeeyuuuh. Eeeyuuuh.*'

'A rising intonation at the end? That's very Australian!

All Mixed Up

But that's how Aunty Anne talks too, that kind of singsongy melodic voice.'

Sarah's family soon returned to Kuala Lumpur. Their Australian dream was never meant to be.

*

Mother and daughter began to correspond in 1987. By then, Sarah was sixteen and had moved out of her father's place, running away to live with a sympathetic uncle who gave her a job at his cleaning business. Her change of address allowed her to communicate with Mum safely and secretly without her father ever finding out.

It was a secret she kept with her uncle and a few others. She stashed the letters away in a hiding place. Sometimes padded packages full of treasures arrived: *I will enclose a Jiffy bag to you with one lipstick from Paris and a powder pack. Also three bangles, earrings and beads.* Over the years, there were purses and eyeliner pencils, Rio brand bras and nighties, and once an Avon necklace. Pens and pencils came too, as well as odds and ends like tea bags. Mum wanted to send packets of Aeroplane Jelly, but while the gesture was well intentioned, the jelly was not halal for Muslims to eat, so Sarah told her not to send them.

Sarah had so many questions, especially about Mum's cultural background as she remembered Mum's fair-skinned features.

Mum was born in Penang. Yes, Mum is a Eurasian.
Mummy's mother and father were born in Penang.
My great grandfather was English and my great
grandmother was French.

> We used to live by the sea. When I was seven years old, we left Penang and went to Singapore. And then from Singapore we went to Kuala Lumpur. And that's where I grew up as a teenager.

Sarah had spent her life haunted by two mysteries: why had her parents divorced, and why had Mum seemingly abandoned her as a baby in Malaysia? When Sarah asked Mum directly, she responded in kind:

Dear Sarah,
Thank you so much for your letter. In your letter you asked me the story about the real thing that happened between me and Dad. Well, one morning Dad had gone to work and I was alone with you in that big house. I felt a sudden nerve attack. You were only one year and three months old. I packed all my clothing and took you to Aunty Anne's house. It means I left Dad.

In the evening, Dad came to look for us. Then he took you off me and went home. The next day in the evening, he came and we had a chat, then he said he divorced me. That was the end.

Sarah pet, no ill-health. Mum is still the same. Very clean and neat and tidy. I have a girlfriend called Afsah, I told her about you, and she sends salam to you.

Next year, I and Narong will be married for 15 years. My marriage to Dad only lasted three years. I met him at 16 years old.

So then darling, I hope you will read this letter carefully. I will send the bras in due time. Have to end with all our love to you. Tomorrow is Christmas Day

and I will use the dress you gave me for a special lunch.
Bye bye, for now.
Love, Mummy XXX.
– 24 December 1987

*

The next day I packed up my laptop and gear, and bade farewell to my view of the Petronas Towers. I had some follow-up questions for Sarah, so I told her I'd call her down the track. With the letters and recordings in my backpack, I boarded my flight back to Sydney.

Chapter Twenty-Four

In my conversations with Dad about Mum, he mentioned one of her old friends from high school, Rosalind. I'd first heard about Rosalind in 2010 when she'd tracked me down by email. I hadn't responded at the time and regretted not following up. Five years later, as part of my inquiry, I trawled through old messages to reconnect with her.

I found her living in Singapore, now in her late sixties. We chatted over Skype, her face appearing fish-eyed on the screen. She had a wavy black bob and wore red-rimmed glasses. I sat on my couch in Sydney while my mum's old friend spoke over the occasional rattling of a construction site opposite her apartment.

Rosalind remembered Mum before her adulthood had brought sorrow upon her. She described a time of laughter, dancing and games, unburdened by disappointment. 'We had chemistry and we became good friends. She was a bubbly, happy girl. She was easygoing, she laughed easily and forgave easily. I can still feel her laugh.'

'What did you two talk about?' I asked.

'Silly things, lah. Boys. Cliff Richard. Elvis Presley. We used to play small records on a player and dance around it.'

Both girls had attended the Catholic boarding school that I'd recently visited. About sixty girls of various ages were housed in two large dormitories. Each morning before class, the girls walked up the hill to say prayers in the chapel.

Rosalind, a Chinese-Malaysian, was two years older than Mum. Their personalities complemented each other. 'I am quite a fastidious fussy girl – you don't mess with me,' Rosalind said. 'Somehow she was able to get onto the good side of me. She was always looking up to me as a big sister. She could see the fun in every little thing I do. If I pulled a long face, she'd come and say, "Oh Chooooooon, what is bothering yooooou?" and she'd make a funny face. Maybe she brought out my happy side because I'm not that easily happy. I still am that way.'

Even though they were good friends, Rosalind knew nothing about Mum's relationship with Adel until they left school. Out of the blue, Mum invited Rosalind to a restaurant, saying, 'I've got a surprise for you, I want you to meet somebody.' As they ate, Rosalind was struck by Adel's good looks and found him suave and well-mannered. Mum was crazy about him but when asked whether she wanted to marry him she denied it, insisting he was 'just a friend'.

Rosalind informed her friend that when a non-Muslim married a Muslim Malay, they had to convert to Islam. Rosalind was sceptical about Mum's true intentions and ribbed her: 'Won't you miss all your pork? Your char siu pork?'

Mum laughed it off.

'I think she was a bit naive to jump into it,' Rosalind recalled, 'and I told her too, "You're a bit naive."'

Mum, who seemed to be testing the waters, possibly perceived her friend's initial misgivings as hostile. She ended up running away from her Catholic family, marrying Adel and having Sarah without telling Rosalind until much later. Rosalind wasn't invited to the extravagant garden reception in Ipoh.

The last time Rosalind spoke to Mum was when she was about to leave for Australia. Rosalind recalled Mum saying, 'I'm going to make the move. I think I'll leave Sarah behind. I have no choice.'

After that the pair lost touch, and by the time Rosalind reconnected with Dad in Australia in the 1990s, it was too late.

'I was pretty shocked at her death because I miss her so much.' Rosalind sighed. 'I support what she did, a hundred per cent. At least she had a second chance, went to Australia and had you. But it's sad she had to have this heart attack and go off so young. It could have been all the stress. I can tell you that she was a very happy lady who turned into a very sad lady later in her life.'

Several months after this interview, while visiting Dad in Melbourne, I found a couple of old black-and-white photos of Rosalind. The first, dated 1966, was a portrait of her with a giant beehive hairstyle. In the second she appeared slightly younger, and was standing irreverently on the base of a tall statue of the Virgin Mary, which bore a striking resemblance to the one I'd seen at Mum's old high school. Staring into the camera, Rosalind held a pair of glasses in a tongue-in-cheek way to her mouth.

On the backs of the photos were the most tender messages I'd ever seen written about Mum. Throughout her life, she'd deserved more of this kindness and gentleness.

All Mixed Up

> To my dearest Patsy,
> Lots of love and warm wishes to you Patsy-girl.
> Always a pal, Rosalind C.

And:

> My dear Patsy,
> Keep this as a sweet remembrance of your friend who will always remember you.
> Lots of love, Rosalind Choon.

*

As I reviewed my notes and pored over Mum's letters, I had to confront an uncomfortable reality: there was evidence supporting whispers within her family that she'd wanted a divorce from Dad.

> Sarah, Mum plan to leave Narong. Mum plan to take my things like my clothing, pots and pans, glasses, cups and mugs. Sarah, also linen. These things could come in handy when you and I rent a house.
> Narong will have the house and Jason. Mum won't take a cent from Narong. Mum has my ticket, one way money. I told a few people in Melbourne that Mum will return to Malaysia. When you get a job, we will rent a place with the boxes of things to start anew. Sarah, I can't live with Narong and Jason any more.
> – 5 April 1992

Each time I read this, it felt like a punch to my stomach. In her mind Mum was already dividing up her belongings, and I was to be left with Dad. It sounded simple: the solution to all her problems was to call it quits and head back to Malaysia.

But several months later, she changed her mind:

Sarah, I love Australia very much. I will not leave Australia. Sarah, put all the dirt down the pothole.
– 28 September 1992

Dad, a staunch believer in the family unit, had always rejected the idea of splitting up. Over a video call, I asked him for his views on Mum's attitude to this.

'When she was angry, she was always, "Divorce, divorce, divorce, I want a divorce,"' he said. 'I say, "Why divorce? Then you have a broken family."'

It seemed that whenever Mum had marital issues, her default action was to reach for the divorce lever but not pull it. Under Australian law, she could have gone to court on her own volition, yet she never did.

'It's not fair, really,' Dad said of Mum's obsession with Adel.

'How did it make you feel?' I felt silly asking the question, but I was testing how far I could probe him. Only moments earlier, he'd tried to wrap up the conversation. The fact we were openly discussing his marriage problems was remarkable.

'I feel upset,' he offered.

Then there was a long, long silence. I kept staring into the screen.

He spat out the words one by one: 'But she's always still thinking of him.'

And there was the sting in the tail for Dad. Perhaps Mum hadn't loved him as much as she'd loved Adel; perhaps she hadn't loved Dad at all. Then Mum had gone and died on him.

'What impact did her obsession with Adel have on your marriage?'

'Bit upset when she talked about Adel. Everything, *Adel, Adel*. But what can you do? You want to divorce, you want to split? You want a broken home?' He looked defeated.

I then revealed to him the contents of the letter in which Mum said she was going to abandon us. 'Were you aware she wanted to pack her bags and go back to Malaysia? Did she ever express that to you?

'No.'

'So she never said to you, "I'm going to pack my bags, I've got my one-way ticket and I'm going to leave"?'

'No.'

'Why did she write that?'

'I don't know.'

*

In Mum's letters, her attitude towards Dad fluctuated. Her assessments lacked nuance: he was either a good man or a bad man, depending on her mood.

Something to tell, Mum is not very happy with Narong.
– 21 July 1987

But then:

Narong and I have been married for 15 happy years.
– 8 May 1988

One source of tension in my parents' marriage would have been the obstacles they faced in trying to adopt Sarah. After the secret meeting at Sarah's high school, it seemed they gave up on seeking custody of her. It was a losing battle, and the years were getting away from them.

In 1987, Mum wrote: *There is a place for you, but the time is not ripe yet.*

But in January 1988, the year Sarah turned eighteen, Mum said Dad was against it. *Between you and me, Narong said that he could not accept you to live with us. But one day sweetheart, on your own, you come to visit me.*

My father disputed this version of events. He maintained he'd always wanted Sarah to be part of our family in Australia.

I asked him, 'Did you ever change your mind about Sarah? Was there a point when you said, "She can't come"?'

'No. Never say that.' He paused. 'Because I wanted more children.'

This was a surprise to me. 'You wanted more children?'

'Yeah.'

'You wanted Sarah in Australia?'

'Yes. And you, and then maybe another child. But because Mummy was sick, she cannot. Too much for her to cope.'

'Is Mum wrong then?'

He let out a moan. 'Yeah. Yeah. We tried to take Sarah here.'

I eased off a bit. 'Say you did succeed in having Sarah with us, were you prepared to look after someone else's daughter?' I asked gently.

He considered this for a moment. 'It's a family. You have to accept that it's her child.'

'How would you bring her up?'

'Like normal, like we bring you up. Go to school or whatever. We have more chance, more life, better life for her. We are a free country, education and all this. So if she is here, she wouldn't be a Muslim.'

I hadn't thought of that. 'Are you sure about that?'

'Yeah, she wouldn't be.'

He meant Sarah may have become a Catholic if she'd come to Australia as a child. Being so young, and with the emotional prospect of finally reuniting with Mum, Sarah may have been more likely to become a Catholic unless she'd desired otherwise. I doubted my parents would have forced her to switch religions. But then, a Muslim living in a Catholic-Buddhist family was possibly haram, forbidden in Islam.

'Did you ever think about how suddenly having Sarah living with us would affect me?'

'You might feel a bit of jealousy. Two kids, always have jealousy. It's normal.'

'In a way,' I said, 'I had to compete for Mum's affections anyway because she –'

He finished my sentence. '– because she loves her. She may love Sarah more than you.'

Mum's love for a daughter out of her reach was a powerful force to reckon with. Dad and I had lived in the shadow of events that preceded us. We'd had to jostle for Mum's affections, and in that respect he and I were the same.

'For all that time she was stuck, wasn't she?' I said to him.

'Maybe ask a psychologist?' He let out a loud yawn. 'Enough for today.'

Dad had carried an immense burden, mostly on his own, in an era before there was help like Beyond Blue; before

Australian politicians and sports stars opened up about their private demons in weekend magazines. In the 1970s and 80s, mental health was poorly understood by the public, and my father was left to fumble in the dark.

He gritted his teeth and pressed on no matter how immovable the obstacle. Mum fell down, he was there. She fell down again, he was there. It happened, according to her medical records, at least five times. Each and every time Mum tripped, Dad picked her up. Caring for her must have required superhuman tenacity, but although my dad was a mere mortal, somehow he managed to persist, and resist falling into a heap himself. He realised his wife needed help, and the only solution was to go to the doctor.

Throughout this, he'd felt abandoned by her family — he said they hadn't lifted a finger to help. Apart from the indefatigable support of his friend Betty, it was all Dad.

My respect and gratitude towards him deepened. All the resentment and blame I'd heaped on him during my teenage years evaporated. I realised he was the link that had held the three of us together as a family, and then the two of us after Mum died. I could see how his persistence must have taken a terrible toll on him, and how his love for Mum may have crumbled under the pressure.

Before they got married, Dad told me, he had no inkling of the magnitude of her despair. It seemed he woke up one day not to the woman he first met under the clocks at Flinders Street Station, not to the woman brimming with optimism in their wedding photos, but to a woman warped by sorrow.

In Mum's letter dated 29 December 1992, I found this strange line: *Sarah, Mum asks Dad's family to forgive Mum.*

Forgive her for what? For failing to memorise the Qur'an? For leaving Islam? For fleeing for her safety and my sister's? Was Mum blaming herself for leaving Sarah?

Among the letters to Sarah were a couple of birthday cards Mum had sent to Adel over the years. She filled in the blank spaces around the generic pre-printed wishes with affectionate comments, and signed on behalf of our family, including me. I doubted Dad was aware of – or would have approved of – these birthday greetings. One of the cards was dated sixteen years after Mum and Adel divorced and Sarah was taken. Why was Mum still sending him best wishes? Did she think that seeking his non-existent affections would prompt him to release Sarah to her, so long after the event?

If so, it didn't work out that way. It was a fantasy.

Mum had been selfish and ungrateful in her inability to appreciate Dad's love. But I couldn't tell if that was part of her reckless character, or if it arose from delusions. She reminisced about Adel with stars in her eyes, overlooking her devastation in an act of appeasement towards her ex, and an egregious failure to acknowledge my father.

After Mum's suicide attempt, Dad moved mountains to pull her out of her illness with little knowledge and few resources. He did all he could to fulfil her desire to have Sarah with her, despite the extreme unlikelihood of success. He organised the flight to KL in 1984 so Mum could finally hold her daughter again. He stuck by her until the end, sitting with her in hospital on the night I called the ambulance. He was still by her side when he gave the nod for her life support to be switched off for the sake of her dignity, then he organised for her body to be buried in a pretty cemetery.

In life, Mum may have seemed like dead weight, perhaps more trouble than she was worth – and yet my father was devoted to her, regardless of her frailties and flaws. She broke down by the side of the road many, many times, and he stood there scratching his head, figuring out how to put the wheels back on. He struggled to verbalise his emotions, but he allowed his problem-solving actions to speak for him.

Much later I came to realise that Adel's act of taking Sarah from Mum, and dangling her daughter over her head, was a form of control. He held that power over Mum from 1972 up until the day she died in 1993: a 21-year stranglehold. The outcomes for each of them were light years apart. Adel went one way, his life in Malaysia uninterrupted, seemingly oblivious to what he'd done to Mum, while denying her existence. Mum went the other, boarding a ship to Australia, annihilated.

The shockwaves from the snatching travelled along the fault line from KL to Melbourne, hitting me and Dad. In that sense, a man I'd never met or even spoken to had deprived me of knowing the real Mum – the woman with the light inside her, which had been sucked out by the time she got to us.

Adel declined to speak to me for my investigation (he died in 2019). Over time, I realised he had occupied our lives for too long, and that as a family we ought to make more space for Mum. I could no longer be an objective journalist and had to be on her side because of what had happened to her. She had no voice in this and I had to speak up for her.

Adel was a blue flame, and Mum was incinerated. Stranded in a burnt landscape, we needed to crouch down in the ashes and extend our hands to help the little green shoots grow.

*

I flew down to Melbourne to spend Easter 2015 with Dad. Sitting in his study, I called Sarah to tie up loose ends. We reflected on how our lives had diverged from the same womb.

Sarah revealed that when Mum had been comatose in hospital, my family had kept her life support on for several days while they tried desperately to have Sarah flown over from Kuala Lumpur. She had applied for an emergency Malaysian passport and was ready to leave, but Adel had forbidden her from travelling to Melbourne to be at our mother's bedside.

She insisted to me that she would have disobeyed her father if she'd had the money to do so. 'I'm a little bit like Mum,' she said. 'I don't care – if I want it, I'll do it.'

But my sister maintained she now understood why she'd been forbidden from travelling to Australia, because she'd developed a better understanding of Islam.

'If I go there and be with Mum,' she told me, 'I would probably be more inclined to Christianity, and that is the thing my family was afraid of. They would be afraid of me, uuuhhh, there is a word for it … Apost … apost … aposty … is it?'

'Apostasy?'

'Yeah. So they were afraid of me going through that. Now I understand in Islam that if I went to Australia and if I wanted to get out of Islam then nobody from my family could help me, not even Allah could help me. So I am grateful and thankful that I am born in this religion, in Islam, because that is the greatest gift that a human being can ever have. That is the understanding I have right now. So, um, yeah. Does that answer your question?'

I was curious. 'Could you have come to Australia and still have been a Muslim?'

'If my iman, my strength in Islam is not strong at that time, I may have gone out of Islam. Because at that time, everything was going wrong in my life. It was always hard for me, my relationship with my father, I was rebelling. So I might have gone out of Islam because my strength in Islam was not strong.'

My brow furrowed. 'Are you saying that according to your faith, you can see that it actually worked out better for you, that if you came to see Mum you would have lost your religion?'

'No. The understanding is that Allah knows everything because he is the Creator.' My sister's voice was clear and assertive, each word emphasised. 'What happened then was Allah's planning. Allah did not allow it to happen that way. Not because my father didn't allow it. No. Because Allah didn't allow it to happen. And why Mum met my dad? It was in the knowledge of Allah. It was fated. And why they divorced? It's all in Allah's knowledge. So I understand things better now, why it happened the way it happened.'

My heart sank. I thought of Mum's interminable sadness. I was sure her life would have been brighter if Sarah had lived with us, regardless of whether she was Muslim.

'I hope you won't be offended about the Muslim thing,' Sarah added, before we said our goodbyes and hung up.

I felt sad, but at the same time I was getting to know my sister better, and how faith shaped who she was.

*

Sarah, I have a girlfriend called Afsah, and she sends salam to you.

During the tumultuous period when Mum wanted to divorce Dad, she turned to a trusted family friend, Afsah, who lived a short drive away. A Muslim from Brunei, Afsah had come to Melbourne on an educational scholarship, and she'd befriended Dad in the 1960s. She eventually settled in Australia, marrying a flame-haired Sicilian man, Ross, who converted to Islam for her. They went on to make their own mixed-up family.

Afsah used to babysit me, and I played with her four children in their overgrown backyard, running among the fig trees and prickly pears. Around the kitchen table, we'd all laugh at Ross's tall stories and jokes. 'Your eyes are bigger than your mouth, Jason,' he said, as I scooped a huge serving of Afsah's boiled potatoes onto my plate. 'One day, they'll be as round as the moon. True! It happened to a man I know.'

When I got back in touch with the family in early 2015, I hadn't seen them in years. They invited me and Dad to join them for Easter Sunday at their house.

Afsah was seventy-two, but she seemingly hadn't aged except for a few grey streaks in her hair. I gave her a hug, and we talked about her long friendship with Mum.

'Such a beautiful thing. I miss her.' Afsah sighed. 'Every time she dropped you off, she would say, "And don't forget that he likes his potatoes and boiled eggs."'

I laughed – I still did.

Afsah revealed that in the lead-up to Mum's death, they were meeting at least once a week. Her already quiet voice fell into a whisper. 'Every time she came here, I saw her hand like this,' Afsah said, putting out her hand, fingers shaking. 'I thought it was the cold or something. So I said, "Come and warm up here."' She demonstrated, rubbing her palms together.

On Thursdays, Afsah visited Mum at our house while I was at school and Dad was away. The women sat on the couch and talked intimately. Afsah recalled Mum bringing out a photo album of her first wedding to Adel but not of her wedding to Dad.

Inevitably, their conversations turned to Sarah, and how much Mum desperately missed her. 'Your mum didn't forget Sarah,' Afsah said. 'I told her to push it to one side, but that one day Sarah would come to see her. That was my comfort.'

Afsah confirmed that Mum had blamed Nan Ruby for forcing her to leave Sarah.

'I kept on saying, "You will see her one day."'

By the 1990s, Sarah was at uni and saving up to come to Australia, and according to Afsah, Mum was planning for her arrival. '"I clean the house if she comes,"' Afsah recalled Mum saying. '"I clean the fridge, all Muslim food, halal food."'

Mum's last letter, four months before she died:

Sarah, Sarah, I can't wait to see you. Sarah, Mum is this way.
    Sarah, I will end with love and kisses to you. I am waiting to see you soon. Bye bye.
    Love, Mum XXX

                                       – 1 March 1993

When my mother had lain comatose in the hospital, a broken heart in her chest, perhaps she'd thought of her baby daughter.

Chapter Twenty-Five

The phone call came out of the blue, breaking one of the long stretches of silence between me and Dad. It was early 2016 and he was calling from Melbourne. I was at work, eating a sandwich on a sunlit terrace above the Harris Street hubbub.

Dad rarely called, so I knew it was important. His voice sounded weak and plaintive, and I struggled to hear him over the traffic below.

'Jeh, I'm getting old now,' he said in his slow Cambodian lilt. 'I want to ask you, would you take a wife?'

It had been fifteen years since I'd come out to him, and not once had he expressed any interest in my love life. Now he was proposing an arranged marriage to a successful young Cambodian woman known to our family in Melbourne. 'I can ask for you.'

I'd first been exposed to Cambodian arranged marriages while growing up in 1980s Melbourne. I remembered standing in someone's house beside Dad and Dit as we watched the bride and groom, both dressed in white, having their photos taken.

Dit observed that the newlyweds had been strangers before that day. 'How can they be in love?' he wondered out loud.

I was thinking the same thing, and asked Dad, who said, 'They will grow to love each other.'

Decades later, this made even less sense to me.

Over the phone Dad continued to make his proposal, explaining how he wanted a big family. He was envious of Aunty Madeleine who showed off photos of her grandchildren.

'Dad, just because you don't have any grandkids doesn't mean your life is any less worthy.'

He wasn't listening. 'You have a wife, then children, then grandchildren. That is a life. I have just a son and that's it.'

That is a life. As if mine meant nothing.

'My life is not complete,' he said with heavy emphasis on each word.

I had little interest in having children unless a future partner wanted them.

By the end of the call, Dad sounded defeated. 'Okay, I will have to stop thinking about it now and live as normal.'

I tried to finish my sandwich but no longer felt hungry. For fifteen years, I had been striding through life independently, confident and open about my sexuality to most of my family, my friends and at work. I didn't shrink away or hide from that, once sending Dad postcards from San Francisco about my gay adventures. So his phone call blindsided me and tipped my world upside down.

My eyes were stinging. I escaped to a stairwell and sank down onto a step, replaying fraught conversations I'd had with Dad over the years. The time I'd explained that I wanted to marry a man if it ever became legal. And the night I'd told him I was gay. 'This is part of who I am,' I'd said repeatedly.

Once, we were looking through some photos on my camera from a friend's wedding. He eyed another friend, Penny, with envy. 'You have a beautiful girlfriend, so why you not attracted to her?'

Penny was indeed stunning, and I liked to joke that I would turn for her.

Later, at the kitchen table, he probed further. 'Do you have girlfriends?'

'What do you mean?'

'Do you have girlfriends?'

'Do you mean, do I have friends who are women?'

'Yeh.'

'Um, yeah. Of course. Why wouldn't I still hang around women? What do you think I am?'

Dad inspected the newspaper and made disapproving noises. 'All mixed up!' he muttered, and continued reading.

'It's not mixed up! Many of us are high profile and have normal lives – Penny Wong, Justice Michael Kirby. Even Peter Hitchener is gay. There are lots of us.' I reeled off a few more names.

Why didn't he accept me?

Memories swarmed through my head, underscored by Dad's words: *My life is not complete*. Slumped in the stairwell, I realised that no matter what I achieved in my life, without a wife I would never be enough for my dad.

*

On Christmas Day 2016, I was shelling prawns at Dad's house. A plastic bag sat on the bench, filled with hefty king prawns from a fish shop in Chaddy. Another bag contained the shells and brains.

'Eat prawns!' Dad said excitedly. *Prrrawns*. His tablet started ringing. 'Jeh, it's cousin Amara in America,' he said, wandering into the kitchen and holding the tablet right up to my nose.

Amara's face appeared on the screen. 'Hi, Jason, how are you doing?!' she asked cheerfully.

Amara was one of my overachieving Cambodian-American cousins who lived in the state of Virginia. Now in her fifties, she was married to a white American man, Bobby, who bobbed around in the background of the video call.

'Merry Christmas!' they cried.

'Yeh!' Dad replied.

We chatted about the lunch Dad and I were preparing, and my plans during my brief holiday in Melbourne. Then the conversation turned to the question that some of my Cambodian relatives asked without fail. Not all of them knew I was gay.

'So Jason, tell me –' Amara began.

The question was coming. I concentrated on the shell of a rubbery prawn, trying to avoid being stabbed by the sharp rostrum on its head.

'– do you have a girlfriend?'

I yanked at another prawn, dismembering it. *Tear off the head and eat the body. Just like all those guys you sleep with in Sydney.*

Dad and I stood frozen under the kitchen skylight. Dad winced. I had no words.

Too many prawns. You'll never find a boyfriend.

Dad opened his mouth: 'It's complicated.'

A white flash. Then …

'It's not complicated, Dad!' I snapped, quickly washing my hands and slamming the front door behind me.

The blaze of summer sunlight. A blur of familiar fences and front yards. The fish and chip shop and the milk bar. A narrow alleyway leading into a wide open park, deserted because it was Christmas: families away on holidays or sitting comfortably in their air-conditioned homes, tucking into lunch. Not a soul to be seen, just mirages shimmering above the scrappy yellowing grass.

I stood, a grown man in my thirties, screaming at the sky. If it had been a movie, the shot would have started on a close-up of my mouth. Aerial. Pulling out slowly until the audience could see me with my arms out wide. No audio, or maybe that ringing-in-the-ears sound effect, because in the suburbs no one can hear you scream.

Everything felt as dramatic as it had been when I was fifteen. It felt like Dad and I were at war again, and I was absolutely exhausted. When would peace be declared? When would Dad accept me for who I was? I'd come out to him in 2001, that world-changing year when the Twin Towers collapsed. He'd had fifteen years to come to terms with reality. Fifteen years!

Dad and I had tap-danced around the issue for too long. It was a twisted performance, yet the show kept going on.

Some people asked me, 'Why does it matter?'

True, many gay men cared little about what their parents thought of them. Some were out and proud, while others preferred to live in silence, hoping their parents would die without finding out because avoidance was far easier than confrontation.

For me, this wasn't about needing my father's approval, or about playing the obedient Asian son, something I'd never been and never would be. It mattered to me because without Mum, Dad was the only parent I had left.

Whenever these issues came up, thoughts of Mum returned to me with a vengeance. I couldn't contain or reconcile my feelings. Everything collided.

On the far side of the park, I sat down and wept on a wooden picnic bench.

If Mum were still alive, I wondered, would she care about who I loved as much as Dad did? I reckoned she probably would have laughed it off, and we'd have proceeded to gossip about handsome guys. But she wasn't there to defend and support me. She'd been gone for more than twenty years.

Luckily, at that moment my seventeen-year-old nephew, Ayman, called me. Speaking from Kuala Lumpur, he told me he was going for his driver's licence. The line was fuzzy with background noise, and I found it hard to follow what he was saying – something about going for a drive with his friends. It sounded like trouble to me.

'Just don't do ...' I was trying to avoid sounding like a paternalistic old man. 'Just don't do, mmm, just do anything illegal.' Ugh. I *was* an old man.

'Okay, I won't,' Ayman singsonged, apparently unfussed. 'How is everything with you, Uncle Jehsen?'

I laughed. 'Er, it's Christmas, so the usual family dramas.'

'Well, I will pray for you, Uncle Jehsen,' he said sweetly. 'I will pray for you!'

'Yes, please do that. I need all the prayers I can get.'

That was my Muslim Malaysian nephew. We'd always lived in different countries and held very different beliefs, and yet there he was, at just the right time, dispensing the kindness I needed – and a teenage boy at that. I thought of

Sarah's belief that everything happens for a reason. *It was fated.*

A calm fell over me. Wiping my eyes, I walked back home in the dry heat. The rest of the prawns needed butterflying. Christmas had to go on.

A few weeks later, Amara told me in an email:

> I'm not trying to be nosy when I asked whether or not you have a girlfriend. :-) I have to phrase it like that when I'm around your dad. :-)
>   Honestly, I just wanted to make sure you're happy and have a companion that you can do stuff with. :-) Or if you'd prefer to be single, I'm still happy and support you just the way you are.

*

By late 2017 the same-sex marriage survey had begun, a postal vote asking Australians whether marriage equality should be legalised by Federal Parliament. I imagined Dad being bombarded by story after story on the TV news. I worried he would vote No. I worried he'd refuse to attend any wedding of mine. I pictured myself taking my vows before a celebrant and breaking down in front of everyone because he wasn't there.

I wrote him an email. *Have you been following the news about the same-sex marriage postal survey? Have you given any thought to how you'll vote?*

I checked my inbox every day.

A week passed before he got back to me. He was circumspect. *It is a controversial issue. It drags on too long now. Wait and see the vote.*

This reply was a non-answer, much like when government departments 'issue a statement'. I was being fobbed off by my own dad.

Weeks later, the Yes campaign released some chirpy advertisements urging Australians to 'ring your rellos' to talk about the survey. One ad showed supportive white parents with their son, hands on his shoulders. If only it were that easy.

The Turnbull Government's survey forced many Australians like me to confront family members who didn't accept them. Despite the Yes campaign's optimistic vision of a modern pluralist society, many LGBTI Australians still lived under a heavy cloak of secrecy and even shame. Some were forced to keep their true self invisible, or have it made invisible for them. They sat quietly at the family table, afraid the mere mention of their sexuality might elicit harsh words or worse.

They were tolerated, not accepted.

*

Weeks went by, and I received a text message from Aunty Madeleine. She came to me with kind words, as always, making me sob in a bathroom at work where I was doing up my tie before walking into make-up. I was about to present the news on TV that night. *I marked it with a YES*, my aunty wrote. *You will understand what I am referring to. Happy day son.* Uncle Johnny, she added, had decided to vote Yes too.

This gave me the courage to email Dad again. And, a friend suggested, perhaps he needed to know how the survey would directly affect me.

So I wrote:

> I got some lovely messages from Aunty Madeleine and Uncle Johnny this week, saying they have voted yes in the postal survey!
>
> I was very touched by their support. It means a lot that they accept me for who I am and understand what it means for many Australians like me.
>
> I want you to know that this postal survey has a direct impact on me. A majority 'yes' outcome would most likely lead to same-sex marriage, meaning one day I could get married like everyone else. I do hope you will vote yes for me.

It took a few days for Dad to reply, and I left the message sitting in my inbox for a while. I dreaded opening it, fearing an angry response.

> Hi Jas, this same-sex marriage [debate] has been going on too long. Politicians don't know what to do about it. So they let the people decide by voting and they won't be blamed. It is nice to hear that Aunty Madeleine and Uncle Johnny vote a yes. I also vote yes to the survey. Everything is okay, and looking to see a warmer weather. Donald Trump gave a very honest and truthful speech at the UN. He spoke his mind.
> Dad.

I was stunned. Why had he changed his mind so dramatically? Had family members persuaded him? I read his words again and held on to the precious moment.

*

The next time I spoke to Dad, I was visiting Melbourne. He drove from the suburbs to meet me at my hotel in the inner city. Over brunch, we talked about his latest home improvement project: staining and polishing some old floorboards. We chatted about the rampant state of the housing market. Finally, we came to the survey.

'So – why did you vote yes in the end?' I asked.

'Times have changed,' he said slowly. 'But they should leave it up to the Parliament. Decide among themselves.' He paused. 'Some Cambodians have voted no. But that is the Asian mind so it's hard.'

Then we were back to talking about housing.

I paid for our meals and helped him to his car, and we drove back to his house.

We stopped at some traffic lights. 'There's only a few weeks left of the survey,' I said. 'I wonder if people will change their mind?'

'It's never too late,' Dad said.

The lights changed, and we followed the road along the Yarra River.

*

My struggle with my father went public after I wrote about it in an article for the ABC News website. In the lead-up, I'd wrung my hands about sharing such a private part of me. As an ABC journalist, I usually avoided discussing the personal. The threat of being dragged through the mud in some newspapers was very real, and I feared I might be blowing up my ABC career. I was also worried about thrusting Dad into the spotlight. But the piece was rigorously reviewed and timed appropriately, and in the end no backlash eventuated. Because it was published on the day of the postal survey result, 15 November 2017, I thought it would get lost among the sea of other joyful stories that day – boy, was I wrong. It exploded, becoming one of the top five stories, with more than 130,000 hits. About a hundred messages of support from the general public, friends and colleagues flooded my inbox. Readers were reduced to tears, crying at their desks. This unexpected reaction was overwhelming, and as my phone continued to ping with text messages, I locked myself in an empty room at work and sobbed.

'Let it all out, brother!' a friend texted.

On the evening of the marriage equality victory, I walked to dinner on Enmore Road with my boyfriend. We passed a house with a rainbow painted on the front. To emphasise the bold statement, its owners had added a large 'Yes' banner in the centre. Tonight the house was glowing and took on a far deeper meaning.

Suddenly, a black car crammed with sniggering young men slowed down beside us. 'Vote yes! Vote yes!' they shouted through the open car windows. They guffawed.

I glared at them and continued walking.

Newtown was alive with crowds enjoying the warm evening. We sat down at an outdoor bench under strings of lights. As we drank beers and tucked into soft-shell tacos, I was suddenly overwhelmed by the emotions of the day. Panic set in. In my mind I replayed the scene of the young men in the car, an innocuous event turned into something more sinister. Catastrophic scenarios ran through my head. There was speculation that 'No' supporters might protest the result and I pictured angry mobs marching up Enmore Road, smashing cars and blocking traffic.

But it wasn't going to happen. I knew I was safe. If the backlash was going to be as mild as 'Vote yes! Vote yes!' shouted from a passing car, then perhaps Australia really had changed.

That day, the Australian values of fairness and equality won out. We were finally accepted. My eyes welled at the thought of my conservative Cambodian father, how much we'd struggled, and how the future for both of us would be brighter. Things would be easier for us from now on.

A few weeks later, I went down to Melbourne to film a follow-up story about my relationship with Dad. It would air on the ABC's *7.30* program and a new digital platform called ABC Life. The idea was to take all the supportive messages I'd received from members of the public and read them out to him while the cameras rolled. Positive reinforcement.

The crew set up in our lounge room – lights, camera, action.

Dad wandered out of the kitchen and took his place in his armchair. 'Aiyah, this is torture!' he said, smiling at the crew and adjusting the cushion behind him.

I sat on the couch. 'Do you mean the interview is torture or just sitting down?'

'The interview. Like a torture chamber!' His face creased into a broad smile.

'I hope not!' I laughed.

The cameras began to roll. Although I'd conducted interviews with Dad in this room a few years earlier, I felt odd interviewing him under bright lights.

'It has opened up – everybody has opened up,' Dad said, reflecting on the same-sex marriage debate in the Cambodian community. 'People didn't talk about the law and about equality until somebody started to talk about it. First I find it a bit odd because we are Asian. We don't talk about it. It's just "shush, shush". I'm glad it's open. No secrets any more.'

'Well, since we put the article out there's been a huge response.' Opening up Twitter on my tablet, I showed Dad the scores of supportive comments.

It was an unfamiliar world to him. 'Mmm. That's good. Good response.' He nodded. 'Yeh.'

'Familiar names?'

'Yeah, Leigh Sales –' He paused. 'It's very emotional. Before – can I mention the name? Penny Wong. I know, somebody told me about her a few years back so I just keep in my mind. She mentioned about her partner. And then the survey came, how happy she was. It shows she keep that for a long, long time. Now, no more secrets.'

My heart was thumping. I cleared my throat, grabbed a tissue and tried to maintain my composure, fearing I might crumble before even getting to the emails. A sip of water. Dad fidgeted his hands in his lap, waiting silently for me to begin.

'I just wanted to read you some of the responses that I got in my email. These are some pretty special responses from people around Australia. So I'll do my best to read this and we'll get through it. This one's from Helen.'

> I'm 62. Cultural and psychological change is very hard. There is a systemic fear of change. From my white Australian female life, I encourage you to seize this opportunity to extend your compassion as a human being to your father for his expression of his deep love for you, his gay son. He is indeed worthy of your love as you are of his.

'Yes, it's a nice email,' Dad said quietly.
'This one's from Christine,' I said.

> My younger brother who lives in the UK has been in a long-term relationship with his male partner for 20 years. Although my brother and dad were very close – because my father was a Catholic and there was concern of what his reaction would be – their relationship was never mentioned. On their last visit before my father died, my dad hugged my brother, shook hands with his partner, and although he would not acknowledge they were gay, was quite emotional as he said he appreciated all the help they gave him and my mum, knew they were good together, and wished them all the best.

As I continued reading the messages, Dad sat forward, looking down, listening carefully to the words with little reaction. Then came the final email.

> Hi Jason, you don't know me but I've known you since you were a baby.

'Hah-hah, who's that?' Dad exclaimed.

> Your dad and I started the Khmer language program on SBS Radio.

'Ah!' Dad said, wringing his fingers.

> I know his way of thinking rather well. I'm so glad for you that he changed his mind and voted yes and I

congratulate you for coming out with your sexuality in this way.

'Do you know who that's from?' I asked.

Dad squinted. 'Maybe – Muntha?' he choked. He quietly took a tissue, lifted his glasses and wiped away tears.

Dad could see me now. It was his coming *to*, not my coming out.

*

Dad's outpouring of feelings was a stunning revelation to me because I'd believed his tear ducts were non-functional. Then I remembered the one time I'd seen a few sniffles.

In 1996, Dad and I had travelled to Rome. At a rustic hotel, he tried to make a phone call at reception, but it wasn't connecting and the Italian staff were indifferent to his plight. The woman in the little counter booth was speaking to an Italian guest as Dad retreated to a couch in the foyer. Incensed, he sat with one leg crossed over the other, muttering to himself.

'Dad!' I said, trying to rattle him out of his funk. He ignored me. I plonked myself on a chair opposite him, wearing a cap, an oversized T-shirt and baggy jeans. More angry mutterings escaped his mouth. 'Dad!' I tried again.

No response. What was wrong with him? *Why is everything like this!?*

'Dad! We can't just sit here in the hotel. How many times are we going to be in Rome? We only have two days, and we have to see the Vatican.'

When I looked back on this now, I realised he'd succumbed to his unacknowledged grief three years after Mum's death. He was struggling to hold back tears.

Somehow I managed to get him off the couch and into the cobblestone street, where we jumped in a taxi. When we got to the Vatican, we discovered that the Sistine Chapel was closed for repairs, so we entered St Peter's Basilica instead. 'Wow,' Dad said with his mouth open, teeth out, nose scrunched as he peered upwards at the spectacular domes.

I pulled out Dad's work diary from 1993, which he'd given to me during my investigation into Mum. Flicking through the pages around that lonely time of her death, I found an entry that said Nan Ruby 'rang to interrogate and scold me'. I then came across an entry that spoke of his private grief, something he'd never shared with me but had with a trusted colleague: *Danielle is back. A talk with her about my sorrow.*

Dad had taken little time off work. A fortnight after Mum had been admitted to hospital, he was back at his job. No one else could carry on his Khmer radio show. *Back to normal*, he wrote in his diary, dusting his hands.

I could see now how Dad had sequestered his feelings inside himself and spewed them out when he blew up, or hidden in his study when it all became too much to comprehend, during my teenage years when we clashed. I didn't ask him what he'd been doing in his room all those times, but I suspected he'd been crying quietly, with no one to pat him on the back. If that were true, there was no chance in hell he'd ever admit it to anyone, let alone me.

This was why I'd needed to go digging through old documents to find the proof of his grief in that one line.

'I read your diary,' I said to him. I was standing at the kitchen bench while he sat at the table facing away from me. 'That entry you wrote about your sorrow, that's a lot to go through.'

He turned his head slightly. Then said nothing.

'Dad, did you hear me? I said, that's a lot to go through.'
Nothing.

*

Dad had once been much gentler towards me. Before Mum died, he used to call me kon, 'son' in Khmer. When I was very young, we hung out together in the old corrugated-iron garage that smelt of oily rags, WD-40 and rusting metal. I followed him around as he did his chores, and watched him dunk a dipstick into the engine of his Toyota Corona. 'Check the oil level,' he explained.

Among the shelves of dripping paint tins, tools and assorted junk, there were a few plastic bags of goodies he'd saved from the potato chip factory where he and Mum worked. Inside were Cheezels and Burger Rings and *Pac-Man* collector cards, which Dad handed out as treats.

We spent long nights spread out on the floral carpet of our small lounge room.

'The cat sat on the mat,' I repeated after filling in the blank spaces of my homework. 'Is that right, Dad?'

He also gave me the answers to mathematical equations.

He helped me put oil into a toy steam-engine train on a circular track, and taught me how to play chess, though that was more like taking lessons in being beaten.

At night, Mum and I listened to the *mwah-mwah-mwah* of Dad's voice speaking in Khmer, a language we didn't understand. But it was Dad! On SBS Radio! We laughed along to the tinkling of the show's theme, a melody in Khmer xylophone.

I used to hold Dad's hand while at the shops in Oakleigh. His fingers felt like the soft sandpaper he kept in the garage.

But one day, I stopped. Something inside my head said I was too old for that, so I let go.

Then Dad stopped calling me kon.

Is that what happens to most fathers and sons? Is there a time when they shut each other off because showing emotions towards each other isn't what it means to be a man? And does a father's fondness for his son stop when that son falls short of his father's ideal?

*

Back in 2013, photos of a friend's grand civil union had appeared on my Facebook feed. Supremely fashionable, influencer-in-the-making Dean was getting hitched to his equally handsome Anglo-Australian boyfriend, Sam. Alongside pictures of them in matching navy tuxedos were shots of Dean's Cambodian father and Filipino mother joining the celebration, the brightness of their smiles dialled up 150 per cent.

I knew Dean from my uni days, while our fathers had known each other in the community since the late 1970s. Given that Dean's parents proudly endorsed the union, I presumed Dean and Sam's relationship was common knowledge, and therefore known to my dad. After all, it was on Facebook. But I never brought up Dean's very public display with him.

Dad never spoke to Dean's father, Ang, about it either. But when Ang read my same-sex marriage story in 2017, he contacted my dad.

'I emailed Narong straight away,' Ang said to me later. 'I told him, "You should be proud of your son. It's a very good article."'

I was curious about why the pair had never spoken about their sons being gay. So, over crispy noodles, fried rice and Chinese tea, I sought answers from them at the restaurant near Chaddy. Ang wore a blue cap and a brown zip-up vest, and he giggled like a baby hyena. Dad sat opposite in his black beret.

'We never talked about our children doing this or doing that,' Ang said. 'That doesn't really interest me.'

'So what did you talk about?' I asked.

'Politics,' he said with his mouth full.

'Which politics? Australian?'

'Cambodian!'

In 2003, Ang had returned to Cambodia to serve as an opposition senator, leaving his family in Australia. He'd come back to Melbourne two years later, at the end of his term.

'So Dean and I didn't even rate a cursory mention: "How is your son going?"'

Ang shook his head and baby hyena-ed. 'Being gay, it's not significant. Sorry to say.' He added, 'I'm Buddhist, and Buddhism says nothing about gay people. It's not a big issue. When Dean came out, I was okay. But my wife cried – she is a Catholic.'

For Dad, my sexuality was no longer a big issue. He relayed a story about a Christmas party he'd attended where a Cambodian woman suggested matchmaking me with her daughter. 'I told her you were gay,' Dad said proudly, 'and she just shut up! She didn't want to know any more. Like, full stop. She always wanted you and her daughter to match as a wife and husband.'

'That's the Cambodian thinking,' Ang joined in. 'But it's not my thinking. Probably, I'm too white in my thinking.' He giggled again. 'Are you okay, both of you now? You should be proud.'

A long pause at the table. My eyes welled up, and I took a sip of white wine.

After I paid the bill, I drove Dad home while thinking our whole sixteen-year ordeal could have been avoided if he'd known about Dean years ago.

That night, my phone pinged. It was Dean on Facebook Messenger. *How was your dad tonight? Did they compare experiences?*

I don't know whether I have a story or not, I thumbed back. *The premise was, here are these two Cambodian dads who never talked about their gay sons, yet when I asked them about it they said they never talked about their kids with each other full stop. They just talked about politics! WTF.*

Face palm emoji from Dean. *I find it odd that they never spoke to one another about it. Dads are weird.*

Yes! I tried probing but they gave the same answer. Surely they would have said, you know, 'How is your son?'; 'Oh, he just had a civil union to a MAN', etc.

He didn't know about me before? Dean asked.

No.

If only we knew they had a purely politics-based relationship. I thought they both would've known? I would've definitely pushed for you to tell him if I had known he had difficulty accepting.

Chapter Twenty-Six

In 2017, the long reign of shame fell and the era of pride began. It started with a celebratory phone call between my father and his older brother in the US, Uncle Chiv.

I'd met my uncle a few times when we'd visited him and my Cambodian-American cousins at their home in Richmond, Virginia, where squirrels ran after acorns in the backyard. With his bald head and big round belly, Uncle Chiv was the spitting image of a happy Buddha statue.

While the same-sex marriage interview footage was being edited in Melbourne, Dad called to tell me about his phone conversation with Uncle Chiv. I walked out of the edit suite at Southbank, where earlier that day a gay colleague had collapsed into tears after watching the rough cut.

'Uncle Chiv wants to know, do you wear a skirt?' Dad asked, probably curious himself.

I paused. One might want to jump down someone's throat for saying something that could be considered by some as offensive. Wearing skirts was a gender stereotype. But in this case, it was clear that honest ignorance, not hate, was at play.

'No, I don't wear a skirt. Some guys like wearing skirts, but it's not my thing.'

More than fifteen years of denial had lifted, and I was happy to let the question slide. By then, my patience was supremely Zen. It was wiser to feed curiosity calmly with facts rather than explode as I'd done in the past. Our differences were being neutralised, and the temperature of our relationship had eased.

'What is LG … LGB … those letters?' Dad asked.

'LGBTI?'

'Yeh.'

'LGBTI stands for Lesbian Gay Bisexual Trans and Intersex community.'

'Intersex? What's that?'

'Intersex people are born with physical sex characteristics that don't fit medical norms for female or male bodies.'

'And transgender, is that like a cross-dresser?'

'No, they're different, though they can overlap. A transgender person has a gender identity that's different to their assigned sex at birth, whereas a cross-dresser likes to wear clothes of the opposite sex.'

'Aaaahhh,' he singsonged.

About eighteen months later, I woke to find a text message from Dad that had come through overnight: *Hi Jas, Bobby SMS telling Uncle Chiv had a stroke last night. He is OK and maybe he stays in hospital for a week. Need to have PT or OT.*

Dad made out as if Uncle Chiv would be okay, saying that while his brother was struggling to speak, he would survive with therapy. I didn't worry too much, and got on with life in Sydney.

A month later, another overnight text arrived from Dad. I woke at 6 am on a Saturday, my body clock still tuned to the *ABC News Breakfast* shift at work that week.

Aunty Touch rang about forty minutes ago, telling that Uncle Chiv passed away. Dad.

Are you okay? I texted back, thinking he was probably still asleep. *Do you want to talk? I'm awake.*

Hours passed, and there was no answer.

I called him up. 'What happened?'

'He got an infection.'

'What?!' I was enraged. 'He got an infection from the hospital?'

'Probably.'

'If I were the cousins, I would sue. People shouldn't be dying in hospital like that.' My heart was racing. I was fired up. 'When's the funeral? Shouldn't we go?'

It would be a marathon flight from Australia to Virginia, which included a stopover in LA or Houston. During the last trip Dad had made, he'd been assisted in a wheelchair between airport terminals.

'Agh,' he moaned, 'it's too long to go. I am worried. Where go to toilet and all that.'

Silence.

'What is the point?' he asked. 'I want to see *him*. If we go, I want to see *him*.'

Uncle Chiv was a corpse. Redundant. One use only. There was no point seeing a man if you couldn't talk to him.

'I'm glad I saw him in 2012,' Dad said softly. 'Now, just memories.'

We fell silent.

'Do you want me to come to Melbourne?'

Dad ignored me. 'What can you do but cry?'

'Dad? Do. You. Want. Me. To. Come. To. Melbourne?'

'It is a loss,' he muttered. 'It is too much.'

More silence. I knew he would never utter the word 'yes' when I asked him if he wanted me to travel from Sydney to take care of him. That was his way. He rarely asked for help. Never would see a counsellor, even when the service was free through work.

'Dad?'

'Mwuh muh agh.'

'Right, I'm coming down.'

*

Outside the Oakleigh train station, Dad was sitting in his souped-up gun-metal 2017 Corolla, looking tiny.

'Are you okay?'

'Yeh,' he murmured, and we were on our way.

At home I fussed over the mess Dad hoarded in the house because he had trouble letting things go. *Keep, still good.*

'You'll need to get rid of these dead flowers,' I insisted, 'the water's all black.'

'Yeh.'

'What about all these empty boxes? Want me to help you clean them up?'

'I clean it up.'

'Put these dishes in the dishwasher.'

'No, leave it. I do later.'

'I'll vacuum later.'

'No, leave it.'

I went to Mum's old room, which was now Dad's bedroom, and opened the timber venetians, but they offered only a meagre light beneath the outdoor awning. In the dimness I changed the sweat-soaked pillowcase and vacuumed layers of dust from the bedhead, the side table and the floor. The room was in desperate need of some fresh air.

At the back of the house, through a glass sliding door, I noticed some movement on the scrappy lawn. 'Dad, there are mice in the backyard,' I said, observing them leapfrogging over some old planks of wood towards a frenzy of pigeons.

'Yeh, I put the bread and rice out and the birds come,' Dad replied quietly. 'The birds come, then the mice.' He went to the window and stood with his hands behind his back, sucking on a tooth, watching them intently.

*

At midnight in Australia, ten o'clock in the morning in Richmond, Virginia, we sat at the kitchen table watching the pixelated images of the funeral service. The ceremony began with prayers and 'Amazing Grace'. The audio was shocking; the one thing that was clear was my cousin Amara's tears as she battled through the eulogy.

After a while, I gave up on viewing the poor-quality connection. The words no longer had any meaning to me. There was nothing to be gained by watching the scratchy and inaudible broadcast, no way to pay tribute to my uncle.

A revelation that emerged at the time of Uncle Chiv's death was the story of how he had heroically led his wife and four children out of Cambodia in 1979.

The extraordinary account of how my extended family had escaped was a secret, a backstory that nobody talked to me about. Not even my cousins in Melbourne had shared it with me – including Dit, whom I'd looked up to and competed with. I'd played tiggy with him in his concrete backyard and fished for yabbies with him, oblivious to his family's traumas. Perhaps my cousins had been too young to remember the details, or they didn't want to remember, casting the terrible events from their minds.

When I asked my Cambodian aunties why they hadn't revealed their stories to me when I was growing up, they said, 'You don't ask so we don't tell.'

*

There was something else I hadn't known as a boy. In the 1970s, Dad's future in Australia was precarious. The federal government had given him notice that he'd have to return to Cambodia after completing his studies. About the same time, the Cambodian government was recalling its nationals overseas to serve in their army. Dad was in his late twenties, fit and eligible to fight.

His future looked bleak: returning to Cambodia would be a death sentence. If Australia wasn't an option, what about Canada?

Dad wrote an urgent letter to Canada's high commissioner in Sydney, filling out a form in neat capitals to apply for permanent residence. About eighteen months later, he received a decision.

> Dear Mr Om,
> Unfortunately, we are unable to process your
> application. This action is taken in accordance with
> information received from the Australian authorities
> that they consider you have an obligation to return to

All Mixed Up

your own country following completion of your studies in Australia.

We realise that this information may be a disappointment to you and wish to thank you for your interest in Canada.

– 21 June 1972

With that door slammed shut, and Dad fearful of being booted out despite his life-threatening circumstances, his trusted tutor, Mr Sharma, came up with an idea. What if Dad married a woman in Australia? It would mean he could stay. And that's how he came to place the dating ad in the newspaper and meet Mum in 1973.

They'd been dating for several weeks before he broke the news: 'If I don't marry someone, I have to go home.'

He proposed to Mum, his life in her hands. By marrying him, she would save him from having to return to the horrors of Cambodia. He would owe his life to her. It would also be an emergency exit for Mum, who, according to Dad, was desperate to move out of Nan Ruby's home.

Dad had no money to buy a ring, so Uncle Chiv – who was briefly living in Japan – went shopping in Tokyo. He bought a gold ring, a pair of gold earrings, and some white pearls to be attached to the jewellery later.

In 1974, Mum and Dad got married in an imposing Catholic church in Oakleigh. The red-brick building was flanked by two towers capped with pale green domes. With little savings between them, the young couple hastily improvised, and in typical Australian fashion they borrowed a friend's car and asked another friend to take photos. Mum wore a sheer sky-blue dress and a matching floppy sunhat with flowing ribbons. Her black hair fell in loose curly waves.

By her side, Dad wore a smart navy suit from Fletcher Jones, a dark red tie, and a white carnation on his lapel.

A Catholic priest officiated. As Jesus's body bled onto a cross that loomed above them, my parents stood before a wooden altar and exchanged rings. They kissed in front of a small group of close friends and relatives sitting in the pews – Cambodians, Malaysians, white Australians, and others.

That night they celebrated at a reception, sitting at a long table of white candles and carnations. The two-tiered cake was modest, with bride and groom figurines on top. As the beer and wine flowed, and speeches were made, the room brimmed with the laughter and voices of family and friends.

*

In 1975 the Khmer Rouge seized power, and in early 1976, Cambodian refugees began streaming into Australia. By that stage, Uncle Chiv had returned to Cambodia from Japan. His fate, and the fates of his wife and four children, as well as those of Dad's two younger sisters, Aunty Touch and Aunty Chan, and their families, were unknown to Dad in Australia. 'I thought they were all dead,' my father recalled.

He heard that refugees were being housed in Melbourne near my parents' new house in Oakleigh. Jumping in his white Corolla, he took a five-minute drive down Warrigal Road to a hostel where the Fraser Government was accommodating families under Australia's humanitarian program. These Cambodians had slogged through the jungle to escape the brutal regime, fleeing to refugee camps in Thailand. From there they'd been transferred to suburban Melbourne, where they now wore donated clothes.

All Mixed Up

Over several months, the refugees confided in Dad, giving him their first-hand accounts of life under the Khmer Rouge. The weeding out of intellectuals had begun with a simple question: 'The first thing they asked was "What did you do in the past?"' the refugees told Dad in Khmer. 'If you were a teacher, they put you in one group. If you were a doctor, they put you in another. If you wore glasses, they thought you studied too hard.'

Intellectuals were deemed unworthy of bullets. 'They whacked these people with a shovel, or a big stick, and then buried them, alive or not.'

Others were forced into arranged marriages. 'The men were lined up on one side, the women on the other,' the refugees said. 'It didn't matter who they were.'

'People starved,' the refugees told Dad. 'They gave you a few grains of rice mixed with lots of water just to keep you barely alive. You had to eat rats, or insects, or grubs, to make up for it.'

The Khmer Rouge were merciless. 'Sometimes they grabbed babies by the leg and smashed them against a tree, or a post, or a wall. Sometimes they threw the baby up in the air and caught it with the end of a bayonet. There was no humanity.'

Dad's eyes widened as these horrors were relayed to him. His home country was burning to the ground, and he couldn't do anything to help. For five years, he fretted about what might have happened to his relatives.

In 1980, a phone call came from a Cambodian cousin in America. Miraculously, it seemed, Dad's family were alive in the Khao-I-Dang refugee camp in Thailand. He sponsored his sisters and their families plus other relatives – a total of twelve men, women and children – to come to Australia, and helped Uncle Chiv and his family make it to America.

Dad shared a disturbing memory with me. Back in the 1950s, many years before the genocide, Pol Pot was known by his birth name, Saloth Sâr. Mr Sâr was a French literature tutor who taught Dad during school holiday classes in Phnom Penh, extolling the virtues of Voltaire and Victor Hugo. 'He didn't speak Cambodian through the class, he spoke French fluently,' Dad recalled. 'He wanted you to learn. When he talked, he was always smiling. He was charming. You couldn't tell he was a bad person.'

*

Uncle Chiv's daughter Amara filled me in about my Cambodian family's struggle in the 1970s. She emailed me her eyewitness account, the first I'd seen.

Amara was twelve when she and the rest of her family managed to flee to a refugee camp in Thailand. One day, buses arrived and everyone happily jumped on, thinking a new future beckoned. What they didn't know was that the Thais were returning them to the Cambodian border, where they were ordered to walk through a mountain valley. Amara wrote:

> Suddenly, I heard a big explosion. My body was pushed to the ground. Dust collected in the air and there was a rancid smell of burning flesh. Many people were dead. The wounded cried and screamed for help. No one knew the mountain valley was a minefield until a boy stepped on one.

Eight months later, the family attempted a second escape from Cambodia, and were interrogated and shot at by Vietnamese soldiers who had invaded the country.

We got off from the side of the road as fast as we could and hid in the bushes. The soldiers fired in our direction. I closed my eyes, listened to my heartbeat, prayed and asked God to save us. They searched us, but couldn't find anything so let us go.

The family took shelter where they could.

We found a big tree to hide under until morning. It was cold and dark as my mother unpacked rice from banana leaves. We slept in the mud. Our bodies soaked and froze. As I lay upon the ground, I could smell body waste and old corpses. No one slapped the mosquitoes because we were afraid of making any sound. We walked in the forest for a whole day to cross the border and reach the refugee camp in Thailand.

They were transferred to another refugee camp in Thailand, and with Dad's help were later given safe passage to America where they became proud US citizens.

Amara wrote, *My brothers and I are grateful to our father. If it weren't for his courage, we would have all died in Cambodia.*

*

On the night of Uncle Chiv's funeral, Dad and I had taken his sisters, Aunty Touch and Aunty Chan, to the Chinese restaurant near Chaddy. We sat at a table in the centre of the dining room with a view of the glowing Shell servo across the road and the flurry of traffic on Princes Highway.

'Jason, you know my life?' Aunty Touch began. 'My life was a hundred times worse than *The Killing Fields*.'

'What?' I struggled to hear over the noise of the restaurant.

'The movie,' Dad clarified.

'Oh, the movie.'

'A hundred times worse,' Aunty Touch said, shaking her head. 'Yeeesss!' She continued in Khmer, explaining how she and my cousins had survived in the Cambodian jungle.

'Rat! Eat the rat!' Dad translated, his voice rising above the restaurant din. *Rrrat*. 'Cricket! Eat the cricket!' *Crricket*. 'Snake! Eat the snake!' *Snek*. 'Anything! Anything for food.'

Aunty Touch and Aunty Chan had led their families through the jungle to the Thai refugee camps, just like Uncle Chiv. Both women's husbands had been high school teachers – intellectuals despised by the regime, presumed murdered.

At the restaurant we bowed our heads and chopsticked fried rice and dumplings into our hungry mouths. Uncle Chiv was gone, so we filled our bellies.

We ate because he wasn't coming back, and there was no purpose in leaving oranges in a bowl at the feet of a Buddha statue at a temple.

We ate because we were alive, knowing that one day we too would depart.

We ate because Mum had been gone for a very long time.

We ate for everyone who had come before us and for everyone who would come after us.

We ate to sustain our bodies, so we would see another day, and another after that.

We ate because Australia was the land of plenty, where in the supermarket you could find ten varieties of the same product on the same shelf.

'We survived! We survived! How did we survive?!' was my dad's frequent refrain when he thought about Mum and the other hardships in our lives.

All Mixed Up

But today, we weren't just surviving. We were living. This was how we as Cambodians celebrated life. This was our life. This was our love, expressed not through sentimental words or hugs but nourishment.

'We live to eat, not eat to live,' Dad declared.

*

My belief about my family's silence on the genocide is that the memories were too painful to revisit. How do you tell your children a bedtime story that begins: 'Gather round, kids, let me tell you about the day we ate rats in the jungle because we were being hunted down by the maniacal Khmer Rouge'?

Perhaps the older generation had wanted to avoid passing down their trauma to us. They'd made sure we couldn't absorb it or run away from it until we were breathless. The indignity of sleeping in the mud with the smell of death all around you. Of forging ahead and not even glancing behind because your husband was probably murdered. Of your family tree being dismembered one branch at a time. Of not knowing whether you'd still be alive in the next five minutes because you might stumble across a Khmer Rouge Communist or a Vietnamese soldier.

My older relatives shut off that world so we kids could go to tennis and piano lessons in the suburbs. So we could enjoy places of natural beauty like the Dandenong Ranges, where we would jump on the Puffing Billy steam train and rattle through forests of tree ferns. So we could eat McDonald's every night and feel sick and get fat.

In Australia we could buy a 'democracy sausage' in white bread and covered in tomato sauce for two bucks while being handed a free vote, which some of our fellow citizens chose to throw away like trash.

After I shared Uncle Chiv's story on Facebook, my gay Cambodian-Filipino-Australian friend, Dean, replied in a post.

> Every story I hear or read from that time is so powerful, horrifying and incomprehensible. We're very lucky to have surviving family, and blessed to be able to live as we do. They are so, so humble. Lost everything and started a new life. They NEVER complained. From the very bottom. Raised good families. They're really inspiring. We should share more of their stories.

Dean's reply made me think of the trip Dad and I had made to his hometown with a family friend when we visited Cambodia in 2005. The journey to Kralanh in north-western Cambodia had seemed never-ending, a bone-jangling drive along a rocky dirt road in which every pothole delivered a jab to my spine.

I sat in the back; Dad was in the front, gripping the handle above the passenger door.

'Are you okay?' I asked.

'Yeh,' he said, which meant he was utterly rattled.

The ute took us along roads the colour of Central Australia, kicking up clouds of red dust in our wake. A flooded landscape of verdant rice paddies rolled past. Men were ploughing their crops with oxen. Women with their heads wrapped in red gingham kramas, bent over in knee-high water the colour of milky coffee, were pulling out and tying together bundles of the long reedy crop. I was immersed in a culture I'd rejected as a child.

We finally came to a halt on a smooth dirt road in the township of Kralanh, where my father was born in the 1940s, a quiet neighbourhood of wooden houses on stilts and a couple of concrete shops. Thin scruffy dogs greeted us with a sniff, while women in colourful sarongs loitered by their front doors to stickybeak.

On the corner of a lane was a large wooden shop that resembled a Wild West saloon. The front doors opened onto a verandah, its walls festooned with colourful advertising. Outside, a mouldy rendered brick trough was filled with murky water.

Gazing at us in curiosity, the shop's occupants emerged: a woman with black curly hair in a sleeveless burgundy top and a lime-green dress, followed by a couple of young girls in pastel outfits.

Dad started waving his hands at the curly-haired woman and talking to her over the trough. The *mwah-mwah-mwah* of Khmer fell from his lips, and I wished I could understand him as he exclaimed, pointing to the shop.

'Chaa!' The woman nodded. 'Chaa!' It was a word I recognised, the feminine version of 'yes'. She was avidly listening to Dad's story while repeating 'Chaa! Chaa!' in the way Cambodians did to show they understood what was being said.

Dad wandered down the lane in his baggy khaki shirt and shorts, his pristine white New Balance sneakers scuffing in the red dirt. We all followed him, scruffy dogs in tow, passing overgrown yards and dilapidated wooden fences until we reached the end of the lane.

'I am looking for the house,' Dad said, brow furrowed. 'Somewhere here.' He was looking for a house on stilts; horses and carts had been kept in the space underneath as part of my grandfather's transport business, a kind of ride-sharing service way before its time. They'd rented out the carts to anyone who needed a lift around town.

Through the trees there were wooden houses on stilts, but none that Dad recognised. 'Maybe here. Or there? Can't find.' He sighed.

A small crowd of locals gathered around Dad – the strange old man from Australia – as he reminisced in Khmer about growing up in the dirt lane sixty years ago.

'Bah, bah, bah,' replied the men, using the masculine version of 'yes'.

'Chaa, chaa, chaa,' said the women as they listened intently with wide eyes.

We asked one of the men to take a photo of us before we walked back past the old shop on the corner. In Dad's day, a Chinese family had lived there. They'd worn their black hair in plaits and made plain sponge 'French cake' to sell at the local market.

'Jeh, this shop still the same,' Dad said in English.

'Really? After all this time?'

'Yeh. Same one. It used to be black.'

Some things still remained the same despite all the upheavals, Kralanh seemingly in a time warp.

Dad had made an incredible journey from his humble beginnings, surviving through tenacity and determination. He was born in a dirt lane in Cambodia, and by extension that's where I came from too, even though I was born in Australia. That was my heritage, that's who I was, and I couldn't have been prouder.

My family may have been all mixed up, but on both sides I had discovered a love and a resilience that ran deeper than any of us could have imagined. Survival was in our DNA.

Chapter Twenty-Seven

Sarah, Mum has been upset for 20 years.
– 2 April 1992

'It's a very sad story,' I said to my father. 'But I don't want it to always be a sad story.'

Dad was sitting in his armchair at his home in Melbourne, quietly listening to me as I lay on the sofa with my legs up on the armrest.

'Surely there must be some happy moments, like your wedding? Wasn't that a very happy moment? Just look at the photos. Mum looks ecstatic.'

Dad nodded. 'Yeah, she's happy – maybe she thought, "Yes, I married the right man,"' he said dryly.

My long journey of discovery into who Mum really was had revealed a tortured life: the violence she faced at the hands of Adel, fleeing for her safety and the devastation of having baby Sarah ripped from her arms by him; a harsh and unforgiving relationship with Nan Ruby; and the resulting war with her own mind, which had caused her irreparable damage. My investigation had also uncovered ugly prejudices.

But the bleakest view was contained in the medical records, which catalogued Mum's darkest moments, and perhaps showed me things not meant for me to see. By their nature, medical records revealed an incomplete picture of a person. People went to see the doctor with their problems and ailments, not their joys and achievements. In Mum's conversations with Dr Chong, they talked about the things that went wrong in her brain.

The records were skewed in a similar way to my painful memories of Mum. Those memories had tended to subsume all of her best qualities: kindness and warmth being two of them.

When Mum told Sarah that she had been 'upset for 20 years', this was partly true, but a more realistic statement might be: 'Mum has been upset *sometimes* over the past 20 years.' Having her baby daughter snatched away was an extraordinarily mind-altering trauma, but even at Mum's lowest ebb – the suicide attempt of 1974 – she had found a reason to press on. Perhaps it was the expectation that she would see Sarah again one day.

If I reversed her statement to say 'Mum has been *happy sometimes* over the past 20 years', that would be accurate too. Saddened by Mum's seemingly endless struggles, I decided to search for evidence of happiness in her life, setting aside the medical records and interviews.

I began by asking Dad to pull out all the photos he had of Mum and send me digital copies. They arrived in dribs and drabs, eventually maxing out my inbox. Other photos came to my phone after I taught Dad how to take pictures of them and send them as text messages.

One day he hit the jackpot, uncovering a box of slides that captured the early years of my parents' marriage. The images filtered through to me. My mother was smiling in most of them: Mum sitting in front of a typewriter with a smirk on her face; Mum and Dad outside the first place they rented together in Melbourne; Mum and Grandpa Leo sitting on a bench somewhere in Melbourne's CBD, Grandpa looking like a giant in a smart grey suit, his brown skin contrasting with Mum's fair complexion.

Another image showed a much younger version of Mum in Malaysia, sitting on the boot of a car parked in the driveway of a house, probably in the 1960s. She wore a white sleeveless top and skinny jeans with the hems neatly rolled up, and she was leaning back on her arms with one leg crossed over the other. Glamorous – and, dare I admit it, sexy – she could have been a catwalk model with her wavy black hair hanging about her shoulders. Young and free, before I knew her.

And then there were photos from the night of Mum and Dad's engagement party at a Chinese restaurant. Nan Ruby sat at the table in a multicoloured paisley outfit; Uncle Johnny was beside her with the mop top that made him look like a Beatle. Next to Dad, Mum was looking sideways at the camera, the ring on her finger glinting in the flash.

Dad had kept the handwritten bill from the King Wah Chinese Restaurant on Lonsdale Street in the CBD. It had been the cheapest and most cheerful celebration:

> Sweet corn soup
> Lemon chicken
> Steak with cashew nuts
> Prawn balls with snow peas
> Sliced fish with black bean sauce
> Sweet and sour pork
> Rice

Sweets
Sweet pork and bean curds
Total $44.00
$1.00 tip
$45.00

– 24 December 1973

*

At some point I realised I'd have to fly down to Melbourne and go through Dad's mountain of photos myself. Over the years he'd amassed hundreds if not thousands of Kodak moments on prints and slides now gathering dust in his metal locker.

'You have so many cameras,' I said, peering inside. 'How many?'

He looked up, squinting. 'Eight!' he said triumphantly.

I lugged the albums out of Dad's locker and laid them on the kitchen table. Most were heavy and about five centimetres thick; others were thin and falling apart. They began in the 1970s when Dad first met Mum and stopped abruptly in 1993.

'Why are there no albums after the early 1990s?' I asked.

'Just a minute,' he said, putting his hands behind his back, his mind ticking over. 'Mmm, maybe no point,' he concluded. 'Yeah, no point.'

There had been little to celebrate for a few years. His photography had resumed in 1996 when we took a trip to America and Europe.

As I flicked through a lifetime of memories, several photos made me wince. A black-and-white snap from 1990 showed me and my parents seated at a dinner table at a wedding reception, looking as if the camera had been forced upon us. My parents wore sour 'we just had a fight' expressions, with me stuck in the middle – a telling family portrait. Mum was squeezed into an ill-fitting dress, the arms of the matching jacket stretched almost to bursting. Her face was bloated by her medication, her gaze startled like that of an animal in the headlights. She looked deeply disturbed as if she wanted to escape. Her eyes pleaded, 'Help me.'

But I kept searching the photos. In my sights was a particular expression of Mum's: the beaming, open-mouthed smile I'd seen in the 1968 photo of her cutting the wedding cake in Ipoh. It represented an unbridled joy in a moment of time, and in this experiment it would be the benchmark for her happiness – the Ipoh smile.

From hundreds of photos, I collected Mum's smiles in the following periods: my parents' engagement and wedding, Mum's pregnancy with me, my babyhood and toddlerhood, and a few of my birthdays in the early 1980s. The rest of the albums were overflowing with photos of me, smiling and showing off for the camera. Dad must have spent hundreds of dollars on film to capture his little boy.

I identified the broad Ipoh smile in my parents' wedding photos, one in particular standing out. Mum and Dad were in the back seat of a car, just wedded, Mum wearing her sky-blue dress and matching floppy hat, her white teeth showing. Dad's hand was blurred as he waved out the window. Their car headed into the future, their fates unknown.

*

The official tagline for Disneyland is 'The Happiest Place on Earth', and on our trip there in 1988, the ersatz happiness seemed to rub off on Mum. She wrote to Sarah on a postcard printed with Snow White and the Seven Dwarfs:

Dear Sarah,
We went to Disneyland. We also went to Hollywood. Was great fun. We are going to New York tomorrow which is the 25th of June. End with love to you. Love Mum XXX.

– 24 June 1988

Here was strong evidence that Mum had enjoyed our visit to California, permitting herself to be happy.

At Universal Studios in Los Angeles, we boarded a trolley that took us past the Bates house in *Psycho*, the lake used in *Jaws*, and a giant mechanical King Kong, who roared as he destroyed New York City amid spectacular bursts of flames. As the trolley rolled on, we arrived at a subway station where an earthquake shook, causing an oncoming train to hurtle towards us. The platform ruptured and pipes burst, splashing water everywhere. We thought we were going to be crushed and killed. It was exhilarating.

The trip to LA was part of a dazzling tour of the US, Paris and Bangkok, which Dad funded by adding to the mortgage. Mum sent Sarah six postcards from our travels.

Dear Sarah,
Did you receive my postcards? Hope you did. Mum arrived home to Melbourne safely this morning, the 30th of July. Mum quite had enough with everything. Very tired.

The house was well taken care of by Uncle Johnny. Yo-yo my cat sort of broke her leg. Poor thing. How are you darling? Hope all is well with your studies. Mum will now try to look for a better job. It's one more month of winter. And it is very cold. You could now write to me.

Pet, Mum is trying to get over jet lag. Have to end now with love to you.

Love, Mum XXX.
– 30 July 1988

Mum's spirits seemed to lift after the overseas trip. On 11 August 1988, she wrote: *We are well and happy.* Variations on this phrase appeared in subsequent letters up until the year she died.

> We are well and happy, sweetheart. Lots of pretty flowers bloom in our garden. It's summer now.
> – 5 December 1988

> Narong, I and Jason are well and happy. The garden is beautiful.
> – 10 November 1989

> Sarah, Mum is well and very happy in Australia.
> – 1 September 1992

I was unsure if *I* had made Mum happy, not that this should be a child's burden. Even so, I searched for evidence, and I found it. Mum had her chest puffed out, swinging her arms as she swaggered. Proud. Boastful. Wide open about her feelings, unlike Dad. She bragged to Sarah about my swimming achievements, my tennis and piano lessons, about the many friends who came to my birthday parties, gathering round a pastel-coloured ice-cream cake at Macca's. Mum lifted me up on her shoulders, holding me in the air for all to see.

Sarah, Jason ask me to tell you that he will be in grade six next year. Jason has won ten tickets in swimming. Sarah, Jason has four more tickets then he leaves swimming school. Jason starts tennis in February next year. Sarah, Jason had a good school report this year.
– 23 December 1991

She barracked for Sarah too:

Pet, darling, Mum is so proud of you. So sweetheart, you got three distinctions of the three students in the class. Real good, pet. Yes, I think all would be happy with your school results. Mum is proud of you.
– 3 November 1988

In a letter dated almost a year before she died, I found the precious words I'd been desperately seeking. It was like stumbling across a gold nugget.

Sarah, Jason starts college next year, 1993. Sarah, Mum loves Jason very, very much because he is a baby boy.
– 24 August 1992

Proof! Words from the past in black and white, absolutely undeniable, unconditional and unequivocal. *Mum loves Jason very, very much because he is a baby boy*. I read the line again and again, and held on to it as if it were a life raft.

*

When my parents inspected the house that would become their home, they were charmed by the camellia trees bursting with pink and red flowers in the front yard. After only a few minutes inside, Mum announced she'd fallen in love with the modest brick-veneer house.

In 1980, when Mum found out she was pregnant with me, she was working at the potato chip factory in Oakleigh. My father had recently become a machine operator there. According to him, Mum went to the production floor and boasted about their happy news, and the mainly Greek workers embraced her.

Because of Mum's Eurasian features, the Greeks initially thought she was Italian, having never met an Asian before. Once they realised she was from Malaysia, they referred to her as a 'kineza', the feminine version of the slur I was called in high school.

'They didn't want the Asians to take their jobs,' Dad recalled.

But upon hearing about Mum's pregnancy, they were immensely proud that *their* kineza, one of their own, an honorary 'wog', was having a baby. For the Greeks, family meant everything.

When I was delivered, I weighed nearly nine pounds, about four kilos. Dad bought a new Minolta for the occasion, loading up the camera with film and snapping off a series of shots: me sleeping in the cot, me asleep in Mum's arms, and even a wide shot of the hospital exterior. But the man at the camera shop revealed Dad had been shooting blanks: the roll of film was loaded incorrectly. The next day he made sure the camera was working, returned to the hospital and reeled off the shots again.

Uncle Johnny saw Mum crying in the hospital bed after I was born. 'I was happy for her,' he recalled, 'because I felt this would get rid of all the loneliness and all the fretting she had for the first child.' As Mum cradled me in her arms, Uncle Johnny thought she was flashing back to the day she'd given birth to Sarah a decade earlier. 'I thought this was a blessing in disguise. This would give her something to think about, something to keep her mind occupied. We were all happy for her.'

As I grew up, Mum found me difficult to handle sometimes, Uncle Johnny said, because I was mischievous. But while my uncle considered me a brat, he said Mum certainly loved me, spoilt or not. 'You filled a gap in her life where she was making up for something she lost.'

I was no substitute for Sarah, but in Australia Mum finally had a child in her arms, and no one could take him away from her.

During one of our video chats, I asked Dad why he'd chosen to stick with Mum and endure such hardship. Lesser men may have thrown it all in. 'Why didn't you just walk away?'

He was sitting in front of his computer in Melbourne, cast in the glow of blue light from the monitor.

'Why didn't you just give up?' I prompted.

He paused and searched for the words. Finally he said it wasn't in his nature to do so. 'That would be cruel,' he added. 'What would happen if I took *you* away from her? She would hang herself. She would end up in an institution.'

My eyes began to well up, and I looked away. I hoped he couldn't see my tears in the fuzzy video image.

Out of all the photos I saw, one that Dad found on a slide shimmered in particular.

It had been shot outside his share house in Caulfield when my parents were first dating. Under a white latticed arch on a back verandah, Mum wore her familiar red blouse with white polka dots and a pair of white slacks. Leaning forward, she rested her arms on the white bannister. Out of focus in the foreground, a magenta flower partially obscured her body, but her ecstatic smile shone through, the excitement of a new life in Australia glinting in her eye. Before the breakdowns. Before the sadness ravaged her.

Dad was behind the camera, seeing the worth and potential in the woman from Malaysia. She noticed the beauty in the simplest of things. A kind, generous and loving person. That's how I would like to remember her. That is the essence of Mum.

Through my investigation, I discovered the light within her, and I promised myself that I would keep it burning brightly, while accepting all her human frailties and flaws, and the choices she made. I freed up more room for her in my heart.

*

When I was eighteen, I emailed a close friend about my grief and pain during high school. Years later, I went looking for that email so I could read my account of what happened on the night I called the ambulance. The email was folded in a journal in my old bedroom. I dusted off the cover and opened the printout.

There was a startling line that echoed Sarah's beliefs: *Things happen because they are supposed to happen.* The email made my stomach churn and head spin, and I had to lie down after reading it. Some things are meant to be avoided. Until that email, I'd kept what happened secret. When my friend hadn't replied, and with no one else to talk to, I again blocked out everything that caused me pain, including Mum.

My investigation and its aftermath gave me plenty of time to reflect on the wall I'd built in my mind. Now, standing back to inspect my defences, I realised I couldn't, and shouldn't, tear all of them down, otherwise I would be overwhelmed. The wall had achieved its purpose, but I'd erred in its design, so I drew up plans for a renovation.

The centrepiece was a brand-new door. That door allowed me to choose what, and who, entered. With open arms, I warmly welcomed Mum through. Anything else that came knocking, or anyone who caused damage, had no place in my life. On my side of the wall, I would grow a garden of flowers in a field with the people I loved.

Epilogue

Dear Mum,
I was on holidays at some fancy place in Byron Bay, lying in a warm bath full of Epsom salts, when I thought about calling out your name. Aunty Madeleine reckons you're watching over me, and I had this idea that maybe, right then, you were sitting by the tub like you did when I was a little boy.

There was no unnaturally blue Mr Matey bubble bath this time, just something called luxury bath tea. A bit posh.

Mum! Are you there? I thought of saying. *Mum!* I wanted to yell out, while my fingers began to prune. It would have been like having a seance in a hot tub.

Can you believe it? A grown man in his thirties, crying for his mummy while having a bath. Not that I believe in spirits!

Mum, I read the letters you wrote to Sarah, and I must tell you this: Mum, I'm very, very sorry about everything. Mum, please excuse me for everything. I thought you didn't love me when the truth was you did.

All this time you loved me when I mistakenly thought I was nothing. For a long time I believed this, but now I know I was wrong.

Nothing stood in the way of your love for your children, no matter the immense obstacles, no matter how your kids turned out. You loved us because we were yours.

As Sarah says, 'The truth will come out.'

I know you and Dad didn't get on well. I can understand how you might have felt unloved by his brand of unspoken emotion (I would know, it's infuriating at times!), but he did love you. He picked you up when you fell down, again and again. Sometimes, I guess, love becomes warped by hardship, and perhaps that's why you couldn't see it.

But Dad can see you now. He has proudly put your wedding photos on a cabinet under the flatscreen TV on the lounge-room wall. He remembers how the two of you went to see Shirley Bassey live in Melbourne in the 1980s. It must have been exhilarating for you to see your favourite singer hit those hip-thrusting bombastic notes in 'Big Spender' on stage.

Yes, Dad can see you now – how you saved his life by marrying him. Mum, it's no small feat to save a man from an impending genocide in Cambodia! If you had rejected his proposal, he would have been slaughtered by the Khmer Rouge. What you did was tremendous.

Sarah probably misses you the most, if it's possible to say such a thing. It's not really a case of missing you more or less, it's just that for her whole life she had nothing but an idea of you: the mysterious woman in the summer dress, the woman in a far-off land who sent lipstick and nighties in the post. All Sarah had growing up were tender words in secret aerograms. As precious as those words were, they did not match up to the warm hugs and strokes on the head I received for twelve years.

I've told Sarah you never let go of her. I know you kicked yourself after she was taken from your arms. Without your baby daughter, life for you was one big tsk. But in reality, you held on to Sarah until the very end, even when your heart gave in.

Your baby girl's all grown up now. You wouldn't recognise her. She has raised two beautiful boys, your grandchildren, while managing a successful career in design. Sometimes I think she doesn't believe in herself, but I try to help her see that she is a strong independent woman.

Yes, *I* can see you now. My memories are rearranging themselves. Your smile of contentment when we all got tarted up to go out. How pretty you looked in your make-up and flowery dresses, your brown leather jacket and the fawn coat that kept you toasty in the winter months, and the shiny jewellery you stored in a wind-up music box. You had a real sense of style, unlike daggy Dad.

You must have felt so good about yourself when you did your hair in the mirror, that black bob Uncle Johnny cut for you under the old lemon tree.

I remember your beaming face when you dressed me in a red flannel shirt and stepped back with pride. You must have been so happy to have a young son to show off.

I can recall the days when you watched me playing in the mud with my Matchbox cars, which I sometimes cheekily placed on the road to see what would happen if real cars ran over them. And the days when you sat on the porch next to the cherry-red camellias while I caught praying mantises in old Monbulk jam jars.

Mum, I can see you now. What about when I was two and we went to the Melbourne Zoo? Dad grumbled at me, and you leapt to my defence: 'See what you did, Narong? Don't provoke him.' You soothed me with a white-bread sandwich and a can of Fanta. You sat and watched me with that benevolent smile.

Or what about when you let me take a sickie from primary school and watch *Play School* on a fold-out bed in the lounge room? You called up the teacher and said I didn't feel well.

I used to ask, 'Do you love me, Mummy?'

You would reply, 'Of course Mummy loves you. I will eat you up.'

You gently rubbed the burning sensation of Tiger Balm into my forehead when I had a headache.

You were kind too – how could I have forgotten? Your kindness showered down on me in the form of meringue animals from the bakery, long john buns filled with jam and cream, mixed lollies, bubblegum and rocket-shaped icy poles.

Aunty Touch remembers how you handed her a pair of earrings after she arrived in Melbourne as a refugee with nothing to her name.

You know that green bowl you used to make cakes in all the time? Well, I still have it. It's travelled with me from Melbourne to Adelaide to Sydney. I think of you every time I mix something up. Sometimes I use the bowl to make your wonderful curry puffs, using a variation of the recipe I pinched from the internet. Coriander and Worcestershire sauce add a little zing, ingredients we didn't use in the 1980s.

I still don't know how to make your kari ayam, but I've eaten it in Malaysia and in many Australian restaurants, wiping my brow as I scoop up the gravy and rice, fondly thinking of you.

Mum, you were always there to back me up a hundred per cent. You were so game when we were walking in the Oakleigh mall and I asked you to buy me a bird I'd seen on the front of a Froot Loops cereal box. I would have been about five.

'What is it called again?' you said, bending down, unfamiliar with the species.

'A toucan.'

'A toucan? Okay.' And you walked into the pet shop and asked the man at the counter, even though the bird was far too foreign and exotic to be perched in a cage in the Melbourne suburbs. You came out looking sheepish when he told you they didn't stock any. We both laughed and wandered off feeling absolutely silly.

Oakleigh's changed now. The Australian children of the Greeks have cleared out the tumbleweeds and set up shops full of cakes. It's like what the Italians did to Carlton, only don't tell the Greeks that. I've taken Dad, Aunty Madeleine and Uncle Johnny for souvlaki at the place that made it into the *New York Times*. I wish you could be there with us where no one would dare call you a kineza any more.

Mum, I can hear you now. And the music you played on our record player. The Seekers, Nana Mouskouri, Bing Crosby and *The Sound of Music*. Do you remember the time we sang that Whitney Houston song about letting the children lead us into the future? 'You make me laugh, Jason!' you cried.

Or that time we were sitting in the lounge room listening to music with Nan Ruby, and I began jigging my knee to the beat? 'Look at him!' you exclaimed, laughing.

Yes, Mum, I can feel you now. Blocking you out is no longer a reflex. The door is open. I can see you now for who you are. The good memories were always there, they were just buried underneath all the dirt. *Push the dirt down the pothole*, as you said in one of your letters.

Mum, about that time when you were waiting at the bus stop for me and I walked off in a huff: I realise now that what you were saying, as you followed me with our little white dog, was, 'Jason, I love you. I love you, Jason.' It sounded insane at the time, but now it all makes sense.

I've come to realise you are not a crazy woman. Calling you 'mental' allowed me to strip you of your humanity, and for that I am sorry.

The bronze plaque on your grave is so weathered that the gloss on the raised lettering has disappeared. We neglected it for too long, and now it's only readable to our fingertips, like braille. Aunty Madeleine has been hassling me to get it fixed, and I will, Mum. We'll get it polished up until it looks brand new, even if the grass around it grows thinly. Down by the lake, we'll lay a fresh bouquet so that you can be beside your 'flowers in the field'. That was one of your strengths, seeing beauty where there is none, as you did on the day in Caulfield when you walked with Dad across a carpet of dandelions. When Sarah asks, 'What was Mum like?' I now know what to say.

I once took Sarah to see your grave, and as we stood together on the grass, a grey honeyeater clasped itself to the low-hanging branches of a nearby gum tree. Eyes shining, Sarah looked at the bird and then at me. We thought it was you.

Mum, I remember you now. While I can't undo the events of the past, I've decided to give you a happier ending, Mum, because as your son I can.

Love,
Jason.
XXX

Acknowledgements

After a few false starts, this work is the proudest of my career so far. Had it not been for my agent Benython Oldfield, ABC Books and HarperCollins, it may have remained a secret to the world. Much appreciation to Kate Goldsworthy, Madeleine James and the marketing and legal team and proofreader, and Jude McGee for her wise guidance. A special thank you to Mark Campbell and George Saad for designing the luminous cover and for incorporating my idea of the dandelion motif.

Thank you to Leigh Sales, Lisa Millar, Marc Fennell and Alice Pung for gifting me your endorsements, to *7.30* and the ABC for allowing me time to work on this project, and to the people behind ABC Life and ABC News who supported the original article about my dad. Much appreciation to members of the public who contacted me.

Many thanks to Dr Chong who kindly found and released Mum's medical records and to Sarah's old school. I am also grateful to the anonymous source in Malaysia who spoke to me despite their fears of a backlash.

To all my friends, thank you for the many, many conversations along the way, and to my 'all mixed up' family members – aunties, uncles and cousins on both sides – who generously shared their stories or took part in some way, I extend my love. Thank you to Betty's daughter, Linda, and Rosalind, Afsah, Dean and his dad, Ang.

To Dad, for your unwavering belief in our story, and for your meticulous fact checking and document fossicking. To Sarah, without you and Mum's letters this book could not have happened. I hope it fills in the gaps.

Finally to Mum, who taught me how fragile and precious life is. I wish the world had been kinder to you.